FUNDAMENTALS OF CRIMINAL INVESTIGATION

Adam J. McKee

Cover designed by Adam J. McKee

Adam J. McKee
Visit my website at www.docmckee.com

Printed in the United States of America

First Printing: July 2019
Forma Pauperis Press

* * *

CONTENTS

SECTION 1

Introduction to Investigations

It must be recognized that all crimes and crime scenes are unique. The legal and political environment of each jurisdiction is different as well. The judgment of the investigator, departmental policy, and the law should be given deference in the implementation of the material in this text. Because of this individuality, no single step-by-step "cookie cutter" process can be devised for conducting criminal investigations. What I have attempted to do in this text is to expound on general principles that, at the time of writing, were considered best practices. This text is not intended as a rigid protocol.

Not every portion of this book will apply to all crimes. It is at the discretion of responding personnel (depending on their responsibilities, as well as the purpose and scope of their duties) to apply the procedures recommended in this book to a particular incident. Some of the procedures described in this book may not be performed in the sequence described or may be performed simultaneously. Nothing herein is intended to constitute legal advice, and no guarantee can be made as to technical accuracy. Always defer to federal, state, and local legal requirements as well as departmental policy.

When most people outside of law enforcement circles hear the term criminal investigation, they immediately think of high technology forensic tools such as DNA, computer-aided video enhancement, and multitudinous chemicals that glow in the dark to reveal invisible evidence. Hollywood has painted a glamorous picture of the criminal investigation process that is largely misleading. To really grasp the true nature of the criminal investigation process, we must proceed to dispel the myths created by Hollywood and get back to basics.

Simply put, a criminal investigation is a systematic search for people, things, and information to reconstruct the circumstances of a criminal act, identify and apprehend the perpetrator, and aid the prosecution of the perpetrator in court.

From this general definition, we can establish several important objectives of a criminal investigation:

- Ensure the safety of officers, civilian support staff, and the public
- Respond to exigent situations at the scene of the crime
- Establish the crime scene priorities
- Identify suspects
- Collect, document, and preserve evidence
- Recover stolen property
- Assist in the prosecution of the defendants

SECTION 1.1

Criminal Law & Investigations

A **crime** is an act or omission that is contrary to law for which there is some sort of formal punishment. From a practical standpoint, crime is simply a violation of some criminal law. **Criminal law** is the branch of law that seeks to prevent harm to society by prohibiting certain acts and omissions and punishing those who commit those acts or omissions. Because criminal law seeks to protect society as a whole, criminal prosecutions are brought forward in the name of the state, not in the name of the victim, as it would be in a *civil law* case. Usually, an attorney called the prosecutor argues the state's case. The person who is accused of the crime is known as the **defendant**.

SOURCES OF CRIMINAL LAW

In the United States, there are three primary levels of government: local, state, and federal. Most criminal cases originate in violations of state law and investigated by local law enforcement. Federal prosecutions make up only a small fraction of criminal cases. Thus, most criminal investigators will need to be concerned with the criminal law on the state level. Most of these laws can be grouped into five major categories:
1. Common law
2. Statutory law
3. Case law
4. Administrative law
5. Common Law

Originally, the **common law** was the ancient traditional legal system of England. When America was founded, the American colonists brought the common law with them to America. That legal tradition is the basis of criminal law in most states (Louisiana being a notable exception). The law was considered common because, being based on precedent, all citizens could expect similar treatment by the criminal justice system under similar circumstances. The common law was first put on paper in the written opinions of judges, so laws originating in court cases are sometimes referred to as common law. Many modern criminal laws have their origins in the common law, as well as many legal ideas that define our contemporary legal system.

Statutory Law

A **statute** is a law passed by some legislative body. This means the U.S. Congress on the federal level and the legislatures of each state on the state level. The ordinances passed by local governing bodies also fall into this category. Many states have moved entirely away from the common law and now make the criminal law a matter entirely of statute. These statutes are referred to as **statutory law**. Statutes are generally passed in no special order by lawmaking bodies. Usually, however, the statutes are organized into a set of books and arranged by topic. Such a topical organization of statutory law is known as a **code**. The section of a state's (or the federal government's) code that contains criminal laws is often called the **criminal code** or **penal code**.

Case Law

When most Americans think of lawmaking, they think of legislatures debating the merits of a proposed law and then taking a vote. Less understood is the fact that American courts are also in the business of making law, albeit indirectly. Appeals courts have the power to interpret previous court decisions, statutes, regulations, and constitutional issues. These interpretations are delivered to us in the form of written decisions called opinions. These decisions taken together form the body of **case law** that is binding on law enforcement and the lower courts.

Administrative Law

While the power of making laws rests in the hands of legislatures, legislators have long recognized the fact that they cannot be experts in everything and cannot adequately regulate certain aspects of our complex society. For this reason, legislatures often delegate their lawmaking authority to administrative agencies that in turn promulgate rules and regulations. Many of these regulations have the force of law and carry criminal penalties (such as fines and jail time) when violated. These agency rules and regulation are collectively known as **administrative law**.

CLASSIFICATION OF CRIME

Most jurisdictions recognize that not all breaches of the law are equal. That is, some offenses are far more serious than others are. The more serious a crime is, the more cost the government is willing to pay to bring the offender to justice and the more severe the punishment. The most serious general classification of crimes is as a felony. A **felony** is a relatively serious crime that is punishable by more than a year in prison. A **misdemeanor**, on the other hand, is a less serious crime that is punishable by less than a year of incarceration, usually in a local jail or regional detention facility.

ELEMENTS OF CRIMES

Criminal law is usually a matter of statute. The statute will set out what act is prohibited and what punishment is warranted for those who commit that act. While each specific crime will be superficially different from another, certain common elements will be found in nearly every crime. Knowledge of these **elements of crimes** is essential to the investigator.

Because the prosecution must prove each element of the crime beyond a reasonable doubt in court, investigators must provide sufficient lawfully obtained evidence for this purpose. Without knowledge of the elements of a crime, the investigator has no idea what evidence is valuable and what is worthless. Most laws follow a general form and have the same general elements in common. Obviously, there must be a criminal act or omission.

An **omission** is something that the law commands and that the defendant fails to do. Common examples of omissions are the failure to pay taxes and the failure of certain professionals such as teachers and nurses to report child abuse. The idea is that *not* doing something commanded by law is a crime. By tradition, the criminal act or omission is known by the Latin legal phrase **actus reus**. Do not be misled by the use of the verb act—it is not necessarily an action verb. Some passive states such as the possession of certain contraband items (e.g., drugs, automatic weapons, explosives) satisfy the criminal act requirements.

In our legal tradition, we generally do not punish accidents as crimes. That is, a person that does not intend the otherwise criminal result of his or her actions is not **culpable**, or worthy of blame. For a person to be guilty of a crime, they must have done it on **purposely**, or at least **knowingly**. The idea of purpose is also known as intent. These words are used to describe the mental state of the perpetrator at the time the act was committed. This mental element of crimes is known by the Latin legal phrase **mens rea**.

Most jurisdictions today punish those who engage in behavior that is likely to result in a prohibited harm even if the person did not actually intend the harm. If the person knew the behavior was very risky and did it anyway, the mental state is considered **reckless** by law. If the behavior was risky, but the actor did not perceive the risk, then the act is considered to be done **negligently**.

Some crimes, usually violations, will not have this mental element. Obviously, it would be detrimental to the working of the criminal justice system if officers had to go to court and testify as to the mental state of a person cited for illegally parking a vehicle. Crimes that do not involve a mental element are known as **strict liability** offenses. Full-scale investigations, however, usually involve serious felony crimes. These types of crimes will usually involve a mental element that must be proven. The task of proving what was going on in someone's head seems daunting, and it sometimes is.

However (luckily for the investigator) there is a presumption of law in most jurisdictions that a person's intent is the likely outcome of his actions. For example, of Joe Doe shoots someone in the head, the law will presume that the likely outcome of shooting someone in the head is to kill them, so it follows that Doe intended to kill his victim. Obviously, the *mens rea* of homicide is much more complex, and we will delve more deeply into that in a later chapter.

For some crimes, the mental element coupled with the criminal act is sufficient to define the crime. If those elements can be proven beyond a reasonable doubt, then a conviction is likely. Some crimes are more complex in nature due to the addition of other elements. Some crimes require that a resulting **harm** occur.

In addition to the prohibited harm, it must usually be shown that the perpetrator's criminal act (*actus reus*) was the **cause** of the prohibited harm. In murder, for example, the resulting harm is the death of a person. If no one dies, then you cannot have a murder (although *attempted* murder is a possible charge).

Keep in mind that if the circumstances of a case are not such that elements of one crime can be proven, then there may well be a less serious offense that can be proven. When the elements of a more serious crime contain all of the elements of a less serious crime, then the less serious crime is considered a **lesser-included offense** of the first crime. In many jurisdictions, for example, breaking and entering is a lesser-included offense of burglary.

Sometimes, even when all of the elements of a crime can be proven beyond a reasonable doubt, the defendant can still be exonerated if he can mount a successful **defense**. Defenses come in three wide varieties. **Procedural defenses** are where the defendant uses some misbehavior by the criminal justice system to nullify a prosecution, such as claiming a speedy trial violation because the prosecutor did not move forward with the case quickly enough.

Sometimes the criminal code will establish certain exceptions to crimes where, when proven, make the act noncriminal. For example, killing another person is usually a criminal homicide. If, however, the killing is done in **self-defense**, the law will not punish it. Such defenses are known as **justifications**. This is why undercover narcotics officers are not committing crimes when purchasing drugs—they are covered under an **execution of public duty** defense. The third and final major category of defenses is **excuses**. Excuses are when circumstances are such that we are willing to forgive the defendant for his or her criminal acts. Insanity is the most well-known of these.

From this simplified overview of criminal law, we can establish several key pieces of evidence that the investigator will be looking for. It is critical to find evidence that establishes:

- That the criminal act (according to some statute) was committed
- That the defendant was the one who committed the criminal act
- That the defendant had mental state required by the statute
- That (if required) the prohibited harm actually occurred
- That the criminal act was the legal cause of the prohibited harm
- That the defendant has no criminal defense available at law

SECTION 1.2

Evidence Law & Investigations

Evidence can be divided into two major types. The first of these major categories is real evidence. Real evidence means any evidence that consists of a tangible item that can be perceived with the five senses. Physical evidence is the first thing that comes to mind when we think of evidence, but documents, photographs, videos, sound recordings, and even computer files fall into this category. Demonstrative evidence also falls into this category, even though investigators usually generate it. Demonstrative evidence consists of aids developed by investigators such as diagrams, sketches, computer simulations, and the like that are intended to help jurors sort through complex evidence and reconstruct a crime in their mind's eye.

The second major type of evidence is *testimonial evidence*. **Testimonial evidence** refers to things that a person communicates to the court under oath. Usually, this means courtroom testimony but can also include things such as affidavits and depositions taken out of court. As a rule, testimonial evidence not given under oath is inadmissible. Certain exceptions, however, do apply.

Another important way to classify evidence is by whether it is *direct* or *circumstantial*. **Direct evidence** is evidence that proves a fact without the need for the jury to make any inferences or presumptions. That is, it *directly* proves a certain fact at issue. Circumstantial evidence, on the other hand, does not prove things directly. Rather, it requires the finders of fact to make inferences and draw their own conclusions.

Direct evidence can be considered the most compelling because, if it is believed, leaves no doubt in the fact finder's mind. A common example of direct evidence is when an eyewitness testifies that the defendant committed the crime. So long as the witness is credible, there can be little doubt as to guilt, and no inferences are required. Crimes being committed on videotape are a good example of direct evidence. Assuming that the person on the tape is clearly the defendant and that the tape is believed to be authentic, then there can be little doubt. Unfortunately, for the investigator, direct evidence is not very common. Most cases are built on circumstantial evidence.

While perhaps less compelling, *circumstantial evidence is still valuable and can be used to secure convictions.* Some circumstantial evidence can be very compelling, being almost direct in nature. For example, if a jury hears compelling evidence that the defendant's fingerprints were found on the murder weapon, then they may conclude that the defendant was, in fact, the person that used the weapon. Often, circumstantial evidence is used to demonstrate the following:

Ability to commit the crime. It is a common defense tactic to try and convince the jury that the defendant could not commit a particular crime based on some personal deficiency. Often, *physical ability*, *mental ability*, and *means* come into play. Investigators must be prepared to combat these assertions in court by offering evidence that the defendant did, in fact, possess the necessary means, as well as the necessary physical and mental ability to commit the crime.

For example, let us say that a school resource officer finds a bomb in a disgruntled high school student's locker. The defense could argue that obviously, the bomb was not the defendants, because he lacked the means to acquire bomb-making supplies and lacked the necessary knowledge to construct the bomb even if he had the means. If the investigators introduce the U.S. Army's "Improvised Munitions Handbook" taken from the student's home into evidence, then the defense's argument crumbles.

Intent. Circumstantial evidence is usually used to show intent because only direct testimonial evidence can reveal the inner workings of the defendant's mind. So, absent a detailed confession, we are forced to piece together his or her mental state using circumstantial evidence. Most commonly, *modus operandi*, *motive*, and *threats* are used for this purpose.

The phrase **modus operandi** (MO) literally means "method of operation." That is, criminals have patterns in how they accomplish their criminal acts. If a new crime is committed using the same behavior patterns that the defendant has used in the past, it is circumstantial evidence that the defendant committed this crime as well. The more novel or bizarre the method, the more compelling the evidence will be. Bizarre behaviors being repeated in multiple crimes are common among sadistic killers and rapists. It can also be important in more mundane crimes, however, such as a burglars signature method of gaining entry into a dwelling.

Motive can also be used to provide the jury with circumstantial evidence of guilt. Usually, the motive is not an element of the crime that needs to be proven to secure a conviction. All that is strictly necessary is that the defendant did it purposely; the reason is of no legal significance. The reason for committing a crime, however, can be a great aid in helping juries determine guilt. Money, especially large insurance policies, is a common motive for murder and arson. Do not, however, limit possible motives to money alone. Depending on the nature of the crime, motives can be almost limitless. Revenge, retaliation, racial hatred, jealousy, and even entertainment can be motives for crime.

Threats are also useful in proving guilt. When a defendant makes a threat to do something criminal, and then that crime happens, a jury may infer that the defendant did the act. This is not as valuable as it first seems. People often make threats in jest or to "blow off steam," never intending to actually carry out the threat. Ultimately, the credibility of a threat or a pattern of threatening behavior is up to the jury.

Acting guilty. If the prosecution can show that the defendant acted in a way that is consistent with a guilty person, then the jury may infer guilt. Flight at any stage in the criminal process is often a sign of guilt. Why would an innocent person run from the police or jump bail? If the jury infers that they would not do so, then they might also infer guilt. Juries may also infer guilt from the defendant trying to conceal evidence. For example, if a knife used in an aggravated battery is found in a dumpster with the defendant's fingerprints on it, the jury may infer guilt. Why else would someone discard a perfectly good knife?

Being caught with the **fruits of a crime** is a powerful indicator of guilt. Juries can reasonably infer, for example, that the possession of a stolen laptop by the suspect reasonably demonstrates that the person in possession stole it. The possession of wealth that has no legitimate origin can also be used to suggest guilt, at least in financially lucrative crimes such as dealing in narcotics.

RULES OF EVIDENCE

As we have seen, evidence serves many purposes in court. However, before evidence can be used in court, it must be admitted. For evidence to be admitted by the judge, it must conform to the *rules of evidence*. The **rules of evidence** are rules that determine the admissibility of evidence at hearings and trials. As a practical matter, almost anything can be admitted into evidence unless there is a specific rule that prohibits it. Obviously, the competent investigator will have a working knowledge of these rules.

The most important rule of evidence to the investigator is the exclusionary rule. The **exclusionary rule** is a rule developed by the U.S. Supreme Court that prohibits the admission of illegally obtained evidence in court. This rule is grounded in the Fourth Amendment, which seeks to protect American citizens from unreasonable searches and seizures.

As a practical matter, investigators must make sure that evidence is obtained within the parameters set forth by the courts in Fourth Amendment cases. The rules about searches and seizures are voluminous and complex. Beyond dedication and long study to learn these procedural laws, the best advice is this: *When in doubt, get a warrant.*

A related rule is the **fruits of the poisonous tree** doctrine. This rule says that when illegally obtained evidence leads an investigator to new evidence, then that evidence (the "fruits" of the original illegal search) is also inadmissible. When these two doctrines are taken together, we can quickly see just how bad it would be if it was determined that a crime scene was illegally searched.

The guilty party would almost certainly go free. Thus, we see that the success of our investigations, the best interest of justice, and the public safety all demand that investigations be conducted "by the book."

Assuming that the police legally obtained the evidence, it is still not automatically admissible in court. To be admissible, the judge must determine that the evidence is 1) *relevant,* 2) *material*, and 3) *competent.*

Relevancy means that a piece of evidence goes to demonstrate the truth or falsity of an issue before the court. What this basically means is that the evidence must be doing something useful in proving a disputed fact. Evidence that is not relevant would waste the court's time and potentially prejudice the defendant.

Materiality refers to the strength or importance of the evidence in supporting or falsifying an alleged fact.

Competency refers to the quality or trustworthiness of the evidence. If the credibility of a piece of evidence or the person offering it is in question, then the value of the evidence is discerning the truth severely diminished. The judge may determine that the evidence is so unreliable that it will not be admitted.

CHAIN OF CUSTODY

Chain of custody is a legal term that refers to the ability to guarantee the identity and integrity of evidence from collection through the presentation in court. It is a process used to maintain and document the chronological history of the evidence. Chain-of-custody documents should include the name of the person collecting the sample, each person or entities subsequently having custody of it, dates the items were collected or transferred, the collection location, a brief description of the item, and an identification number.

Evidence is considered to be in your custody when:

- The evidence is in your physical possession;
- The evidence is in your view, after being in your physical possession;
- The evidence is in your physical possession and then locked up so that tampering cannot occur;
- The evidence is kept in a secured area, with access restricted to authorized personnel only.

The exact chain of custody requirements will vary from jurisdiction to jurisdiction. Most departments and crime labs will have developed protocols that must be followed. The following are some general rules to keep in mind:

- Keep the number of people involved in collecting and handling the evidence to a minimum.
- Only allow people associated with the investigation to handle evidence.
- Always document the transfer of evidence from one person to another on chain-of-custody forms.
- Always accompany samples and data with their chain-of-custody forms.
- Give evidence items positive identification at all times that is legible and written with permanent ink.

Chain of custody is one of the most important tasks of the criminal investigator because if the chain of custody is broken, the evidence cannot be used in court.

LINKAGE CONCEPTS

Comparison samples are a generic term used to describe physical material/ evidence discovered at crime scenes that may be compared with samples from persons, tools, and physical locations. Comparison samples may be from either an unknown/questioned or a known source. Samples whose source is unknown/questioned are of three basic types: Recovered crime scene samples whose source is in question (e.g., evidence left by suspects, victims).

Questioned evidence that may have been transferred to an offender during the commission of the crime and taken away by him or her. Such questioned evidence can be compared with the evidence of a known source and can thereby be associated/linked to a person/vehicle/tool of a crime. Evidence of an unknown/questioned source recovered from several crime scenes may also be used to associate multiple offenses that were committed by the same person and/or with the same tool or weapon.

Samples whose source is known are of three basic types:

A **standard/reference sample** is material of a verifiable/documented source which, when compared with evidence of an unknown source, shows an association or linkage between an offender, crime scene, and/or victim (e.g., a carpet cutting taken from a location suspected as the point of transfer for comparison with the fibers recovered from the suspect's shoes, a sample of paint removed from a suspect's vehicle to be compared with paint found on a victim's vehicle following an accident, or a sample of the suspect's and/or victim's blood submitted for comparison with a bloodstained shirt recovered as evidence).

A **control/blank sample** is material of a known source that presumably was uncontaminated during the commission of the crime (e.g., a sample to be used in laboratory testing to ensure that the surface on which the sample is deposited does not interfere with testing. For example, when a bloodstain is collected from a carpet, a segment of unstained carpet must be collected for use as a blank or elimination sample).

An **elimination sample** is one of known source taken from a person who had lawful access to the scene (e.g., fingerprints from occupants, tire tread impressions from police vehicles, footwear impressions from emergency medical personnel) to be used for comparison with evidence of the same type.

SECTION 1.3

Preliminary Investigations

One of the most important aspects of securing a crime scene is to preserve the scene with minimal contamination and disturbance of any physical evidence present. This, as important as it may be, must be a secondary concern. Officer and public safety must be the first priority.

ARRIVAL AND APPROACH

The investigation begins the moment an officer is dispatched to the scene. The first responding officer should begin by making a note of all dispatch information, including the address, time, date, type of call, and any information known about parties involved. The officer should be alert from the onset, taking care to note any vehicles or persons leaving the vicinity of the crime scene, and those remaining near the crime scene that may be involved. The actual scene must be approached cautiously. Scan the area thoroughly, noting any possible secondary crime scenes. The officer should make an initial observation of the entire scene, assessing the scene for potential dangers to safety.

DEALING WITH EXIGENCIES

The initial responding officer must treat each crime scene as a crime in progress until he or she is sure that it is otherwise. The first priority is always to ensure there are no immediate threats to the officer's safety and the safety of other responders. The officer should carefully scan the area for sights, sounds, and smells that may indicate danger to personnel. These can include hazardous materials such as gasoline, anhydrous ammonia, and chemical solvents.

In cases where a safe response is beyond the reach of the responding officer's agency, an appropriate agency should be contacted immediately. Assistance from another agency is frequently required in cases of clandestine drug laboratories, biological weapons, and radiological or chemical threats. *Do not enter a scene if you have not been trained in proper safety procedures for that kind of scene.*

Aside from environmental threats, the perpetrator, accomplices, and other potentially dangerous individuals may be present at the scene. The environment must be considered hostile until a security sweep has proven otherwise. If the situation requires it, summon and wait for backup to arrive before entering the scene.

Once it has been determined that the scene is safe or has been made so, then other emergencies should be considered. Emergency medical treatment of those at the scene should be a second priority. Every effort should be made to reduce the risk of scene contamination during the administration of medical assistance. The officer should guide medical personnel through the scene, pointing out possible physical evidence and instructing them to make minimal contact with it.

Remember that bullet holes, knife tears, and so forth in clothing are potential evidence. Instruct medical personnel to cut *around* these potentially valuable sources of evidence. Any potential source of contamination or alteration of the appearance of the scene by emergency medical personnel should be documented. EMTs will usually move the victim, and this should be noted. They should be asked not to alter the scene in any way, such as by cleaning up.

If medical personnel were the first responders, make sure to note the name, unit, and contact information for all personnel at the scene. If the victim is removed, make sure to obtain information about where he or she is being taken from emergency medical personnel. If there is a chance that the victim may die, try to obtain a "dying declaration." If the victim or the suspect is transported to a hospital, attempt to send an officer with them to document any statements made and to preserve any evidence. If no officers are available, request that the ambulance personnel preserve evidence and document any comments.

HAS A CRIME BEEN COMMITTED?

An alleged crime scene should be treated as such until it can be determined otherwise. This issue should be carefully considered before time and resources are allotted to a potentially unnecessary investigation.

SECURITY AND CONTROL

The first responding officer has the challenging task of controlling *all* individuals at the scene. Individuals must be prevented from altering or destroying evidence. This is best accomplished by restricting movement through the scene unless necessary, such as with emergency medical personnel. The officer is also responsible for the safety of those at the scene.

The officer must also identify *all* individuals present at the scene. All nonessential personnel should be excluded from the scene. This includes officers not working the case, politicians, and the media. Bystanders should be removed from the scene, but only after determining that they are not witnesses. Victims and the family and friends of the victim must also be controlled, but with tact and compassion. Witnesses and suspects should both be secured and separated.

Before the scene can be properly protected, it must be identified and boundaries established. Crime scene perimeters are usually established by working outward from the focal point to include:

- Where the crime actually occurred
- Likely points of entry and exit of suspects and witnesses
- Places where the victim and evidence may have been moved

Where existing boundaries are available, such as walls, doors, and fences, they should be used. Where no preexisting boundaries exist, they should be established using anything available, from personnel and vehicles to cones and crime scene tape. Once the boundaries have been established, any person entering or leaving the scene should be documented.

Another early priority is to effect measures designed to protect evidence that may be lost or compromised. The elements can destroy evidence, as well as the activity of humans and animals. Rain, wind, sun, snow, vehicle traffic, footsteps, can all potentially destroy valuable evidence.

It is important to maintain the integrity of the scene from the very beginning. Often, contamination of the scene is done by police officers, mostly without thinking about the consequences. No one within the boundaries of a crime scene should engage in behaviors that alter or modify the scene. Examples are: Smoking, chewing tobacco, spitting, using telephones and bathrooms, eating, drinking, moving items, adjusting thermostats, opening windows and doors, touching things unnecessarily and without precautions (such as gloves), and littering.

CHANGE OF CONTROL

In most jurisdictions, investigators, not the first responder, will investigate the scene of serious crimes. When turning over control of the scene to investigators, the first responder should:

- Brief the investigators taking charge
- Assist in controlling the scene if necessary
- Turn over documentation such as entry/exit logs
- Remain at the scene until relieved of duty

An important consideration for the lead investigator is the composition of the crime scene team. In many cases, a lone investigator can do an adequate job of processing the scene. In others, however, the scope and complexity of the scene may dictate that additional human resources are required. Additional personnel will often be necessary when there are multiple scenes, multiple victims, or numerous witnesses.

Circumstances where forensic evidence dictates the assistance of additional resources often arise. Keep in mind that the scene must remain secure, and entry and exit documentation must still be maintained. Specialized tasks should be performed by persons with expertise in those areas. Even basic tasks such as photography, sketching, print lifting, and evidence collection require specialized skills. When specific team members are assigned to specific tasks, the lead investigator should document those assignments.

FIRST RESPONDER DOCUMENTATION

The initial responding officers should carefully document their actions before and upon arrival at the scene. It is critical that these things be documented as quickly as possible after the event such that the information is preserved. Observations about the scene, such as the location of items and persons within the scene and the appearance of the scene upon arrival should be recorded. It is also critical to note things that are time-sensitive, such as the temperature, weather, and time of day.

Conditions that may have changed or deteriorated with time (such as smells and the presence of ice) should be noted. Also important are things that have changed or been contaminated by the first responder, such as whether doors were initially open or closed. Personal and contact information form victims, witnesses, and suspects should be recorded, along with any statements or comments they made. Finally, the initial responding officer should record his or her own actions at the scene, as well as those of others present, such as emergency medical personnel.

INVESTIGATOR SCENE ASSESSMENT

Once the scene has been turned over to the investigators (or it has been decided that the initial responder will be conducting the investigation), the investigators must make an initial assessment of the scene. The first priority will generally be to talk with the first responder regarding his or her observations about the scene. Second, the investigator should verify that the first responder has conducted a protective sweep of the scene, and that it has been properly secured. Following this, the investigator should survey the scene for environmental hazards, such as the presence of blood that may contain blood borne pathogens.

Once the scene has been determined to be safe and all medical emergencies have been taken care of, then the exigency exception to the search warrant requirement has ceased to be valid. Investigators should evaluate the search and seizure issues carefully and determine the necessity of obtaining either consent or a search warrant. Contrary to popular belief, *there is no general "crime scene exception" to the search warrant requirement. When in doubt, obtain a warrant.*

Once it is determined that a search of the scene will be lawful, the next order of business is to establish a path of entry and exit to the scene to be used by authorized personnel. The initial boundaries of the scene should be reevaluated and expanded if necessary.

The investigator will also want to establish a secure area within close proximity to the scene for the purpose of consultation and equipment staging. In the same or a slightly different area, a temporary evidence storage area should be established. This must be done with consideration of the rules of evidence, with special attention being paid to chain of custody issues. If there are multiple scenes, then communication must be established between the investigators at all scenes.

During the scene assessment by the investigator, the need for additional investigative resources must be considered. During this phase of the assessment, consider the need for legal consultation (usually the prosecutor's office), specialized scientific consultation (such as crime lab requirements and capabilities), and the investigative aid of another agency. If an investigator realized that he or she lacks the necessary training and equipment to adequately investigate a particular crime, then the assistance of another should immediately be sought.

The investigator must also continue to maintain the integrity of the scene. The entry and exit of authorized personnel must still be documented, and unauthorized persons must be kept out of the scene. The area around the scene should be canvassed, and the results should be documented.

SCENE WALK-THROUGH

Conducting a walk-through provides the investigator with an overview of the entire scene. This knowledge is necessary to effectively manage the evidence collection process. Fragile and perishable evidence must be collected first. Evidence that may be compromised must be given first priority for documentation, photographing, and collection.

During this walk-through, the investigator must take care to use the established entry path, taking care to avoid contamination. Preliminary documentation of the scene should be prepared as the scene is being observed. It is important to document how the scene was found before any evidence is moved or collected.

CONTAMINATION CONTROL

After safety, contamination control is one of the most important things for the crime scene investigator to consider. In fact, these issues are intricately related. Physical, biological, and chemical hazards at the scene threaten the health and safety of the investigator. Contamination of the evidence by personnel at the scene will generally result in the inability to use evidence in court. Thus, the prevention of contamination is essential for the safety of personnel and the integrity of evidence.

The easiest culprits to eliminate are nonessential personnel. As previously indicated, all nonessential personnel must be kept out of the scene. Those that are essential must follow the established entry and exit routes. When contamination is likely, such as when EMTs have been at the scene, the investigator should consider collecting elimination samples from these individuals. Elimination samples are samples such as fingerprints and DNA taken those known to have been at the scene and known not to have been involved in the crime, such as victims, investigators, and emergency medical personnel.

The use of personal protective equipment (PPE) is essential to the prevention of contamination of both the scene and personnel at the scene. PPE consists of a wide variety of equipment designed to protect the user from hazards in the environment, such as gloves, respirators, and safety goggles. The use of gloves (usually latex or nitrile) is recommended at every scene.

Gloves protect the user from hazards in the environment (such as blood borne pathogens), and protect the integrity of evidence by preventing the transfer of fingerprints and DNA. It must be remembered that in performing its function, PPE becomes contaminated. Equipment must be sanitized between uses, or else disposed of and replaced. Most experts agree that single-use equipment should be used for the direct collection of biological samples.

Scene Arrival Procedural Summary

- Note or log dispatch all dispatch information.
- Be aware of any persons or vehicles leaving the crime scene.
- Approach the scene cautiously; scan the entire area, assessing the scene.
- Note any possible secondary crime scenes.
- Be aware of any persons and vehicles in the vicinity that may be related to the crime.
- Make initial observations (look, listen, smell) to ensure officer safety.
- Remain alert and attentive.

19

- Assume the crime is ongoing until determined to be otherwise.
- Treat the location as a crime scene until assessed and determined to be otherwise.
- Safely direct additional responding units into the area.

Officer Safety Procedural Summary

- Ensure that there is no immediate threat to other responders; scan the area for sights, sounds, and smells that may present danger to personnel (e.g., hazardous materials such as gasoline, natural gas).
- If the situation involves a clandestine drug laboratory, biological weapons, or radiological or chemical threats, contact the appropriate personnel or agency before entering the scene.
- Approach the scene in a way calculated to reduce the risk of harm to officers while maximizing the safety of victims, witnesses, and others in the area.
- Survey the scene for dangerous persons and control the situation.
- Notify supervisory personnel and call for assistance and backup as necessary.

Emergency Care Procedural Summary

- If victims are present, assess them for signs of life and medical needs, and provide immediate medical attention.
- Call for medical personnel.
- Guide medical personnel to the victim in a way that minimizes contamination of the crime scene.
- Point out potential physical evidence to medical personnel, instruct them to minimize contact with such evidence (e.g., ensure that medical personnel preserve all clothing and personal effects without cutting through bullet holes, knife tears), and document movement of persons or items by medical personnel.
- Instruct medical personnel not to "clean up" the scene and to avoid removal or alteration of items originating from the scene.
- If medical personnel arrived first, obtain the name, unit, and telephone number of attending personnel, and the name and location of the medical facility where the victim is to be taken.
- In some instances, fingerprint and shoe impressions of medical personnel may need to be taken for elimination purposes.

- If there is a chance the victim may die, attempt to obtain "dying declaration."
- Document any statements/comments made by victims, suspects, or witnesses at the scene.
- If the victim or suspect is transported to a medical facility, send a law enforcement official with the victim or suspect to document any comments made and preserve evidence. (If no officers are available to accompany the victim/suspect, stay at the scene and request medical personnel to preserve evidence and document any comments made by the victim or suspect.)
- Safeguard evidence, such as a weapon, that is taken into custody.
- Follow chain-of-custody procedures as soon as the evidence is confiscated.

Scene Control Procedural Summary

- Control all individuals at the scene—prevent individuals from altering or destroying physical evidence by restricting movement.
- Identify all individuals at the scene.
- Suspects and witnesses should be separated, and bystanders should be questioned to determine if they are witnesses.
- Victims, family, and friends need to be controlled, but in a way that shows compassion.
- Exclude unauthorized and nonessential personnel from the scene (e.g., law enforcement officials not working the case, politicians, media).

Boundary Procedural Summary

- Establish boundaries of the scene(s), starting at the focal point and extending outward to include Where the crime occurred, potential points and paths of exit and entry of suspects and witnesses, places where the victim or evidence may have been moved (be aware of trace and impression evidence while assessing the scene).
- Secure the scene. Set up physical barriers (e.g., ropes, cones, crime scene barrier tape, available vehicles, personnel, other equipment) or use existing boundaries (e.g., doors, walls, gates).
- Document the entry/exit of all people entering and leaving the scene, once boundaries have been established.
- Protect the scene. Control the flow of personnel and animals entering and leaving the scene to maintain integrity of the scene. Institute measures to preserve/protect evidence that may be lost or compromised (e.g., protect

from the elements (rain, snow, wind) and from footsteps, tire tracks, sprinklers).

- Document the original location of the victim or any objects that you observe being moved.
- Consider search and seizure issues to determine the necessity of obtaining consent to search and/or obtaining a search warrant. Remember: *There is no crime scene exception to the search warrant requirement.*

Chance of Control Procedural Summary

- Brief the investigator(s) taking charge.
- Assist in controlling the scene.
- Turn over responsibility for the documentation of entry/exit.
- Remain at the scene until relieved of duty.

Documentation Procedural Summary

- Document observations of the crime scene, including the location of persons and items within the crime scene and the appearance and condition of the scene upon arrival.
- Document conditions upon arrival (e.g., lights on/off; shades up/down, open/closed; doors and windows open/closed; smells; ice, liquids; movable furniture; weather; temperature; and personal items.)
- Document personal information from witnesses, victims, suspects and any statements or comments made.
- Document your own actions and actions of others.

REFERENCES AND FURTHER READING

Technical Working Group on Crime Scene Investigation. (2000). *Crime Scene Investigation: A Guide for Law Enforcement.* Available:
https://www.ncjrs.gov/pdffiles1/nij/178280.pdf

SECTION 1.4

The Investigator at the Crime Scene

T In most cases, the investigator will arrive at a crime scene after first responders have conducted a preliminary investigation. The investigator will often be the senior officer on the scene and will be the most experienced and best-trained officer on the scene. While the scene is still active, it falls on the investigator to provide leadership to junior officers, review the tasks completed by the first responder, and ultimately to conduct the in-depth investigation.

CRIME SCENE DEBRIEFING TEAM

The crime scene debriefing enables law enforcement personnel and other responders to share information regarding particular scene findings before releasing the scene. It provides an opportunity for input regarding follow-up investigation, special requests for assistance, and the establishment of post-scene responsibilities.

Establish a crime scene debriefing team, which includes the investigator(s) in charge of the crime scene, other investigators and evidence collection personnel (e.g., photographers, evidence technicians, latent print personnel, specialized personnel, and initial responding officer(s) if still present). Determine what evidence was collected. Discuss preliminary scene findings with team members. Discuss potential technical forensic testing and the sequence of tests to be performed. Initiate any action(s) identified in the discussion that are required to complete the crime scene investigation.

Brief person(s) in charge upon completion of assigned crime scene tasks. Establish post-scene responsibilities for law enforcement personnel and other responders. Summary: The crime scene debriefing is the best opportunity for law enforcement personnel and other responders to ensure that the crime scene investigation is complete.

FINAL SURVEY OF THE CRIME SCENE

A final survey of the crime scene ensures that evidence has been collected and the scene has been processed before release. Also, a systematic review of the scene ensures that evidence, equipment, or materials generated by the investigation are not inadvertently left behind and any dangerous materials or conditions have been reported and addressed.

The investigator in charge should ensure that each area identified as part of the crime scene is visually inspected. All evidence collected at the scene is accounted for. All equipment and materials generated by the investigation are removed. Any dangerous materials or conditions are reported and addressed. The crime scene is released by jurisdictional requirements. Consider taking photographs depicting the condition of the scene at the time.

Conducting a scene walk-through ensures that all evidence has been collected, that materials are not inadvertently left behind, and that any dangerous materials or conditions have been reported and addressed.

CRIME SCENE DOCUMENTATION

Compiling reports and other documentation about the crime scene investigation into a "case file" provides a record of the actions taken and evidence collected at the scene. This documentation allows for an independent review of the work conducted.

The investigator in charge should obtain the following for the crime scene case file:

- Initial responding officer(s') documentation.
- Emergency medical personnel documents.
- Entry/exit documentation.
- Photographs/videos.
- Crime scene sketches/diagrams.
- Evidence Documentation.
- Other responders' documentation.
- Record of the consent form or search warrant.
- Reports such as forensic/technical reports, when they become available.

The above list is limited to crime scene documentation. This should not be considered a comprehensive list of the documents involved in an investigative case file.

This procedure will ensure that reports and other documentation about the crime scene investigation are compiled into a case file by the investigator in charge of the crime scene and allow for an independent review of the work conducted.

SPECIAL CIRCUMSTANCES

While all crime scene investigations pose their individual complexities, some situations may involve atypical crime scene locations or requirements for which law enforcement personnel and other responders should be aware. Crime scene investigators should adjust their approach to an investigation to warrant specific needs of the investigation, which includes:

- Crime Scenes in correctional and custodial facilities
- Crime scenes in which the safety of the crime scene investigators must be considered in the approach to the time spent at the scene.

CRIME SCENE TIME LIMITS

In some instances, deteriorating security or environmental conditions limit the amount of time available for the investigation of the crime scene. While these time limits will not allow for a thorough crime scene investigation to be conducted, the following procedure will maximize the use of the limited time on site. In such circumstances, preparation before staging or entry into the crime scene area is paramount. This could include a site survey (e.g., in-person, photographic, photogrammetric or videographic) before the team's arrival at the scene or conducting extensive interviews of any witnesses from the area.

Elements of this preparation and execution are designed to:

- Determine the time available to remain at the crime scene based on knowledge of time-limiting factors.
- Determine the most critical objective of being on the site of the investigation (e.g., removal of a deceased body, identification of a suspect, collection of explosive residue)
- Determine the equipment needed to fulfill the objective.
- Pre-package from established crime scene collection kits a ready-kit for this specific event.
- Determine any specialized personnel that may be needed on-scene for this investigation.
- Develop a documentation and collection plan to include:

    1. Type and nature of documentation expected
    2. Priority of evidence collection
    3. Responsibility for onsite collection
    4. Responsibility for evidence custody

COMMAND POST

The investigator in charge should set up a temporary command post in a location where media can take necessary photographs without jeopardizing the scene (and evidence) security. If circumstances and policy dictate transfer of the scene to another investigator, the investigator in charge should notify investigators or appropriate departments (such as Homicide) of information gathered at the crime scene. Details of the scene are discussed in this step.

The investigator in charge should notify the Communications Department (Dispatch) of phone numbers at the command post. The Communications Department should be asked to notify surrounding agencies and send teletypes regionally and nationally when a suspect has fled the scene.

These alerts should include a description of the suspect, vehicles involved, and contact information for the person these agencies should contact if they locate the suspect. The investigator in charge should brief the supervisor as required by departmental policy. The first responder, as well as any other officers at the scene, should be debriefed.

When crime scenes are large and complex, necessary procedures will dictate that the investigator will need assistance processing and securing the scene. The investigator in charge should make necessary duty assignments and record each on a formal assignment sheet. The assignment sheet should be updated to record assignment updates throughout the investigation. The assignment sheet should be available to all personnel working on the case. Typical assignments include an evidence recorder and an entry/exit recorder (who is also responsible for keeping event timetable).

An early priority should be to establish the status and locations of victims and suspects. Also, the status of bulletins that have been broadcast regarding victims and suspects should be established. The investigator in charge will also want to ensure that missing suspect alerts are broadcast.

The investigator in charge will also want to establish a schedule for investigative team meetings (including all uniformed officers), during which status will be given, assignment updates will be made, and other key information will be shared.

Witness Management Procedural Summary

- Interview any witnesses at the scene separately to best use their reported experiences to benefit the overall investigation.
- Obtain written/recorded statements from each witness at the police station.
- Transport each witness to the police station separately from other witnesses or suspects.
- When possible, the following tasks should be performed by the Supervising Officer:

1. Establish the status and locations of each victim and suspect.
2. Establish the status of bulletins that have been broadcast regarding each victim and suspect.
3. Ensure that any necessary missing suspect alert is broadcast promptly.

Scene Assessment Procedural Summary

- Converse with the first responder(s) regarding observations/activities.
- Evaluate safety issues that may affect all personnel entering the scene(s) (e.g., blood-borne pathogens, hazards).
- Evaluate search and seizure issues to determine the necessity of obtaining consent to search and/or obtain a search warrant.
- Evaluate and establish a path of entry/exit to the scene to be utilized by authorized personnel.
- Evaluate initial scene boundaries.
- Determine the number/size of the scene(s) and prioritize.
- Establish a secure area within close proximity to the scene(s) for the purpose of consultation and equipment staging.

- If multiple scenes exist, establish and maintain communication with personnel at those locations.
- Establish a secure area for temporary evidence storage by rules of evidence/chain of custody.
- Determine and request additional investigative resources as required (e.g., personnel/specialized units, legal consultation/ prosecutors, equipment).
- Ensure continued scene integrity (e.g., document entry/exit of authorized personnel, prevent unauthorized access to the scene).
- Ensure that witnesses to the incident are identified and separated (e.g., obtain valid ID).
- Ensure the surrounding area is canvassed, and the results are documented.
- Ensure preliminary documentation/photography of the scene, injured persons and vehicles.

Walk-through Procedural Summary

- Avoid contaminating the scene by using the established path of entry. Consider whether personal protective equipment (PPE) should be used.
- Prepare preliminary documentation (e.g. notes, rough sketches) of the scene as observed. Identify and protect fragile and/or perishable evidence (e.g., consider climatic conditions, crowds/hostile environment).
- Ensure that all evidence that may be compromised is immediately documented, photographed and collected.
- When involved in the initial walkthrough, note the condition of the scene. Record relevant observations, which may include things such as Ceilings, doors, including entry and exit points. Are they open, closed, locked or forced? On which side was the key?
- Windows: Are they open or closed? Is there broken glass? Were they locked or forced open?
- Lights: On or off? If left on, which lights were on?
- Shades or shutters: Open or closed?

- Floors/Rugs
- Interior lighting conditions
- Odors: Cigarette smoke, gas, powder, perfume, etc.
- Description of perpetrator (when present)
- Description of crime-related people present
- Description of emergency medical or search-and-rescue personnel present
- Weapons observed
- Furniture present, including location relative to victim, as applicable and overall scene
- Signs of activity: Meal preparation, dishes in sink, condition of housekeeping (clean, dirty or items in disarray), appliances left on, television/stereo left on (note the channel), etc.
- Date and time indicators: Mail, newspapers, dates on milk cartons, stopped clocks, spoiled foods, items that should have been hot or cold, but are at room temperature
- Temperature of the room and environmental conditions
- Develop a general theory of the crime

Team Composition Procedural Summary

- Assess the need for additional personnel.
- Be aware of the need for additional personnel in cases involving multiple scenes, multiple victims, numerous witnesses or unique circumstances.
- Assess forensic needs and call forensic specialists to the scene for expertise and/or equipment.
- Ensure that scene security and the entry/exit documentation are continued.
- Select qualified person(s) to perform specialized tasks (e.g., photography, sketch, latent prints, evidence collection).
- Document team members and assignments.

Contamination Control Procedural Summary

- Limit scene access to people directly involved in scene processing.

- Follow established entry/exit routes at the scene.
- Identify first responders and consider the collection of elimination samples.
- Designate a secure area for trash and equipment.
- Use personal protective equipment (PPE) to prevent contamination of personnel and minimize scene contamination.
- Clean/sanitize or dispose of tools/equipment and personal protective equipment between each item of evidence collection and/or scenes.
- Utilize single-use equipment when performing a direct collection of biological samples.

SECTION 1.5

Crime Scene Procedures

I f you ask any experienced detective or crime scene technician to identify the top five most serious and common problems they find at crime scenes, you will inevitably hear the same response within those five: Curious officers, supervisors, and detectives contaminate crime scenes with disturbing regularity.

The inadvertent contamination of crime scenes is a serious problem that will not go away without effective departmental policies that are explained and reinforced through rigorous training. This training needs to include all police officers and support staff, not just crime scene technicians and detectives. First responders are obviously the first on the scene, and they will frequently contaminate scenes if they are not trained in proper protocols.

Hollywood has generated a multitude of myths about criminal justice, and crime scene investigation has not escaped the trend of misinformation. Television murder scenes are always staffed by a dozen or so uniformed officers, several detectives, an (often angry) lieutenant, and a few crime scene technicians wandering around snapping random pictures and dusting (haphazardly) for fingerprints. This is precisely the opposite of what should occur. Absolutely no one who is not necessary to carry out the investigation should be allowed into an active crime scene.

A horde of curious officers stampeding a crime scene is a recipe for disaster. Few things can damage an investigation more seriously and irrevocably. The more sensitive the type of evidence, the more serious the problem of contamination becomes. DNA analysis, blood splatter interpretation, and the analysis of trace evidence becomes much more difficult if not impossible.

Collecting hair samples, for example, becomes an exercise in futility when twenty officers have passed through the search space. Footwear, tire tracks, and other impression evidence can become worthless, even on the fringes of the crime scene when many unnecessary personnel are mulling about.

SUPERVISORY ROLE

The first line of defense for crime scene integrity comes from supervisory personnel setting good policy and good examples for line officers. Ultimately, supervisory personnel, including detectives, are responsible for investigations. Investigators who severely curtail access to active crime scenes do so to preserve the scientific integrity of forensic evidence, as well as preserving the legal integrity of the evidence so that it will later be admissible in court.

The behavior of supervisory personnel can go a long way in teaching curious officers to stay away from crime scenes to avoid contamination. Leaders must be self-disciplined enough to follow departmental policies (which need to be based on best practices) such as rigorously maintaining entry and exit logs, not entering a crime scene without a legitimate investigative purpose, and so forth. Peeking in cabinets and digging around in drawers sets the opposite example, and ultimately degrades the overall professionalism of the department.

WRITTEN POLICIES

Another major responsibility of departmental leadership is to develop clear policies concerning crime scene protection and preservation. The policy cannot be taken lightly; it needs to have the same force as other departmental policies, and supervisory personnel needs to make sure that the policy is carefully followed by all officers. It is easy to forget that patrol officers are the first ones on most scenes and that they need to be trained and guided into correctly securing, protecting, and preserving crime scenes.

It must be made known to all officers, regardless of rank, that inquisitiveness is no excuse for entering a crime scene without an investigative role to play. When formulating policy, administrators would be wise to consult district attorneys that have lost cases due to crime scene contamination. Also, crime laboratory staff should be considered as well.

A key goal of a crime scene policy should be to provide a set of uniform procedures to restrict unnecessary access to active crime scenes. A necessary element of such a policy is that a single point of entry should be established and that the officer assigned to that main entrance must log every person entering and exiting the scene, along with the time of the entry or exist.

Along with the person's name and rank, the reason for the visit should be recorded. A policy (and the related standardized form) that asks the purpose of entering the scene serves as a reminder that only persons with legitimate investigative roles should enter. The policy must absolutely prohibit entry by all undocumented persons.

The policy should direct all officers (and civilian support staff if applicable) entering the scene to write a standardized report detailing what they did at the scene. Anyone entering the scene must make themselves available to produce elimination samples (e.g., hairs, fingerprints, and saliva).

To eliminate "tourism" at crime scenes, many departments have adopted a policy that requires the highest ranking officer to enter the scene to take responsibility for all personnel at the scene. This means that high-ranking officers wanting to "have a look around" cannot leave the scene until all other officers and technicians have finished their work or an officer of higher rank arrives.

Often, the officer tasked with security of the scene will be a patrol officer who is placed in the untenable position of telling higher-ranking officers not to enter the scene. Clear, written policies can go a long way in protecting the integrity of the scene. Senior staff should keep those power dynamics in mind when drafting policies that not only look good on paper but which can be implemented by officers in the field.

Ultimately, even the best-designed policies are useless if they are not properly implemented in the field. Every officer within a department, not just detectives, must understand the high cost of crime scene contamination. Best practices dictate that rookie officers be trained on crime scene protection and the preservation of evidence at the academy and that these important lessons be reinforced through in-service training at periodic intervals.

REFERENCES AND FURTHER READING

Technical Working Group on Crime Scene Investigation. (2000). *Crime Scene Investigation: A Guide for Law Enforcement*.
Available: https://www.ncjrs.gov/pdffiles1/nij/178280.pdf

SECTION 2

Crime Scene Documentation

Physical evidence has the potential to play a critical role in the investigation and resolution of a crime. For this potential to be realized, action must be taken early on at the crime scene. It is critical that physical evidence is properly collected, documented, and preserved. Increasingly advanced technologies have given investigators a much wider array of tools, but have also place added importance on proper collection and preservation techniques.

For evidence to ultimately have a significant role in court, it is critical that investigators follow an "objective, thorough, and thoughtful approach" (NIJ Technical Working Group on Crime Scene Investigation, 2000, p. 1).

To understand what evidence is used for and thus what is appropriate evidence to collect, the uses of evidence must be considered. Physical evidence can be used to help **reconstruct** the crime scene, help determine if a crime has actually occurred, help link a suspect to a victim, help link a suspect to a crime scene, help link **serial crimes**, provide investigative leads, and provide facts to a jury. Note the prevalence of the term *link*. It is safe to say that a major function of physical evidence is to provide linkages that, taken together, indicate guilt. It is rare that an investigator will encounter a crime where there is direct evidence of a suspect's guilt.

Rather, the proof beyond a reasonable doubt necessary in court is established by a series of circumstantial evidence items demonstrate guilt only when taken together as a whole. For example, a suspect's fingerprint on a gun does not prove guilt directly. Standing alone, this evidence is not very compelling. But if we add to this the fact that the bullet removed from the victim's body came from that gun and the facts that the suspect had the motivation and opportunity to kill the victim, the overall picture becomes much more convincing.

Physical evidence can be categorized in several ways. One particularly useful way to do this is to consider the physical nature of the evidence. This often dictates which type of forensic science specialist will analyze the evidence when an investigator sends it to the crime lab. Common categories include **drug evidence**, **friction ridge** evidence (fingerprints, palm prints, footprints, etc.), **firearm evidence**, **biological evidence** (blood, semen, etc.), **trace evidence** (microscopic transfer evidence), document evidence (paper, inks, handwriting, etc.), **physical matching** evidence, and **toxicology** evidence.

As the old saying goes, "it's not what you know; it's what you can prove." For the investigator, this means that no amount of keen observation and brilliant analysis is worth anything if it is not properly documented for presentation in court. A part of the investigator's initial assessment of the scene should be to determine what kind of documentation will be necessary. Remember another important rule of criminal investigations: **"If it ain't on paper, it didn't happen."**

Crime scene processing involves more than merely taking photographs and locating trace evidence. A good detective (or crime scene technician) evaluates the scene to discover what precisely happened, the sequence of events, and if those findings corroborate the statements of victims and witnesses. In addition to these basic tasks, the detective must be alert to *anything* that may connect the suspect to the crime. This requires a very high level of awareness and hyper-focused attention to detail.

DOCUMENTATION SUMMARY

- Review the assessment of the scene to determine the type of documentation needed.
- Coordinate photographs, video, sketches, measurements, and notes.
- Photograph (see Photography section for details the scene utilizing overall, medium, and close-up coverage.
- Photograph evidence to be collected with and without measurement scale and/or evidence identifiers.
- Photograph victims, suspects, witnesses, crowd and vehicles. Consider photographs with additional perspectives (e.g., aerial photographs, witness's view, the area under the body once the body is removed).
- Record video as an optional supplement to photographs
- Prepare preliminary sketches that include measurements of the immediate area of the scene, (noting case identifiers and indicating north on the sketch).
- Sketches should show the relative location of items of evidence, correlating evidence items with evidence records before movement.
- Sketches should show rooms, furniture, or other objects.
- Sketches should show the distance to adjacent buildings or other landmarks.

- Generate notes at the scene that document the location of the scene, time of arrival, and time of departure.
- Notes should describe the scene as it appears.
- Notes should record transient evidence (e.g., smells, sounds, sights) and conditions (e.g., temperature, weather).
- Notes should document circumstances that require a departure from usual procedures.

SECTION 2.1

Crime Scene Photography

A series of poorly planned, poorly executed, and poorly displayed photographs have the potential to directly affect the success of other facets of the crime scene investigation. Therefore, crime scene photography is a major component of the entire investigation process. The most basic purpose of crime scene photography is to create a visual record of the crime scene, which ideally includes all pertinent features. In other words, the pictures should tell the "story" of the crime scene; they should recreate the scene in the mind's eye of the finder of facts. In keeping with this purpose, it is important that the scene is recorded (as much as reasonably possible) before it is disturbed. Good crime scene photography depicts the original, uncontaminated features of the scene.

Completeness is of critical importance. In days gone by, the cost of the film was a factor in deciding what to photograph and how many photographs to take. Training manuals stated that this factor should be placed as a secondary consideration after completeness. In the modern era of digital photography, there is no excuse for insufficient photographic documentation.

If a potential photograph has the slightest possibility of being useful later in the investigation, take it. Always remember that crime scenes are tricky and your initial theories about what is important may later prove incorrect. When your theory of what happened at a particular scene is reevaluated, what at first glance seemed inconsequential may become critically important to the investigation.

Crime scene photography will utilize overall (long-range), medium (mid-range), and close-up coverage. That is, the compilation of photographs will progress from the very general to the very specific. These ideas should be applied to the crime scene as a whole, as well as to each individual segment of the crime scene.

Thus, a long-range photograph of a large building would constitute an overall or long-range shot, as would a photograph of a long hallway leading to the particular room within that building where a crime took place. In other words, the meaning of the various range descriptors used in crime scene photography is fluid, and the exact meaning will depend on the nature of the overall scene as well as the particular segments of that scene that are important to recreating the story of what happened there. The use of the term "segments" suggests that crimes generally happen in multiple steps, and each step should be considered and photographed separately.

Long-range photographs should provide the viewer with an overall impression of the scene as if they were viewing it from a standing position. In other words, it should record as accurately as possible what the first responder saw when she first arrived at the scene. This is usually best accomplished by taking photographs from eye level. The camera should be a sufficient distance from the scene to capture as much of the area of interest as possible in a single photograph.

Mid-range photographs are usually taken from a range of ten to twenty feet from the subject matter. The range is dictated by what the photographer is trying to accomplish: The mid-range photographs should establish the location of the subject matter within the larger crime scene. Thus, enough of the area surrounding the subject matter must be included to achieve this effect.

Close-up photographs are usually taken within five feet of the subject matter. The purpose of close-up photographs is to provide details about items of interest that were not readily apparent in the mid-range and long-range photographs.

Each item of evidence to be collected should be photographed twice: Once without measurement scales and evidence identifiers, and again with those investigative tools present. The photographs taken with measurement scales present are critical in facilitating the recreation of size and spatial relationships. The photographs without scales are "uncluttered," and may be demanded by the court.

Many investigators find it valuable to include the vantage point of each photograph within the sketch of the scene. In this way, disputes about camera angles that arise in court can easily be sorted out. Some authors recommend attaching such a sketch to each photograph with the camera location clearly marked in colored ink on that sketch.

The question of what exactly to photograph can be answered by keeping several facets of the investigative process in mind. Photographs must answer questions about the location of the crime, the nature of the crime, the results of the crime, the evidence existing at the scene, and follow-up tasks that are not directly related to the crime scene.

The location of the crime photographs should depict the overall crime scene, placing points of entry, potential exit points, and specific areas of interest within an overall picture. Aerial photographs, exterior pictures of buildings, and the like are examples of this idea. Extend this idea into a dwelling or other building to place rooms in relation to each other, such as the progress of a crime from a living room, down a hall, and into a bedroom.

The nature of the crime photographs should provide information to the investigator as to what type of crime occurred. They should also differentiate between types of crimes as well as differentiate between crimes and acts that are not actually crimes. For instance, investigators are often called upon to determine if a death was the result of homicide or suicide. Pictures that show the trajectory of bullets and the nature of the wound will be vital in this determination.

The results of the crime may be simple and straightforward or they may have several elements. For example, in a rape case, the rape may have been preceded by a breaking and entering, an assault, vandalism, and myriad other acts by the perpetrator. The photographs must present the results of each of these acts in a logical progression that recreates the sequence of events that occurred during the commission of the crimes.

The physical evidence of the crime is arguably the most important series of photographs that the investigator will take. These are necessary to facilitate the connection between the evidence, the accused, and the crime scene in court.

The follow-up photographs can be considered an extension of the crime scene investigation. Autopsy photos and photographs of bruising on living victims are common examples of this type of forensic photography. In addition, victims, suspects, witnesses, crowds, and vehicles should be photographed.

The need to photographically document additional perspectives should be considered. The perspectives of witnesses may be useful in court. Aerial photographs may be useful, especially with large, outdoor crime scenes. The area under a body should always be photographed once the body is moved.

A shoebox full of photographs is obviously not useful in court. The courtroom presentation of crime scene photographs must be organized and logical. Items of evidence must be related to photographs. To accomplish these organizational and relational goals, it is critical that investigators keep a log of all photographs taken at a crime scene. The log should contain a complete record of the record of all photographic efforts at the crime scene.

To be admissible in court, photographic evidence must meet four legal standards: It must provide accurate representations, it must be free of distortion, it must be material and relevant, and it must be unbiased. In addition, the photographs must follow what has been informally called the maggot rule. The idea is that the probative value of the photograph must outweigh its prejudicial effect against the defendant. If a particular photograph depicts the gruesome nature of the scene and is likely to "excite" the viewer, it may be thrown out by the court because the prejudicial effects of such a photograph outweigh its value as a source of truth.

PHOTOGRAPHING THE DECEASED

Before the body of a deceased person is moved, it should be photographed. Take photographs from all possible angles. Show a facial view, and the positions of the hands and feet when possible to do so without altering the body, its clothing or position. Wound photography should be conducted at close-up range. Take photographs while moving around the body and from an overhead perspective.

Photograph the body from two perspectives, when possible: As though looking at the body from a standing position From the same level as the body is lying, such as at ground level when the body is lying on the ground. Use oblique lighting to show wounds on the body, such as bite marks, with and without a scale. After the deceased has been removed from the scene, photograph the area where the body was. Signs of activity can include:

- TV and room lights turned on
- A glass holding a cold beverage (ice melting or still frozen) and a plate with fresh food on it
- Scattered clothing, magazines, or other objects
- A landline phone that was in use and is making a loud notification sound
- Misplaced furniture, as with a tipped stool beside a body
- Cigarettes, lit or remains piled in an ashtray
- Tool marks in an unusual location or near entry/exit
- Shoeprints and/or fingerprints
- Drug paraphernalia

Include the time that photographing was begun and completed in the notes. Remove the film or download the digital images and store in a secure location according to departmental regulations.

IMPRESSION EVIDENCE

Tire Impressions: For tire impressions, take a series of overlapping photographs showing the tire's entire circumference.

Impressions on Glass: When the impression is on glass and when possible: Protect latent prints Position a colored card or piece of cloth that contrasts with the impression behind the glass Include in notes that this approach was used for contrast purposes to obtain the photograph.

Impressions on a Mirror: When the impression is on a mirror, hold the flash to the side (oblique lighting); use a tripod to avoid being in the photograph.

Dust Impressions: When photographing a dust impression or an impression in a soft material (e.g., wax or putty), use reflective lighting (also known as oblique lighting). When using reflective lighting, if a detail does not appear sufficiently, block the ambient light and then experiment with positioning the light or flash in other locations until the desired result is achieved.

Impressions on a Porous Surface: When the impression is on a porous surface, position the light or flash wherever the best results or contrast can be achieved, such as at a 90-degree angle from the impression. Photograph bloodstains or other bodily fluid stains using color film or digital camera. Carefully place the camera plane perpendicular to the plane of the stain and ruler. Stay alert to the location of the bloodstains, so equipment is not inadvertently touched to the stain.

It is extremely important that the ruler is on the same plane as the impression. If the stain is on a wall, use an adhesive label with a ruler on it. Otherwise, tape a ruler beside the stain, or have an assistant hold the ruler beside the stain. Indicate upward direction. Ensure that the camera lens is perpendicular (90 degrees) to the subject. Adjust lighting when photographing the stain to obtain the best contrast and result.

When the stain is on glass, position a colored card or piece of cloth that contrasts with the stain behind the glass, making sure to protect latent prints; include in the notes that this approach was used for contrast purposes of obtaining the photograph. When the stain is on a mirror, hold the flash off to the side (oblique lighting) and use a tripod to avoid being in the photograph. The camera will show in the photograph when the mirror is 90 degrees from the lens.

CLOSE UP PHOTOGRAPHY TECHNIQUES

If not using a digital camera, photograph wounds using color film. Carefully place the camera perpendicular relative to the wounds to obtain accurate measurements. Photograph the body of a deceased person before moving it and also photograph it at the morgue. Include scales where appropriate. Adjust lighting when photographing the wounds to obtain the best contrast and result.

Take multiple shots with the light held or placed at different angles to the subject to achieve the best results. Retake photographs of wounds such as bruises at different intervals to capture changes, such as in color, over several days. Photograph serial numbers on weapons or VIN numbers on vehicles: Carefully place the ruler, camera and placard relative to the item to obtain accurately scaled photographs. Place placard and ruler on the same plane as the weapon.

It is extremely important when the photo needs to be accurately scaled, that the ruler is on the same plane as the subject. The camera lens should be perpendicular (90 degrees) to the subject. Position the lighting to obtain the best possible contrast and results. Take multiple shots with the light held or placed at different angles to the subject to achieve the best results. Photograph vehicular damaged areas, the license plate and the registration decal. Include the time that photographing was begun and completed in the notes. Remove the film or download the digital images and store in a secure location according to departmental regulations.

AERIAL PHOTOGRAPHY

Take aerial and/or overhead photographs of a scene to show geographic relationships of locations or objects and aid identification of objects shown in other photographs. Obtain aerial photographs by taking the pictures from a helicopter or plane. News footage can sometimes be a useful source of aerial photographs. Overhead photographs, in this context, are taken from above the scene, such as from a ladder, a second story, a cherry picker; they are not taken from the sky, as from a plane. Aerial and overhead photographs must be overlapping. Remove the film or download the digital images and store in a secure location according to departmental regulations.

VIDEO

Today, investigators often choose to use video recordings as a useful supplement to still photography.

Plan the video shoot carefully. Take a video of the scene in its original state from multiple angles and distances. Take a video of fragile evidence first. Avoid disturbing the scene. Always take a video of the scene before and after alteration, such as when placards and scales are placed near evidence. Exclude officers, bystanders, and others at a scene from the video. Turn audio off. Take overall (long-range) video to show where the crime occurred, midrange video to show relationships of evidence and other points of interest, and close-up video to show individual items and their characteristics.

Use a sturdy tripod whenever possible to reduce movement while taking video. Take video from angles that result in the best representation of that scene. Avoid panning side to side or up and down. Avoid zooming while out of focus. Always use the designated safe route when moving through the scene. When applicable, include the names of those assigned to specific tasks in your notebook.

Plan the videography route. Take a video of transient objects, such as bloodstains or latent prints, as soon as possible. Move from the exterior to the interior of the crime scene, and from general to specific focus. The videography session should occur in an uninterrupted, systematic, focused manner. When planning the route, ask: How did the victim or suspect arrive at or leave from the scene? How was the crime committed? Which items were handled? Which items were moved? Which items are broken or stained? Have potentially flammable vapors been detected at the scene?

Go beyond boundary markers to take video only when necessary. Plan and prepare lighting for each scene and camera angle. Front lighting places the camera lens at a 90-degree angle to the recorded object. It is often the most appropriate type of lighting to use at crime scenes. Side lighting places the lighting source at a 45-degree angle to an object.

It is used to show details such as tool marks, surface irregularities or textures to show vehicle accident damage when videotaping in closets or other small spaces when videotaping polished surfaces. Control the use of lighting by manually changing the focus settings and turning on/off flash settings. It is important to have a detachable flash or, if the flash is not detachable, another light source. Turn audio off.

Record overall video of the house/building exterior, vehicles, other structures at the crime scene, including entrances and exits, and bystanders. Slowly pan in one directional sweep; never move the camera side to side or up and down. The overall video should include a 360-degree view of the entire scene, including landmarks, entrances and exits, and identifying marks, such as a house number or license plate.

Always use slow camera movements such as when panning and zooming. Use a tripod whenever possible, unless using it will disturb either the scene or other team members. When recording a long, narrow area, such as a side yard or train tracks, use a tripod and slow zooming.

Always avoid walking while taping these shots Record entry/exit points from all possible angles. Show any paths used during the crime, when possible. While taking a video of a scene, record related information in notes. Specify any changes made to a scene while taking video, such as when a light was turned on or the tripod left a mark. Film midrange and close-up exterior video (within 5 feet of the subject) immediately following the overall recording of a scene. Record in a systematic, focused way.

When recording video, use slow camera movements such as when panning and zooming. Before zooming, stop filming, zoom, focus, then start the filming. Use the tripod whenever possible. When recording a long, narrow area, such as a side yard or train tracks, use a tripod and slow zooming unless using it will disturb either the scene or other team members. Always avoid walking while recording a long, narrow area.

A high camera angle, such as with an overhead view, may be required to show individual objects that are on similar planes. Record entry/exit points from all possible angles. Show any paths used during the crime. Move to the interior and take overall, midrange, and close-up video. When recording interiors: Always use slow camera movements such as when panning and zooming. Use a tripod whenever possible, even though it takes more time to set up unless using it will disturb either the scene or other team members.

When recording overall video in tight spaces, such as a closet or bathroom, use a high camera angle from a corner. When recording a long, narrow area, such as a hallway or porch, use a tripod and slow zooming. Always avoid walking while recording these shots. When necessary and possible, use artificial lighting to get the best possible clarity.

Consider using a blue filter over artificial light to achieve similar lighting as daylight. Complete note taking. Include in the notes such items as events that occurred while recording and the time recording was completed. Remove the videotape from the camera or download the digital video before storing the camera in a secure location according to departmental regulations.

A well-documented scene ensures the integrity of the investigation and provides a permanent record for later evaluation.

REFERENCES AND FURTHER READING

Bureau of Justice Assistance. (2014). *Video Evidence.*
Available: https://it.ojp.gov/gist/164/File/Video%20Evidence_LE%20Guide%20to%20Resources%20and%20Best%20Practices1.pdf

National Institute of Justice. (2013). Technical *Advances in the Visual Documentation of Crime Scenes.* Available: https://rti.connectsolutions.com/p48gn4fh4wi/

SECTION 2.2

Crime Scene Sketching

Sketching is extremely important to the reconstruction of crime scenes in the minds of both investigators and finders of fact. Sketches have the advantage of removing the potential clutter inherent in photography as well as providing exact distances between environmental elements and evidence items. Photographs are often not as clear on important details as are sketches. Both photographs and sketches are usually necessary in cases involving serious offenses.

The rough sketch is the first sketch drawn at the scene. In some cases, multiple rough sketches will be required. This will depend largely on the scope of the crime scene. The sketch includes a scene outline with the location of objects and evidence clearly marked. A finished sketch is derived from the rough sketch.

Preliminary sketches should be made of the immediate area of the scene, complete with case identifiers and an indication of north on the sketch. The location of all evidence items should be included in the sketch, as well as accurate measurements sufficient for later reconstruction of the scene. It is important that evidence items within the sketch are paired with the same items in the evidence records. Remember that initial photographs and sketches must be done prior to moving evidence items. That is, sketches should be drawn after photographs are taken, and before anything is moved or destroyed. It is critical not to alter the scene.

For most cases, rough sketches will include measurements that can be used to recreate the crime scene. These measurements should be as precise as possible, never deviating more than a quarter of an inch from the true measurement. Include measurements for dimensions of rooms, furniture, doors and windows, and distances between objects, entrances and exits, bodies and persons. For indoor scenes, large objects (such as furniture and appliances) and room characteristics (such as windows and doors) should be included in the sketch.

Depending on the crime, draw one or all of these types of sketches: a sketch showing the surrounding areas, a sketch showing only measurements, and a sketch showing locations of objects, such as the locations of evidence, the victim(s), etc. Measurements should be accurate to within ¼". Include, outside of the drawn crime scene, measurements for dimensions of rooms, furniture, doors and windows, and distances between objects, entrances and exits, bodies, and persons. Draw details, such as object size, proportionally in a rough sketch.

Take measurements from a fixed location reference point, such as walls or curbs, or from stationary appliances. Include as much information as possible in the sketch: streets, plants, entry and exit points, location of bullets and cartridges, etc. Do not alter a rough sketch after leaving the crime scene. If changes are required of the rough sketch, photocopy the original rough sketch to preserve its integrity. Newer technology makes use of laser scanning devices to perform crime scene sketching.

The employment of these devices should be reserved to investigators trained in their use. Information That Should be Documented Record the time, date, name of the person who contacted the authorities, and incident information as soon as notification of a crime is received. These notes should be kept separate from the sketch. Initial notes about the incident should answer the who, what, when, where, why and how questions.

Incident information includes: who reported the incident when the incident was first reported, the crime scene location, a description of incident and participant names. Gather information to use when sketching by talking to others at the scene. Record that information in the notes.

Questions that can provide valuable information include:

- How did the victim or suspect arrive at or leave from the scene?
- How was the crime committed?
- Which items were handled?
- Which items were moved?
- Which items are broken or stained? Have potentially flammable vapors been detected at the scene?

While sketching the scene, record related information in the notes. It is critical to use a systematic approach to note taking while sketching to maintain a record of your activities and the order of sketches made. Specify the changes made to a scene prior to sketching, such as when objects were moved or placards added. Note who made the changes and why they occurred.

DETERMINING SCALE

Determine the scale to use for all sketches. The usual scale for outdoor scenes is one inch equals twenty feet. The usual scale for indoor scenes is one-eighth inch equals one foot. Select which standard units of measurement will be used: metric (meters, centimeters) or English (feet, inches). An important consideration when determining the scale is fitting the scene to the sketch paper.

To calculate the scale, determine the longest measurement at the scene. Divide this measurement by the longest measurement of the sketch paper. The resulting number establishes the largest measurement end of the scale.

Often graph paper is used for scale drawings. When using graph paper, assign a specific number of squares to the measurement identified in Step 2. Use this method to establish other measurements by substituting the actual measurement in place of the longest measurement in Step 1.

Create a title block on the graph paper being used for the sketch in the lower right corner of the paper. The title block typically includes:

- Case number
- Crime type
- Victim name
- Name and ID# of sketcher
- Name and ID# of person verifying measurements
- Location of sketch
- Date completed

Create a legend for the sketch on the graph paper used for the sketch. Each sketch must include a legend that is specific to it. A legend identifies:

- North-facing direction (usually points to the top of page)
- Identification symbols used for information in sketch
- Sketch ID#
- Scale used

51

An accepted practice for assigning identification symbols is to use compass points to identify walls. Use evidence numbers assigned to objects to identify them in the sketch. The legend will be updated after drawing the sketch to ensure accuracy and completeness. The legend will be updated after drawing the sketch to ensure accuracy and completeness, and to include:

- Measurements for dimensions of rooms, furniture, doors, and windows
- Distances between objects, entrances and exits, bodies, and persons

CATEGORIES OF SKETCHES

There are four categories of sketches:

Perspective – A perspective sketch contains a vanishing point and depicts objects of evidence as they would appear to the eye concerning relative distance and depth.

Projection – A projection sketch usually contains only one viewpoint and depicts objects on one plane. The overview sketch (of the horizontal plane) is the most common type of sketch and is usually done from a bird's eye view; it shows the floor plan. Less common is the elevation sketch (of the vertical plane), which shows a side view typically of landscapes or buildings. One extrapolation of the projection sketch is the "Exploded" view sketch that contains more than one wall from one viewpoint. It combines the overview and elevation sketches.

Schematic – The schematic sketch is used when it is desirable to represent a sequence of events such as following the trajectory of a bullet through a crime scene location.

Detailed – The detailed sketch is used when describing a small area that is not easily incorporated into the overall drawing due to the scale chosen for the rough or finished scale drawing. This is especially useful for large crime scenes.

CREATING A PROJECTION SKETCH

Determine the view to be shown in the sketch: *overhead* or *exploded*. The **overhead view** shows a floor plan. This is the most frequently used view in sketches. The **exploded view** shows a floor plan with walls laid out flat. Objects on the floor and on walls, such as bullet holes or bloodstains, are shown in their relative positions in the exploded view sketch.

Draw an outline that is to scale of the area of interest, including locations of approaches and accurate measurements of the perimeter. The size of the outline should fill as much of the paper as possible. Draw the rough sketch before anything is moved or destroyed, and after photographs are taken. Do not alter the scene. Show locations of windows and doors. Use a curved line to indicate the direction that each door opens.

Use only the selected units of measurement. The sketch or accompanying notes should indicate where a measurement of an object was taken (e.g., middle of the object, near corner, far corner, etc.). Measurements of bloodstains are often done on a metric scale (e.g., millimeters). Whenever possible, have another officer or crime scene investigator observe measurements for confirmation purposes.

OBTAINING MEASUREMENTS

There are four measuring techniques used to obtain accurate measurements for the sketch:

Triangulation Method – The triangulation method utilizes two fixed permanent objects within the crime scene. Measurements are taken from each fixed point to each piece of evidence.

Rectangular Coordinate Method – The rectangular coordinate method is used when measuring the distance to an object from two mutually perpendicular objects, such as walls that meet at a 90-degree angle.

Polar Coordinate Method – The polar coordinate method is more appropriate for an outdoor scene in which only a single fixed or reference point is present. Measure both the distance and direction (angle) an object is from a known reference point. The angle can be measured with either a large protractor or an optical device such as a transit or a compass. The protractor technique with a 360-degree protractor is useful for underwater scenes.

Transecting Baseline Coordinate Method – The transecting baseline coordinate method is used to measure items of evidence when there are numerous objects in the crime scene and other measuring techniques will not work. This is accomplished by laying a tape measure down so that it crosses the entire room or area to be measured. This first tape measure becomes the baseline for all other measurements in the crime scene. Measurements are then made perpendicularly from this tape by laying another tape measure at a 90-degree angle to the first tape and measuring out to the evidence.

Take accurate measurements of the exact locations and relative positions of evidence using the triangulation method when there are at least two fixed points within the outlined area.

Use triangulation indoors or outdoors; it is an especially good method to use in areas lacking straight lines. Take measurements from fixed locations, such as a wall or curb, or from a stationary appliance. Identify these locations in your legend. Measurements should be accurate to within a ¼ inch. Include height measurements to show how far off of the ground an object was found.

When determining distance based on triangulation:

1. Select two fixed points within the outlined area, such as walls, curbs, or street signs.
2. Draw a baseline between the two fixed points.
3. Select another object within the outlined area.
4. Measure the distance to that object from each of the baseline's fixed endpoints, creating a triangle.

Use a measuring tool to ensure accurate measurements are taken. Take accurate measurements of the exact location and relative position of evidence using rectangular coordinates and the baseline method when there are two known points, or accurate measurements are needed for an object located on or perpendicular to the line between those two points (the baseline).

Use the baseline method in outdoor areas that are irregularly shaped and where no natural baseline is present. This method is useful in situations such as scenes that occur in the desert or on farmland. Take measurements from fixed locations, such as a lamp post or curb, or from a stationary appliance. Measurements should be accurate to within ¼ inch. Include height measurements to show how far off of the ground an object was found.

When determining distance based on the transecting baseline coordinate method, select two fixed points within (at the outer edges of) the outlined area, such as a kitchen appliance, a door, a window, a corner or wall (a wall is preferred). Then, take the following steps:

1. Create the baseline by drawing a line between the two selected fixed points.
2. Measure the length of the baseline.
3. Select an object within the outlined area.
4. When the object is on the baseline, measure from one of the fixed end-points to the object.
5. When the object is not on the baseline, draw a straight line from the object at a 90-degree angle to the baseline.
6. Measure the length of the line drawn.

Measure from one of the fixed end-points to the point where the new line meets the baseline. Ensure that all identification symbols used on the sketch are included and defined on the legend. Include descriptive details related to the sketch in notes such as lighting conditions, names of people in the area, colors of objects, odors, weather. Include updates such as distances between objects and dimensions of rooms, windows, doors, and so forth. Until all rough sketches for a crime scene are complete, repeat the previous steps. Do not update any rough sketch after leaving the scene.

Finish note-taking at the scene. Include the time that sketching was completed in the notes. Note taking should occur throughout the sketching activities. Finished sketches can be completed either by the originator of the rough sketches or by another staff member, such as a draftsperson or artist.

When a sketch is complete, prominently write "Not to Scale" outside of the sketch, then update related documentation, such as the legend and notes. Note: Although accurate measurements were taken, potential courtroom controversies related to those measurements may be avoided by placing the "Not to Scale" disclaimer on the rough sketch.

Sketching Equipment Summary

- Graph paper
- Paper
- a 50- to a 100-foot retractable measuring tape
- 1000-foot walking wheel

- Folding rule
- Ruler
- Oversize clipboard with a storage pocket
- Eraser
- Magnetic compass
- Personal protective equipment (when needed)
- Flashlight
- Notebook
- Pencils

SECTION 2.3

Note Taking

Accurate and thorough notes are a critical part of good crime scene documentation. As previously indicated, note taking should begin the moment the call comes in to dispatch. The time of the call, the person making the call, and all other relevant information should be documented. The location of the scene, the time of arrival at the scene, and the time of departure from the scene should all be documented.

These notes provide a permanent written record of the facts of a case that can be used in further investigation, in writing reports, and in prosecuting the case. Detailed notes can make or break a case.

Notes are defined as any initial written documentation of investigative activity created as part of a criminal investigation. This would include, but not be limited to, initial documentation of crime scenes, interviews, surveillance, record searches, analytical notes regarding evidence or records examined or seized, or any other matter of evidence obtained during the investigation of the offense. Additionally, notes would include written documentation of investigative processes such as the development of **lead sheets** and completion of pertinent forms utilized during the investigative process.

Initial observations about the scene should be noted. Remember to include all five senses: Smells and other sense impressions can often be just as important as visual observations. **Transient** evidence—things likely to move, change, or disappear—should be given careful consideration at this point. Also, any circumstances that require a departure from the standard operating procedure should be documented.

Begin taking notes as soon as possible after receiving a call and continue recording information as it is received through the investigation.

Remember that taking notes often involves recording the statements of witnesses. Interviewing is a critical skill of the investigator. If possible, have witnesses write out statements.

Take notes on everything you do in an official investigative capacity. Record all facts, regardless of where they may lead. Remember that establishing a suspect's innocence is just as important as establishing guilt—you don't want to waste time "barking up the wrong tree."

Be sure to record the time and date of the call, the location of the call, the officer assigned to the call, and the time of arrival at the scene. Make notes even if this basic information is recorded by dispatch.

There are several critical questions that will apply to all crime scenes: Who? What? When? Where? Why? How? Any information that helps answer any of these questions should be recorded. What follows are some general questions along these lines that apply to almost every case. Other questions will be case specific.

When Questions

- When did the incident happen?
- When was it discovered?
- When was it reported?
- When did law enforcement arrive on the scene?
- When were the suspects arrested?
- When will the case go to court?

Where Questions

- Where did the incident happen?
- Where was evidence found?
- Where was evidence stored?
- Where do victims, suspects, and witnesses live?
- Where do suspects frequent most often?
- Where were suspects arrested?

Who Questions

Concerning the Suspects:

- Who are suspects?
- Who are accomplices?
- COMPLETE descriptions: gender, race, coloring, age, height, weight, hair (color, style) eyes (color, glasses) and any distinguishing characteristics such as a unique walk or an accent.
- Who had a **motive**?

Concerning Victims and Witnesses:

- Who were the victims?
- Who were the witnesses?
- Who saw or heard something important?
- Who reported the incident?
- Who made a complaint?

Concerning Law Enforcement:

- Who was assigned the case?
- Who else investigated the incident?
- Who marked and received evidence?
- Who was notified?

What Questions

- What type of crime was committed?
- What was the amount of **property damage** involved?
- What happened? (Narrative reports from all sources)
- What evidence was found?
- What preventive measures had been taken?
- What skills, knowledge, and strengths were required to commit the crime?
- What was said?
- What did law enforcement do?

- What further information is needed?
- What further action is needed?

How Questions

- How was the crime discovered?
- How does this crime relate to other crimes?
- How was evidence found?

Why Questions

- Why was the crime committed? (**intent**, consent, motive)
- Why was certain property stolen?
- Why was a particular time selected?

INVESTIGATIVE CONCERNS

The acronym **MO** means *modus operandi*. Modus operandi, (Latin: "operating method"). In investigations, there is often a distinct pattern or manner of working that comes to be associated with a particular criminal. Criminologists have observed that, whatever his specialty—burglary, auto theft, or embezzling—the professional criminal is very likely to adhere to his particular way of operating. If, for example, a burglar begins his career by entering houses from the roof, he will, in all probability, continue this method for as long as he can work. Some burglars become so attached to their modus operandi that they burglarize the same places or people again and again.

A criminal investigation is a reconstructive process that uses **deductive reasoning**, which is a logical process in which a conclusion follows from specific facts. Deductive reasoning is a way of reasoning that relates two or more general concepts or conditions to a specific case. For example, a child learns that birds fly south in October and that a robin is a bird, he will use deductive reasoning to conclude that a robin will fly south in October. Deductive reasoning is often confused with **inductive reasoning**, which uses a specific observation to reach a general conclusion.

Note Taking Procedural Summary

Detailed entry/exit logs should be created. An **entry/exit log** is used to document the people who come to and go from a crime scene during the investigation. People who were at the crime scene before the investigation began are also noted in this log. The officer monitoring the log, the "Log Officer," is assigned the task by the Supervising Officer and is responsible for completing this task and monitoring the log at all times.

The Log Officer is responsible for ensuring that the log is filled out thoroughly and anyone entering the scene has a stated purpose there. Always position the log so that it is clearly visible. Set up the log for people to use when arriving to and departing from the scene. Record the following information about the crime scene:

- Crime scene location
- Name of witnesses
- Name of victims
- Name of persons taken into custody
- Name of first responders and approximate arrival times
- Name of Supervising Officer and approximate arrival time (approximate time should be used if arrival time was before the log was established)

Record the information below for each person at the scene. If not using an official logbook or forms, leave spaces where this information can be recorded:

- Arrival date
- Time of arrival
- Name
- Identification
- Unit numbers
- Organization (if not with the investigating department)
- Reason for being at the scene

Log information should include the arrival and departure times of all personnel at the crime scene, including the **Coroner** or **Medical Examiner**, crime scene technicians, and **State's Attorney**. It should also contain information about who is at the crime scene and why they are there, incident number, first responder names,

Log Officer name, Supervising Officer name, shield numbers, Unit numbers, location of the crime scene; the name of the victim(s).

Before making it available to crime scene visitors, record logistical data (time, crime scene location, names of victims and witnesses, etc.) in the entry/exit log. Ensure that the departure time for any person departing from the scene is recorded before that person actually leaving.

If someone exits the scene without reporting to the Log Officer, that officer can enter an estimated departure time along with a note stating the rationale for it being estimated. Store the log in a secure location and as mandated by departmental regulations.

REFERENCES AND FURTHER READING

"Deductive Reasoning." *Gale Encyclopedia of Psychology*. Retrieved July 09, 2019 from Encyclopedia.com: https://www.encyclopedia.com/medicine/encyclopedias-almanacs-transcripts-and-maps/deductive-reasoning

SECTION 2.4:

The Case File

When a crime scene investigation concludes, the lead investigator must compile a **case file** for the investigation (depending on the department, the final collection of documents may be called the **final report** or **prosecution report**). The case file is simply a systematic collection of all pertinent documents regarding a particular case. The following documents from the crime scene and other investigative activity should be included in the case file:

- complaint
- preliminary investigation report
- follow-up reports
- statements
- admissions/confessions
- laboratory reports
- photographs
- sketches/drawings
- summary of negative evidence

Complaint. All crimes known to the police came to their attention in some way. Most often, this is a phone call to 911 or another dispatch number. However that initial complaint was made, the record should be included in the final report. At a minimum, it should contain the date and time of the complaint, the address of the incident, details of what the person making the complaint said, and the identity of the officers dispatched to the scene, and the time that they were dispatched.

Preliminary Investigation Report. The first responder to a crime scene should conduct a preliminary investigation, and the results of and facts surrounding that investigation should be recorded in a formal written report. This report can provide important information such as when officers arrived on the scene, conditions (e.g., weather and persons present) at the scene, and the actions of the first responders.

Follow-up Report. Each time a significant lead is followed in an investigation, the actions taken by investigators and the results of those actions should be recorded. Such reports should be added chronologically to the final report.

Statements. Assemble all witness statements gathered during the investigation. If witness statements were not obtained, then provide summaries of oral statements made during interviews.

Admissions/Confessions. All documentation of admissions and confessions should be included as a separate part of the report.

Laboratory Reports. Documents resulting from **forensic** laboratory analysis and the follow-up investigation should be added when they become available. All laboratory reports should be included in the final report. Generally, investigators will want to include information about how these reports relate to other elements of the report.

Media. All relevant photographs, drawings, and sketches should be included in the final report. Photographs.

Summary of Negative Evidence. Any evidence that tends to hamper the state's case must be included in the report. This is necessary for the prosecutor to adequately argue against such evidence (e.g., witness statements that provide an alibi). Also, failure to reveal exculpatory evidence to the defense can result in a mistrial as this is legally required as part of the discovery process.

ORGANIZING INFORMATION

A key to clarity in report writing is organization. Logically and as a matter of time tested tradition, police reports are written in **chronological order**. This usually means starting off with an explanation of how an incident came to the attention of police and ends with the final disposition in the case. One way to view an incident is as a story, and all good stories have a beginning, a middle, and an end.

It is difficult to provide a generic outline of a good report since the complexity of reports will depend largely on departmental policy and the complexity of the case. A report on a "fender bender" may be as short as a few sentences, while a homicide investigation may result in a case file that contains thousands of pages of reports and supporting documents. Different departments have different standardized forms, and those forms must be used and organized per policy.

Police report writers are advised to begin with a simple (informal) outline of what will be covered in the report. Some departments will aid in this process by developing in-house checklists of things to include in specific types of reports.

KEY ELEMENTS OF A GOOD REPORT

Reports are a critical part of policing because they record important details of an event and are used to help further investigations and as evidence in court. Therefore, police reports must be *clear*, *factual*, and ***concise***. One often-difficult part of the police report for officers to write is the **narrative**. This is a section in which an officer describes everything that she observed at the scene. Victims are identified, perpetrators are described based on witness statements, the scene (time and place) is recorded, and the situation is summarized. The narrative consists of ***facts***. A key element of good report writing is to stick to factual information and not include **speculation** or opinion.

Witnesses should be identified, and important details from their interviews may be included. If you have **verbatim** statements from a victim or witness, write exactly what he or she said in quotation marks.

Grammar, Style, and Spelling. Use correct spelling, punctuation, and grammar. Police reports become part of the public record and may be used in court. You want to make a good impression in order to be considered knowledgeable and reliable.

The "never-ending sentence" is a common problem. A sentence goes on and on and on leaving the reader gasping for breath. An example: "I asked the victim if he could identify the robber and before he could answer, he was interrupted by his mother, who was urging him not to say anything because she was afraid that if he answered, he might find himself in harm's way and end up hurt somehow" (Hart, 2017).

This is not an efficient or effective way to communicate. It would be far better to break that sentence down into several shorter sentences. Besides being easier for the reader to digest, it will probably cause the author to omit some of the "fluff" that gets included in such sentences (Hart, 2017).

A corollary to this is to avoid the "never-ending paragraph." An amazing number of police reports go a full page or more using just one paragraph. Your readers expect a break every now and again. These pauses help the reader comprehend your message clearly and logically.

Simplicity proves to be the key to success. Officers encounter trouble when they try to make reports fancy. Intricate writing works for an English class; however, it wastes time and enables errors when writing reports. Police officers must remember that they write to inform, not to impress.

Audience. Other officers often read police reports, but sworn personnel are not the only people that read reports. *Consider your audience.* Use **Standard English** (not **slang**, police "ten codes" or "signals," abbreviations) so that anyone reading the report understands the meaning clearly.

Clarity. A lot of report writers force the reader to search for information. For example, many officers include the date and time in the heading of their reports. Then they begin their report like this: "On the above date and time..." This causes a disruption in the reader's flow, because the reader must now look elsewhere to find out which date and time the author is referencing.

Similarly, authors often put the names and addresses of suspects, witnesses and victims in the heading, assigning each one a number. Then the author continually refers to each person described in the report as "Subject #1" or "Victim #2." This is extremely confusing and causes lots of searching for the reader. It is better to identify each person by name in the report so that such confusion is minimized. Do not make your reader hunt for information. Make it easy for them to follow your narrative logically and clearly.

It is important to include all relevant actions, statements, and observations in your report. A lack of detail means a lack of clarity.

Always Proofread. Your computer's spell checker will not report improper use of a word that is spelled correctly. Most spell-checkers offer you several options when an unrecognized word is encountered. Typical options would be "Change," "Ignore" or "Add to Dictionary." If you accidentally press "Change" when you meant to press "Ignore" – as when encountering a proper name – you could have some disastrous results.

The best way to proofread a report is to give it to somebody else to read. It is always better to have fresh eyes look for mistakes. Encourage them to point out anything that looks wrong or sounds awkward. Then read it yourself and see if you can improve it. One of the best features of a word processor is that mistakes are easily corrected, without having to type the whole thing over.

Accountability matters. Usually, the people in charge determine the level of writing in classrooms and agencies. If they demand quality, the people they are teaching or supervising will slow down, proofread, seek assistance, and submit superior reports. Nevertheless, if those in charge tolerate mistakes and mediocrity, individuals will produce poorly written reports.

TIPS FOR AVOIDING COMMON ERRORS

Begin sentences with a noun—person, place, or thing. Writing simple, straightforward sentences often eliminates fragments, run-on sentences, dangling modifiers, and other **syntax** errors.

Do not tolerate "text speak" (e.g., u instead of you, or omitted capital letters). Refrain from fixing those errors. Return the report to the writer for corrections.

Avoid unnecessary transitions, like *upon hearing the gunshot* or *whereupon she ran out the door*. Keep it simple.

Use everyday language, such as I, me, saw, heard, and house instead of this officer, ascertained, or residence.

Resist the temptation to flaunt your skills. Writing *extinguish the illumination* instead of *turn out the light* sounds pompous and does not impress anyone.

Remember that possessive pronouns—his, hers, ours, theirs, yours, and its—never use apostrophes. Link its and his and remember to omit the apostrophe when using the possessive form (e.g., he doubled his speed or the car doubled its speed). Never put an apostrophe after the *s* in its.

Be careful with woman and women. Writers often use women to refer to a single female: I spoke to a women who witnessed the assault, instead of I spoke to a woman.

Use apostrophes only to show ownership (Linda's car) and omission of letters in contractions (didn't, couldn't). Avoid decorating plurals with apostrophes (e.g., I saw bruise's on Tom's left cheek).

Develop the habit of using resources—a dictionary, Internet search, or quick question for a fellow officer who writes well.

Narrative Checklist

_____ Narrative clearly states the crime/event that occurred.
_____ Narrative identifies the scene (time and place).
_____ Narrative summarizes the crime/event in chronological order.
_____ Narrative includes details about what was *seen*.
_____ Narrative is factual (objective).
_____ Narrative is of adequate length to tell the "entire story"
_____ Narrative contains correct spelling.
_____ Narrative contains correct capitalization.
_____ Narrative contains correct punctuation and grammar.

TESTIFYING IN COURT

For many officers, one of the most stressful duties they must perform is testifying in court under both **direct examination** and **cross-examination**. All law enforcement officers, regardless of their rank or assignments, are going to find themselves testifying on the witness stand at some point. Testifying in court may be the most difficult and important task an officer faces in his or her career. No other assignment subjects an officer and his/her department to more intense, microscopic scrutiny than the officer's credibility, competency, and conduct in the courtroom.

Be honest. When testifying in court, your job is to help the criminal justice system with truthful and accurate testimony. You are there to present evidence on behalf of the state or government to win a conviction. Just provide answers to questions that you can. Do not ever try to make up answers to questions that you do not know the answer.

Do your homework. Make sure that you write a good, concise case report. If you are not good at report writing, check out the reports of other officers who do write good reports. Read those reports and see how they structure their narratives. Learn from them and make adjustments in your reports. Always write your reports from the perspective of a defense attorney. When you are writing your reports, imagine that you are going to be the defense attorney defending this case. If you write your reports with this mindset, you are going to give the defense attorney less opportunity to "work you over" on the witness stand.

What would you be looking for when exploring areas to attack? What are the weaknesses in this police report? Do not lie about anything. Do not be afraid to admit any mistakes that you have made during the case—nobody is perfect. There is often an issue of police officers overreaching in their efforts to obtain a conviction.

Look professional. Dress for your court appearance with the same attention to detail you would in going before a promotion board. You should be exceptionally neat— fingernails clean, hair trimmed, clothes pressed, shoes shined. Carry only the essentials—avoid items that jingle, jangle, flash, shine, or otherwise distract. Your department policy may dictate whether you wear a uniform or civilian clothes when you testify.

Often, on-duty officers will wear a uniform, and off-duty officers will wear civilian attire. In state and local courts, you may be armed whether you are in uniform or not. (In federal courts, you generally will not be permitted to wear your firearm into court.) Be aware that some jurors are distracted by the sight of a witness in civilian clothes armed with a gun and carrying bullets, handcuffs, etc. even if they are testifying as a police officer. Discuss this possibility with the prosecutor before your appearance to decide what you should and should not carry.

Establish your competence and expertise. Look and be attentive. This communicates that you care about being accurate and responsive. Take the time you need to fully understand the question and give the proper response. It does not hurt to appear thoughtful. Organize your thoughts; do not be hasty. It is tempting to add information to your answer that you think helps advance the prosecution's case. Resist this temptation. This is the prosecutor's job; let the prosecutor develop your testimony. Do not jump ahead, do not anticipate, just answer the question that is asked.

When you elaborate heavily for the prosecution and then are very reserved in your testimony when cross-examined by the defense, you appear biased. This undermines your credibility as an objective reporter of the facts. Adding extraneous information to your answer opens up other areas for cross-examination.

Trials are serious matters for everyone involved. Refrain from wisecracks and clever remarks. On the other hand, do not hesitate to laugh at yourself or an unexpected occurrence, if appropriate. Avoid appearing frozen, calculated, or devoid of emotion.

Keep the jury interested. Speak a little louder and slower than you think is necessary. Do not inject long pauses between words, phrases, or sentences but do concentrate on making each word clearly heard and understood.

Maintain your composure. It's normal to be nervous and anxious on the stand. You might sweat, shake, have trouble focusing, forget everyone's name, speak too rapidly, speak in a monotone voice, your voice may involuntarily raise or lower. All of these symptoms are normal.

Some pointers to help you compose yourself: Sit up straight, but not stiffly. A normal reaction to the stress of being on the stand is slouching in your chair. Do not let yourself start slouching as it may progress as your testimony continues.

Orient yourself in the courtroom. Look at each of the walls within your vision without turning around. Look at each person or groups of persons in the courtroom.

Mentally prepare yourself for the fact that when you enter the courtroom, everyone—jurors, judges, spectators, attorneys, the defendant, the court staff—all will be watching your entrance. Stay poised and remind yourself that this is how every witness is viewed. Do not avoid looking at the judge or jurors; look back at them as you would a person speaking with you.

Do not look like an advocate for a conviction. Juries can sense when you appear not to be completely neutral. Defense attorneys will use this against you. As a witness, you are going to be in the spotlight. You are going to be cross-examined about all the activities you have been involved in surrounding the case. Do not try to get cute or cocky with the defense attorney. You are not there to try to outsmart a defense attorney, just to present the facts of the case, as you know them to be.

Remember you do not have to have an answer for every question asked. Do not be afraid to say, "I don't recall" or "I don't remember." You are not supposed to remember everything.

A defense attorney is likely to try to show a judge or jury that you can be very aggressive. They will try to get under your skin and get you aggravated. Do not fall into that trap. They are playing a psychological game. Your job on the witness stand is to convince a judge or jury that you are just doing your job, that you do not have a personal stake in whether or not the defendant goes to jail. Your personal stake is that you did your job and acted professionally.

Your credibility is going to be attacked on the witness stand. Often, that is all a defense attorney has to work with. It is important that you understand that our criminal justice system is set-up to be **adversarial**. Do not take it personally. As they say, "You win some and you lose some." It is just an unpleasant fact, accept it, learn from the experience, and move on.

If you, as a law enforcement officer, lose your cool on the stand, no matter what kind of case, you lose all credibility with the jury. The jury, as citizens, have authorized you to carry guns and granted you a power and use of force they do not permit themselves. If you cannot control yourself in a courtroom, they are justified in being gravely concerned about your ability to control yourself on the streets, where you are subjected to much greater stress and no one is watching.

Your patience and temper will be sorely tried with interruptions, delays, argumentative questions, and attacks on your character. Do not allow yourself to become arrogant, flip, antagonistic, impatient, or excited. The worse it gets the greater an opportunity you are being handed to impress the jury with your strength of character, your integrity, your dignity.

Like it or not, as a law enforcement officer, jurors hold you to a higher standard than they do lay witnesses and they expect you to be able to take more abuse on the stand and still remain professional. Be aware that experienced prosecutors know this and may not come to your defense as quickly as they might a lay witness with an objection that the defense is "being argumentative" or "harassing the witness." Take this as the compliment it is. The prosecutor knows your credibility will shine through such challenges and knows the jury will become frustrated, impatient, and finally angry with your attacker.

REFERENCES AND FURTHER READING

Bennett, W. W. & Hess, K. M. (2004). *Criminal Investigation*, 7th Ed. New York: Thompson.

Baltimore City Police Department Academy Report Writing Manual. Available: http://brittneealford.com/wp-content/uploads/2014/01/Alford_BCPDA-Report-Writing-Manual.pdf

Hart, F. (2017). 10 steps to improve your written police reports. *PoliceOne.com.* Available: https://www.policeone.com/police-training/articles/44385-10-steps-to-improve-your-written-police-reports/

McCarthy, P. (2010). Turning testimony from stressful to successful. *PoliceOne.com.* Available: https://www.policeone.com/legal/articles/2006910-Turning-testimony-from-stressful-to-successful/

North Carolina State Bureau of Investigation. (2010). *Report Writing Manual.*
Available:
http://www.ncids.com/forensic/labs/Lab/Policy/SBI_Report_Writing_Manual(1.15.1
0%20Edition).pdf

SECTION 2.5:

Searches

The first steps in the collection of evidence are to prioritize such that valuable evidence is not lost, contaminated, or destroyed. This evaluation process consists of conducting a careful and methodical evaluation of all potential evidence items at the scene.

SEARCH PATTERNS

Generally, searches should be conducted such that areas that are easily accessible and in open view are searched first. After these areas are searched, then move on to out-of-view locations. Most criminal investigators will choose a systematic **search pattern** based on the size and location of the scene.

There are four types of search methodology that can be considered to search a crime scene:

1.   Lane or strip search
2.   Grid search
3.   Zone Search
4.   Spiral search

The size of the lane of the search should be approximately the arms' length of the searcher. As the search of an area is completed, some marking should be made to indicate that the area has been completed. A mechanism should exist for the

73

circumstance when potential evidence is found (e.g., who is called over, what path they should take, whether the other searches should halt moving until this finding is resolved).

Lane or Strip Searches are accomplished by the searchers walking in parallel along defined lanes in the same direction.

A **Grid Search** is a lane search that is conducted by completing a lane search in one direction and then completing a lane search in a perpendicular direction. While it takes twice as long as a lane search, it provides a more thorough search of an area.

A **Zone Search** involves dividing the area to be searched into adjacent zones. The smaller the size of the zone, the more methodical the search can be. Zone searches may be done by multiple searchers per zone.

A **Spiral search** involves a spiral into (inward) or out from (outward) a crime scene. A practical disadvantage with outward spiral searches is the evidence may be destroyed as the searchers move to the center of the crime scene area to begin their outward search.

EVIDENCE COLLECTION

It is important to choose a progression of collection and **processing methods** so that initial techniques do not compromise subsequent techniques. As a rule, focus on transient evidence first and move to the least transient forms of physical evidence. Likewise, move from the least **intrusive processing methods** to the most intrusive. It is also important to reassess continually any relevant environmental factors (e.g., sunlight, wind, rain, and approaching darkness) that will affect evidence and the investigator's ability to process the scene. It is also important to maintain security throughout processing.

Perhaps the most important aspect of evidence collection is documentation. For each piece of evidence, you must record its location at the scene, the date, and time collected, and who collected it.

Remember that chain of custody concerns begin the moment that the evidence is identified as such.

It is also important to collect **reference samples**, **control samples**, and **elimination samples** from the scene.

Immediately secure electronically recorded evidence from the vicinity of the crime scene. Computers, answering machine tapes, and security camera video can easily be erased and altered.

Evidence should be stored in appropriate containers and labeled at the crime scene. It is critical that evidence containers be properly labeled. When packaging items, it is critical to consider the nature of the evidence as it relates to proper packaging. Improperly packaged evidence can be lost, destroyed, and contaminated.

When evidence must be altered before submission to the crime lab (such as making a firearm safe for transport), it is critically important to document the original condition.

As a rule, you should avoid excessive handling of the evidence after it is collected.

When transporting evidence and submitting it for secure storage, always keep in mind the safety of the officer, the integrity of the evidence, and maintaining chain of custody.

CRIME SCENE DEBRIEFING TEAM

When an investigation of a crime scene is completed, it is released back to the persons who routinely control it. Once this happens, any evidence not collected during crime scene processing will most likely be lost or destroyed. To prevent this catastrophic state of affairs, it is imperative that a **crime scene debriefing** is conducted. The debriefing enables law enforcement personnel and other responders to share information regarding scene findings. Everyone involved gets a chance to discuss the need for a follow-up investigation, the need for special assistance, and the establishment of post-scene responsibilities.

The first order of business is to establish the **debriefing team**. This should include the investigators in charge of the scene, other investigators, evidence collection personnel, and the initial responding officer. The team should consider the following things:

- What evidence was collected?
- What are the preliminary scene findings?
- What forensic tests should be performed?
- What further actions should be taken?
- Who will do what next?

FINAL SCENE SURVEY

Once it has been determined that the scene has been adequately processed and is ready for release, a final survey of the scene is in order. This last examination accomplishes several functions. The first goal is to make sure that all evidence has indeed been collected and that no useful evidence remains at the scene. Second, it ensures that the investigative team leaves behind no equipment or materials. Finally, it ensures that no dangerous materials or conditions remain unaddressed.

In conducting the final survey, all areas identified as part of the crime scene are visually inspected. All equipment and materials generated by the investigation are removed. Any dangerous materials or conditions are reported and addressed.

RELEASE OF THE SCENE

The investigator should ensure that the scene is not released until all reasonable efforts have been made to identify and collect all evidence for further examination and that all of the physical characteristics of the scene have been properly documented.

Evidence Prioritization Procedural Summary

- Identify roles of the team members (e.g., scribe, collector, packager, etc.)
- Conduct a careful and methodical evaluation considering all physical evidence possibilities (e.g., biological fluids, latent prints, trace evidence).
- Focus first on the easily accessible areas in open view and proceed to out-of-view locations.
- Select a systematic search pattern for evidence collection based on the size and location of the scene(s).
- Select a progression of processing/collection methods so that initial techniques do not compromise subsequent processing/ collection methods.
- Concentrate on the most transient evidence (e.g., most susceptible to environmental conditions) and work to the least transient forms of physical evidence.
- Move from least intrusive to most intrusive processing/collection methods. Continually assess environmental and other factors that may affect the

evidence. Be aware of multiple scenes (e.g., victims, suspects, vehicles, locations).

- Processing one scene at a time to avoids cross contaminating these various scenes
- Recognize other methods that are available to locate, technically document, and collect evidence (e.g., alternate light source enhancement, blood pattern documentation, projectile trajectory analysis).

Evidence Collection Procedural Summary

- Maintain scene security throughout processing and until the scene is released.
- Document the collection of evidence by recording its location at the scene, date of collection, and who collected it.
- Collect each item identified as evidence.
- Establish chain of custody.
- Obtain standard/reference samples from the scene.
- Obtain control samples.
- Consider obtaining elimination samples.
- Immediately secure electronically recorded evidence (e.g., answering machine tapes, surveillance camera videotapes, computers) from the vicinity.
- Identify and secure evidence in containers (e.g., label, date, initial container) at the crime scene.
- Different types of evidence require different containers (e.g., **porous**, **nonporous**, crush-proof). Package items to avoid contamination and **cross-contamination**.
- Document the condition of firearms/weapons prior to rendering them safe for transportation and submission.
- Avoid excessive handling of evidence after it is collected.
- Maintain evidence at the scene in a manner designed to diminish degradation or loss.
- Transport and submit evidence items for secure storage.

SECTION 3

Physical Evidence

Physical evidence has the potential to play a critical role in the investigation and resolution of a crime. For this potential to be realized, action must be taken early on at the crime scene. It is critical that physical evidence is properly collected, documented, and preserved. Increasingly advanced technologies have given investigators a much wider array of tools, but have also place added importance on proper collection and preservation techniques. For evidence to ultimately have a significant role in court, it is critical that investigators follow an "objective, thorough, and thoughtful approach" (NIJ Technical Working Group on Crime Scene Investigation, 2000, p. 1).

To understand what evidence is used for and thus what is appropriate evidence to collect, the uses of evidence must be considered. Physical evidence can be used to help **reconstruct** the crime scene, help determine if a crime has actually occurred, help link a suspect to a victim, help link a suspect to a crime scene, help link **serial crimes**, provide investigative leads, and provide facts to a jury. Note the prevalence of the term *link*. It is safe to say that a major function of physical evidence is to provide linkages that, taken together, indicate guilt. It is rare that an investigator will encounter a crime where there is direct evidence of a suspect's guilt.

Rather, the proof beyond a reasonable doubt necessary in court is established by a series of circumstantial evidence items demonstrate guilt only when taken together as a whole. For example, a suspect's fingerprint on a gun does not prove guilt directly. Standing alone, this evidence is not very compelling. However, if we add to this the fact that the bullet removed from the victim's body came from that gun and the facts that the suspect had the motivation and opportunity to kill the victim, the overall picture becomes much more convincing.

Physical evidence can be categorized in several ways. One particularly useful way to do this is to consider the physical nature of the evidence. This often dictates which type of forensic science specialist will analyze the evidence when an investigator sends it to the crime lab. Common categories include **drug evidence**, **friction ridge** evidence (fingerprints, palm prints, footprints, etc.), **firearm evidence**, **biological evidence** (blood, semen, etc.), **trace evidence** (microscopic transfer evidence), document evidence (paper, inks, handwriting, etc.), **physical matching** evidence, and **toxicology** evidence.

SECTION 3.1:

Evidence Handling

Recall the importance of maintaining a chain of custody. It is a critically important legal requirement for the introduction of physical evidence in court that the evidence item is identified as the same item collected at the scene and that the item has not been altered in any significant way. Thus, any person in physical control of the evidence, no matter how briefly, must be recorded so that they can testify in court that the evidence was not altered. *Any break in the chain of custody will likely result in the exclusion of the evidence in court.*

All personnel responsible for the chain of custody of evidence items should maintain written records documenting the sample number, a description of the evidence, the date, and the location where the evidence was found, the name of the person collecting the evidence, and any other information required by policy. All transfers of custody should be documented, including the name of the recipient as well as the date and manner the evidence was transferred. The final disposition of the evidence should be documented as well.

Another critically important element in the scientific validity of the analysis of physical evidence is preventing **contamination** of the evidence. *Contaminated evidence is useless in court.* This is why securing the crime scene is a critical responsibility of the first responder. Also, it is critically important that evidence is protected from environmental factors that may cause damage to it, and the evidence must be packaged properly. Proper packaging and storage ensure that the evidence remains in the state that is was found at the crime scene.

It is also important to remember to collect **comparison standards** where appropriate. The analysis of many types of evidence involves comparing something found at the scene with something that is known to see if they are the same. A fingerprint found at a crime scene, for example, is useless without having a comparison standard taken from a suspect. The crime scene investigator must always remember to collect comparison standards when necessary for comparison by the crime lab.

Preventing changes in the condition of a sample after it has been collected requires carefully controlled packaging and transportation. The investigator should ensure that packaging, transportation, and storage procedures are followed to prevent any destructive changes in the condition of samples.

PERSONAL SAFETY

Many different types of evidence can be hazardous, and precautions should be taken when dealing with dangerous substances. If you do not know the proper safety precautions for a particular type of evidence, defer to someone who does. Note that *all biological materials (blood, semen, saliva, etc.) should be considered hazardous*. It is best to assume that all biological materials are contaminated with **pathogens** such as HIV, hepatitis, and others. Protective eyewear, protective gloves, respirator masks, and protective clothing should be worn when dealing with biological materials.

In addition to biological hazards, criminal investigations involve exposure to **chemical hazards** as well. Clandestine drug laboratories are a prime example. Many **forensic chemicals**, such as those used to develop latent fingerprints, are dangerous. Be sure to read the labels on all of the chemical supplies that you use, and obtain and read the **chemical safety data sheets**.

Biohazards are more common at crime scenes than many realize. Officers often enter scenes where people have been hurt or killed, and blood is a common denominator. A basic forensic principle that whenever two things come into contact, something from one object is always transferred to the other and vice versa. This idea can be generalized to the transfer of biohazards such as blood. If an officer steps in blood at a crime scene, then there is blood on the officer's boot. That blood may well be contaminated with dangerous pathogens, and anything the contaminated boot touches is contaminated.

In this way, biohazards can come into contact with people who were never present at the crime scene. Besides the obvious public health nightmare that this situation can create, there is also the specter of departmental liability to contend with. If it can be shown that police personnel negligently or recklessly caused harm to someone, then that person has the basis for a lawsuit.

The cure for all of these potential harms (as with many in policing) is adequate training and good policies that are rigorously enforced. Officers must understand the risks posed by biohazards, and they must be properly trained to **mitigate** those risks by properly using **Personal Protective Equipment (PPE)**. Officers must also be trained in the proper (safe) disposal of PPE. The use of **biohazard bags**, **sharps disposal containers**, and so forth represent a nuisance for officers and an expense for departments, but those costs in officer time and public money pale in comparison to the potential harms that can be caused if the issue is ignored.

While the proper disposal of PPE such as gloves, shoe covers, face shields and the like is important, it is also important to realize that many "tools of the trade" need to be properly **cleaned** and **sterilized** or safely discarded. Swabs, **pipettes**, razor blades and a host of other equipment are routinely contaminated with biological materials. At the end of a long night, it is tempting just to toss those used tools into a kit and forget about them.

This creates a real threat to officers from biological contamination, and it also creates a problem that materials from one crime scene may be transferred to a future crime scene via transference from unclean tools and equipment. Because of these dangers, departments need to carefully design and implement safety protocols for dealing with contaminated equipment. A potential source for good advice (and possibly training) is the crime laboratory.

Occupational Safety and Health Administration (OSHA)

OSHA, established by the Occupational Safety and Health Act of 1970, authorizes the Secretary of Labor to develop and promulgate occupational safety and health standards, to develop and issue regulations, to conduct investigations and inspections, to determine the status of compliance with safety and health standards and regulations, and to issue citations for noncompliance with safety and health standards and regulations. The Act also requires that states with an approved state plan provide for the development and enforcement of safety and health standards. Twenty-one states operate their own job safety and health programs (three additional states cover only state and local government employees). States with approved programs must set job safety and health standards that are "at least as effective as" comparable Federal standards. In most cases, states adopt standards identical to Federal ones.

EXPOSURE CONTROL PLAN

Crime laboratories, property and evidence rooms, and other locations where biological evidence is stored should have **exposure control plans** in place that are designed to minimize or eliminate occupational exposure to **bloodborne pathogens**. An exposure control plan is an employer's written policy that outlines the protective measures the employer takes to eliminate or minimize employee exposure to blood and potentially **infectious diseases**.

At a minimum, the plan must contain the following: an exposure determination that identifies job classifications and, in some cases, tasks and procedures that involve occupational exposure to blood and potentially infectious diseases procedures for evaluating the circumstances surrounding an exposure incident a schedule of how and when other provisions of the standard will be implemented, including methods of compliance, communication of hazards to employees, and recordkeeping (OSHA 2012). Each employee handling biological evidence must be trained on all related requirements and exposure risks.

Agencies should strictly limit the number of employees with exposure to these types of hazardous materials, either through staffing or through segregation of biohazardous materials.

IS IT EVIDENCE?

Once a crime scene investigation ends and the property is released back to the owners, the window for officers to find evidence quickly and irrevocably closes. Investigators must take care to identify and collect all items of evidential value. The costs of overlooking a useful evidence item can be very high in terms of the legal outcome of the case.

In general, it can be said that it is better to collect items that can later be discarded if they turn out to have no evidential value than to not collect them and lose valuable evidence. The failure to identify and collect evidence at the crime scene is the most commonly cited facet of the evidence identification problem, but the converse can also be an issue. In other words, "overkill" can also be a problem for investigators.

Some departments have adopted standardized checklists of potential evidence, and these can be useful as a reminder of what types of things have the *potential* to become evidence. If investigators "bag and tag" every item on the list, however, the likelihood of having several boxes of useless evidence becomes quite high. This comes at the cost of inordinate amounts of the investigator's time that could be better spent performing more fruitful tasks to move the investigation along. Also, laboratory analysis is expensive and time-consuming. If labs accepted all possible evidence from all crime scenes, the backlog would quickly stretch into years.

The obvious way to eliminate both extremes is to develop the ability to "read" the scene and evaluate the evidence related to the case. Once a narrative of what transpired at the scene takes shape, certain types of evidence can be eliminated because they do not fit the narrative. For example, let us say that a victim was shot by a sniper at long range. It would be senseless for investigators to collect **fingernail scrapings** in such a case. Since the narrative suggests that the victim never came into physical contact with the perpetrator, there is no logical reason to suspect that any evidence would be found on the victim's body.

EVIDENCE DOCUMENTATION

Ensure that the portion of the area or object with the stain has been documented as it was found. When photographing the object, include a scale and an identification label. Take one or more location photographs that show the object where it was found. Show the relationship of the object to other evidence in the photograph. Label a container such as a paper bag or envelope with your initials and identification number, the date and time, case number, evidence number, location, and evidence description.

Each piece of evidence must have a unique number. This number should correspond to the placard next to the evidence.

The evidence description should include:

- Type of item (e.g., victim's shirt, glass, carpet fibers)
- Location of the stain
- Whether the stain is wet or dry
- Location of the item at the crime scene

Mark the envelope with your initials and identification number, the date and time, case number, evidence number, location, and evidence description.

Ignitable Evidence

Accelerants and **ignitable liquids** recognition and collection are best performed by specialized personnel. For scene personnel, evidence may be observed through smell, sight, and sound, and should be recorded in notes.

Never attempt to collect any evidence until you have spoken with an accelerant and ignitable liquids investigator or specialist. Ensure the safety of people at or near the scene. Follow the instructions provided by the accelerants and ignitable liquids investigator or specialist with whom you speak.

BLOOD EVIDENCE

Blood evidence is present in many types of crimes and can provide important information useful in reconstructing a crime.

Possible substrates with bloodstains:

- Clothing
- Entire portable object
- Part of a non-portable object
- Stain on a nonporous surface

Equipment needed for bodily fluid collection includes:

- Paper bags, boxes, and envelopes
- Cotton-tipped swabs
- **Paper bindles** or other sterile swab storage container
- Distilled water or one-time use sterile water
- Scalpel, utility knife, or scissors
- Clean paper
- Waterproof pen
- **Evidence tape**
- Protective gloves
- Face protection

Commercial products are also available for crime scene collection of stains. Blood and other physiological fluids are fragile, and certain best practices must be maintained. *Do not package bloodstained evidence in plastic bags.* If possible, collect the entire stained garment. Avoid altering the stain or transferring blood from one portion of the garment to another; do not fold or crumple the garment. Be careful not to lose or contaminate any remaining trace evidence on the garment.

Avoid excessive heat when collecting, transporting, or storing blood evidence. Avoid moisture, water, or other liquids. Avoid exposing the bloody evidence to strong light, especially UV light. Avoid touching, taking off gloves, or coughing/sneezing over or near the evidence. Describe the stain as a "red stain" or "apparent bloodstain." Do not label it as blood if the stain has not been forensically identified as such. Mark package with appropriate cautions about contents, such as "Store Frozen" or by affixing Biohazard stickers.

Caution: Leaving evidence exposed at a crime scene can lead to contamination. It may not be possible to dry an item at the scene without risking contamination.

Storing Blood Evidence

Ideally, bloodstained items should be stored in a temperature-controlled environment (between 60–75 degrees, with less than 60% humidity). If stored at ambient temperature, place the container in a secure, dry storage area. Never expose the container to extreme heat, such as from a heater vent. Avoid exposing the container to direct sunlight.

SEMEN AND BODILY FLUID EVIDENCE

Ensure that the portion of the area or object with the stain has been documented as it was found. When photographing the object, include a scale and an identification label. Take one or more location photographs that show the object where it was found. Show the relationship of the object to other evidence in the photograph.

Locating Semen Stains

Unlike bloodstains, semen stains are not always obvious to the unaided eye at a crime scene. Semen stains are difficult to see under room and ambient lighting conditions. They may appear as a slightly yellow stain on light-colored fabrics or a whitish stain on dark-colored fabrics. Semen stains may also appear "crusty." Still, many stains will be missed by normal or unaided visual examination; therefore, it is best to collect any item that may have semen stains.

Common items to collect are:

- Victim's clothing, especially underwear of sexual assault victims
- Suspect's clothing
- Bedding (e.g., blankets, sheets) where an alleged sexual assault took place
- Towels
- Tissue paper
- Car seats

Detecting Semen Stains

Items that are impractical to submit to the laboratory (e.g., vehicles, carpets) can be screened using special lighting techniques. All visual lighting techniques are screening tests that can fail to detect semen stains; detection varies depending on the type of fabric or material on which the stain may be deposited. Visual tests will not discriminate between many possible physiological fluids or fluorescent contaminants.

A forensic light source is an **alternate light source (ALS)** that may cause semen stains to fluoresce when viewed through an appropriate color filter. Optimal **wavelength** is dependent on surface characteristics of the item. Certain surfaces appear to quench the fluorescent reaction. Argon ion laser causes a similar reaction as ALS.

Long-wave Ultraviolet (UV) Lamp. As a precaution, analysts must wear plastic UV eye protection and cover any bare skin that will be exposed, such as hands and arms, during the UV examination or viewing. Semen stains may appear on a dark background. It should be noted that some clothing could **fluoresce** due to such materials as detergents and food stains.

Collection of Semen Stains

Minimize disturbance, transference/swiping, and contamination of the stain. Gloves should be worn during the collection and handling of the swab. *Always collect a control sample.* The preference when collecting dry semen stains should be to collect the entire item bearing the stain. Ensure that the stain will not flake off or become dislodged. Cut the stain from carpet, upholstery or other items that cannot be collected. Moisten a sterile swab with distilled water, swab the suspected semen stain, and air dry before packaging.

Saliva

Label a container that will be used to collect the item. Document the location of the item with photography, measurements, and sketching, where appropriate. Cigarette butts and used beverage cans or bottles are common types of saliva-containing evidence found at crime scenes.

In sexual assault cases, consider swabbing the breast or other body areas to collect any potential saliva evidence if case circumstances dictate. Use a dry swab or moistened swab depending upon the circumstance of the stain. Use gloved hands or forceps to collect the item to prevent contamination. Do not lick the envelope flap or cough/sneeze on the sample, or contamination of the sample may occur.

Standard Sample for Body Fluid

To compare DNA types from the suspect(s) and victim(s) to evidence analysis results, a standard/reference sample must be collected. In cases involving semen as evidence, it is not necessary to obtain a semen reference standard. Saliva or buccal swab standards are recommended. Be sure to adhere to legal standards for search and seizure, if any, for your jurisdiction.

Cellular material obtained by buccal swab is sufficient for DNA analysis. The preferred method is to collect buccal or saliva swabs with several clean swabs. Finger-pricking the suspect and placing the blood drops on filter paper, or specialty paper designed for this purpose, is acceptable. This reference material should be handled and processed as evidence.

REFERENCES AND FURTHER READING

Michielsen, S. (2019). *Transfer of Bloodstains from Textile Surfaces: A Fundamental Analysis.* Available: https://www.ncjrs.gov/pdffiles1/nij/grants/252773.pdf

SECTION 3.2:

Forensic Science

Understanding the capabilities of the **crime laboratory** is critical to the success of an investigation. Knowing what can be analyzed and something about how it will be analyzed aids the investigator in sending quality samples to the lab. No matter how good the lab, the quality of analysis can be no better than the quality of the samples submitted by the investigator.

While **lab protocols** vary from jurisdiction to jurisdiction, we can use the FBI's submission protocols as a general template.

Requests for evidence examinations by the FBI's laboratory must contain the submitting contact person's name, agency, address, and telephone number. Previous case-identification numbers, evidence submissions, and communications relating to the case should be provided. Descriptions of the nature and the basic facts of the case as they pertain to evidence examinations should also be provided. The name(s) of and descriptive data about the individual(s) involved (subject, suspect, victim, or a combination of those categories) and the agency-assigned case-identification number should be included. The name of the prosecutor assigned should be provided, if available.

A list of the evidence being submitted **"herewith"** (enclosed) or **"under separate cover."** "Herewith" is limited to small items of evidence that are not endangered by transmitting in an envelope. Write on the envelope before placing evidence inside to avoid damaging or altering the evidence. The written communication should state: "Submitted herewith are the following items of evidence."

"Separate cover" is used to ship numerous or bulky items of evidence. Include a copy of the communication requesting the examinations. The written communication should state: "Submitted under separate cover by [list the method of shipment] are the following items of evidence."

In addition to the above information, what types of examinations are requested should be specified. The lab should also be notified as to where the evidence should be returned and where the Laboratory report should be sent.

FORENSIC SCIENCE PRINCIPLES

Trace evidence is any tiny fragment of physical evidence such as hairs or fibers from clothing or carpeting, small particles of glass, and so forth. These minuscule items can help tell the story of what happened at the crime scene. Trace evidence can be transferred when two objects come in contact with each other or when some small particles are dispersed by action or movement. For example, paint can be transferred from one vehicle to another when a collision happens. Similarly, hair can be left on a cloth during a physical attack, such as in rape cases.

Reconstruction of an event can be done with the aid of such evidence, or the evidence may indicate that a person or thing was present. Therefore, trace evidence provides crucial information in solving cases. Collection of materials from a crime scene can yield information about where the various sample came from and help demonstrate how the evidence aids investigators in reconstructing the story. **Forensic scientists** in the crime laboratory analyze the physical, **optical**, and chemical properties of trace evidence and use a variety of tools to find and compare samples and then look for the sources or the common origin of each item.

Most test methods require **microscopy** and/or **chemical analysis** because samples are often very small and because important properties are not readily apparent. Using advanced laboratory methods, even the smallest piece of evidence is enough to provide information about what happened at a scene such as whether an item or body was moved, or whether someone was assaulted from the rear, side, or from the front.

Some laboratories consider fire accelerants as trace evidence, and others will include them in chemistry even though the same tests are conducted in both the laboratories. Suspects often interact with the victim while committing a crime as well as interacting with the environment of the crime scene. These interactions are very important to keep in mind.

Trace evidence becomes very important during such interactions because the exchange of physical evidence can occur when anyone or anything comes into contact with something or someone else. Edmond Locard, a French scientist, first discovered the significance of trace evidence in the investigation of criminal cases. According to **Locard's exchange principle**, wherever a criminal perpetrator steps, whatever he touches, and whatever he leaves behind will serve as a silent witness against him. Not only his fingerprints and footprints can link him to the scene and the victim, but his hair, the fibers from his clothes, the glass he breaks, the toolmarks he leaves, the paint he scratches, the blood or semen he deposits, can prove valuable to the investigator's case.

All of these and many more may be "a mute witness" against him. Trace evidence does not forget, the excitement or terror of the moment does not confuse it, and it is not subject to the limitations of human memory. According to the exchange principle, there is *always* a transfer of evidence when two things come into contact.

If it is absent, it is because the investigator failed to find it, or lacked the tools and technology to detect it. It is up to the investigator to find relevant trace evidence, and it is up to the laboratory technicians to correctly analyze it before it can ever be used as evidence in a criminal trial. Between detection and analysis is the all-important task of *preservation*.

Trace evidence is important in accident investigations. Such investigations usually involve the movement of one part against another. When there is such contact (as in an automobile collision), telltale marks are left behind. For example, fibers, glass, paint chips, fingerprints, tire impression, glove prints, hairs, cosmetics, plant fibers, soil, and other materials can be present as used to demonstrate linkages between people and things. For example, in the case of a hit and run, investigators can use such evidence to link a suspect vehicle with the vehicle belonging to the victim.

Modern technology has worked wonders for investigators attempting to identify the characteristics of trace evidence. **Comparison databases** from scientists and manufacturers contain a growing number of samples of items such as paint, glass, and even soil. These databases allow for a forensic sample (a sample from a crime scene) to be compared against known standards to provide solid and consistent classifications. For example, the **National Automotive Paint File** is an FBI database containing more than 45,000 samples of automotive paint from manufacturers dating back to the 1930s.

Law enforcement and forensic agencies are not the only ones that maintain databases of useful information. Paint manufacturer Sherwin-Williams maintains a large database which can be very helpful in identifying a vehicle's year, make, and model based on color. Trace investigators must stay abreast of advances in manufacturing techniques, materials, coatings, and processes. Every item that can be touched or transported has the potential to become trace evidence. Investigators and analysts must consider the potential that a product may have a new or updated version available.

COLLECTION OF TRACE EVIDENCE

The collection process begins with documentation of the crime scene and analysis of evidence locations. Several materials are used for collecting evidence items. These materials include containers such as bags and envelopes. Non-breakable, leak-proof containers are used for the transportation of liquids. Evidence such as blood and plants (which are moist or wet) are usually collected in plastic containers and sent back to the area where evidence is stored.

Once wet evidence reaches a secure location, it is removed and allowed to dry completely. It is then repackaged in a new dry paper container. Note that the wet evidence should not be packed in plastic or paper containers for more than two hours because microorganisms start growing in it and destroy the evidence. The investigator responsible for packaging and transport to the evidence room or laboratory should take precautions to prevent contamination of evidence packages. How investigators should "bag and tag" evidence items depend on the characteristics of the items and the conditions in which they are found.

ANALYSIS OF TRACE EVIDENCE

Trace material analysis usually starts with a visual examination of the evidence using macro photography followed by microscopic analysis. There are different analytical methods based on the different type of material available for analysis. Common analytical equipment includes **stereo microscopes**, **scanning electron microscopes (SEM)**, and x-ray machines.

Chemical analyses can be done using **mass spectrometry**, **high-performance liquid chromatography (HPLC)**, and **infrared spectroscopy (IR)**. For example, such methods may be used to identify a small amount of explosives, volatile hydrocarbons, and other chemicals. It is important to protect such samples from damage by using non-destructive testing. That is, non-destructive methods should always be used *before* making use of destructive methods. Such analyses are usually conducted by technicians trained in **forensic chemistry**.

HAIR

Microscopy allows for the forensic examination of hair samples. A key type of class evidence is the structure of the hair in question. Forensic examination of hairs helps in the determination of origin, such as determining whether the hair is animal or human. If a sample is of animal origin, the species and possibly breed of the animal can be determined.

When hairs are of human origin, racial characteristics, length, area of the body and any treatment or damage can be determined. Samples can be tested to determine the color, shape, and chemical composition of the hair. The presence of toxins, dyes, and hair treatments are also detectable. This information can assist investigators in including or excluding particular individuals.

If the hair still has a follicle root attached, DNA testing may be used to identify a particular individual. Otherwise, hair comparison is typically considered as class evidence and is most useful to exclude innocent suspects.

Collected samples are sent to the laboratory along with **control samples** from a suspected individual. Control samples should include hair from all parts of the head. Pubic hair should also be collected. The pubic area should be combed for foreign hair before sample collection. Hair samples are primarily collected using tweezers.

Hair samples are tested primarily by microscopic comparison and chemical analysis. The microscopic comparison identifies the shape, color, texture, and other visual aspects of the sample. Chemical analysis indicates the presence of toxins, drugs, dyes, and other chemicals.

FIBERS

Fibers are thread-like elements from fabric or other materials such as mattresses. Fibers fall into three categories. **Natural fibers** come from animals (e.g., wool) or plants (e.g., cotton). **Synthetic fibers** are completely man-made products, including polyester and nylon. Fibers that are manufactured by heavily processing natural materials to create fibers can also be classified as synthetic, such as rayon.

Fiber examination helps in determining the origin of the fiber, and whether it is natural or synthetic. Fibers are useful in the crime-scene investigation because their origin can often be identified. For example, a carpet fiber on a person shoe can indicate the individual's presence at a crime scene. Fibers are very mobile and can become airborne, get brushed off, or fall from clothing. This mobility makes timely collection crucial to prevent loss of material or cross contamination.

Fibers tend to cling to other fibers and hair, but may be easily brushed off. When approaching a scene, investigators should try to pinpoint the most likely locations for deposited fibers. For example, clothing from the victim or a suspected weapon is likely places to find fibers. Common collection methods include individual fiber collection using tweezers and vacuuming an area and sorting the materials at the laboratory.

Trace evidence can also be gathered by tape lifting, but this is not an ideal method of collection due to the destructive nature of adhesives. Samples that potentially hold fibers should be separately bagged to prevent cross-contamination.

Trace evidence analysts often have only mere strands to work with. From these strands, fiber testing can be done using a high-powered comparison microscope to compare texture in a side-by-side assessment. Chemical analysis can determine the chemical composition of the fibers. In the case of synthetic fabric or carpet, this information can be used to trace the product to the manufacturer using standard databases, further enhancing the probative value of the evidence.

GLASS

Source determination of glass requires the comparison of a known with the questioned sample to identify the type and source of the glass. A variety of material is used in making of glass. These materials make it easy to differentiate one glass sample from another. The properties of glass vary with the temperatures to which it was exposed during its manufacturing. Some basic properties of glass that can be observed without specialized equipment are color, thickness, and curvature. The **optical properties** of glass, which require more sophisticated analysis, depends on the methods used in the manufacturing process.

Glass, then, can be used as evidence, and it can also be the location of evidence. For example, investigators often find fingerprints and blood evidence on broken windows. Broken glass fragments are very small and can be found in shoes, clothing, hair, and skin. Collecting glass fragments from a crime scene can be valuable in connecting people and objects to places. For example, windshields have a different color and composition than a drinking glass, so glass fragments on a suspect's clothing could be compared to those collected at a hit-and-run scene to determine if that individual was present.

Investigators (and examiners in the lab) often use magnification and light to find glass fragments on clothing.

"JIGSAW" MATCHING

When things break or tear, they usually do so in a random way rather than in straight lines (or other predictable, uniform patterns). When the pieces of a broken object (or a torn one) are large enough to observe, unique patterns may emerge such that the original shape can be reconstructed. When the pieces of a broken object can be reconstructed like a jigsaw puzzle, the pieces can be regarded (beyond a reasonable doubt) as coming from the same source.

This type of **pattern matching** is possible with several types of evidence, but it is perhaps most commonly used with glass evidence and is often called **fracture analysis**. Glass characteristics are usually considered as class evidence, but the presence of a demonstrable fracture pattern raises it to the level of individualized evidence. Glass, then, can yield valuable information from fracture marks lines and patterns.

REFERENCES AND FURTHER READING

Federal Bureau of Investigation (2019). *Handbook of Forensic Services*. Available: https://www.fbi.gov/file-repository/handbook-of-forensic-services-pdf.pdf/view

SECTION 3.3:

Biological Evidence

Biological evidence refers to samples of biological material—such as hair, tissue, bones, teeth, blood, semen, or other bodily fluids—or to evidence items containing biological material. This biological evidence, which may or may not have been previously analyzed at a forensic laboratory, should be retained in an appropriate storage facility until needed for court or for forensic testing. Such evidence is frequently essential in linking someone to or excluding someone from crime scene evidence. The criminal justice system depends on presenting evidence to judges and jurors to help them reach a conclusion about the guilt or innocence of the defendant.

All criminal justice stakeholders, including law enforcement officers, lawyers, forensic analysts, and fact finders, should be certain that the biological evidence they are considering has been properly preserved, processed, stored, and tracked to avoid contamination, premature destruction, or **degradation**. Also, individuals who come into contact with biological evidence, such as evidence custodians, need to be confident that it has been packaged and labeled in a way that will allow them to efficiently locate relevant evidence for a case. To establish this confidence, all handlers of biological evidence should follow well-defined procedures for its optimal preservation.

SAFETY

Contact with bodily fluids can spread disease such as those caused by bloodborne pathogens, and individuals handling biological evidence should treat it as hazardous to ensure safety. This section offers recommendations on various aspects of biological evidence handling, including the use of personal protective equipment.

IDENTIFYING BIOLOGICAL EVIDENCE

Existing state laws vary in their definitions of what constitutes biological evidence in the context of **evidence retention**. A review of the National Institute of Justice's list of items from which biological evidence can be found for criminal cases illustrates the variety of items that can be successfully tested with current technology. Further, **touch DNA**, or DNA contained in shed skin cells that transfer to surfaces that humans touch, can be sampled from countless objects and surfaces.

Requiring the retention of all physical evidence that can potentially contain DNA would result in the retention of all evidence collected unless it was screened to determine the possible presence of genetic material. Law enforcement organizations must attempt to balance the interests of justice with practicable storage concerns and to offer a minimum threshold for biological evidence retention.

BULKY ITEMS

To facilitate forensic testing for trial and **post-conviction proceedings**, it is essential to store and track as much of the evidence as necessary. However, it may be extremely difficult to maintain large or bulky items of evidence from which biological material is derived. For the long term, agencies might find it sufficient to retain samples taken from a large item as opposed to the large item on which biological evidence may have been located.

Other examples of bulky evidence include a car, the wall/ceiling of a house, carpet, or another large piece of furniture such as a bed. If the origin of a sample is well documented (such as through photographs or case files), it may not be necessary to store the entire couch for testing and future re-testing.

CASE STATUS

When determining the duration of time that biological evidence must be held, it is essential to understand what is meant by "**case status**" for criminal cases. Generally, there are four categories of case status:

- Open Cases (i.e., no suspect, but investigation continuing)
- Charges Filed (i.e., suspects charged and court proceedings active)
- Adjudicated (i.e., conviction, dismissal, or acquittal)
- Unfounded/Refused/Denied/No Further Investigation

Open cases. Open cases are those in which one or more suspects have not yet been identified or charged, a suspect has been identified but not yet charged, or the investigation is ongoing. As a standard practice, it is recommended that the evidence be maintained by the holding agency for as long as the statute of limitations for the crime or as applicable by law. Biological evidence that is collected in the course of an open investigation should be retained indefinitely for homicides and, at a minimum, for the length of the statute of limitations for all other offenses.

Charges filed. Standard practice dictates that all evidence in any case being prosecuted is maintained in the event that the evidence is needed for laboratory analysis or court proceedings. When charges are filed, a person has been charged and court proceedings have been or will be initiated. Evidence custodians should be notified if charges have been filed to

1. communicate case status for evidence release requests and
2. assist evidence custodians in determining disposition status

A communications link should be established between investigators, prosecutors, and the responsible custodial agency to be able to determine if charges are filed.

Adjudicated. A case is adjudicated when a final judgment has been rendered in a legal proceeding. The disposition of evidence in adjudicated cases varies according to the crime category. Knowledge of the retention statutes in one's state is essential. Biological evidence should be preserved through, at a minimum, the period of incarceration in the following crime categories, as defined in NIBRS, regardless of whether or not a plea was obtained: homicides, sexual assault offenses, assaults, kidnapping/abductions, and robberies. For all other Group A and B offenses, biological evidence may be disposed of upon receipt of authorizations.

Unfounded. In cases categorized as unfounded, refused, or denied, or for which no further investigation will be conducted, evidence can be disposed of upon receipt of disposition approval from the assigned investigator unless such disposal is prohibited by law. This category includes instances in which the victim chooses not to press charges, the prosecutor decides not to file charges, the investigator determines no arrest will be made, or the case is exceptionally cleared. After it is determined that charges will not be sought or filed, evidence, including any biological evidence, need not be retained unless destruction is prohibited by statute.

STORAGE OF BIOLOGICAL EVIDENCE

The packaging and storage of evidence are of paramount importance in forensic investigation. However, requests to produce evidence have demonstrated inadequacies in the packaging and storage of some evidence. Further, studies call for greater care when packaging and storing evidence to prevent contamination and to ensure reliable analysis in the future.

Multiple underlying factors affect law enforcement's ability to appropriately store evidence for optimum preservation, including limitations in the management and capacity of the storage facility, insufficient materials available for packaging, inadequate or improper temporary storage, changes in technology, and the lag between evidence collection and transport of the evidence to the evidence storage facility.

Jurisdictions should place greater emphasis on the needs of their property rooms and staff members. The jurisdiction must ensure that the agency has sufficient resources and must apply appropriate methods and procedures to ensure that evidence is maintained in a condition suitable for future analysis. In tandem with state or local legislatures, managers in law enforcement and relevant stakeholders should advocate for additional resources and funding to ensure the integrity of biological evidence through prioritizing the packaging, storage, maintenance, and security of the evidence in their jurisdictions.

WET VERSUS DRY EVIDENCE

There are two physical states in which biological evidence is submitted: wet and dry. Certain types of evidence, such as blood-draw samples or some of the contents of a **sexual assault kit**, must remain in liquid form. In most cases, these types of evidence are obtained from the crime laboratory or medical facility. All other evidence that is wet should be dried to be properly stored and tested in the future. Drying wet items of evidence, such as a blood-soaked garment, should be the first task of anyone handling wet biological evidence once it has been collected.

Temporary Storage of Wet Items

At times, the evidence handler may have to temporarily store evidence in its wet state because the facilities or equipment necessary to dry it properly are not available. In such a case, the handler should place the evidence in an **impermeable** and nonporous container (i.e., packaging through which liquids or vapors cannot pass), such as a metal can or glass jar, and should place the container in a refrigerator that maintains a temperature of 2°C to 8°C (approximately 35°F to 46°F) and that is away from direct sunlight. The handler may leave the evidence there until it can be air dried or submitted to the laboratory.

Plastic bags can be used temporarily to store wet evidence but must not be used for long-term storage because of the possibility of bacterial growth or mold. Exceptions include plastic bags that contain desiccant, a drying agent that prevents condensation and the subsequent growth of fungi or bacteria and breathable plastic bags (Tyvek) that can be used for damp items and swabs.

Drying Wet Evidence

If evidence with wet biological material is not correctly air-dried, there is a high probability that the biological material will be destroyed by bacterial growth. This could potentially preclude the generation of DNA results. Here are a few examples of low-tech and high-tech methods for properly drying evidence.

Agencies that do not have sufficient funds or a need (i.e., they do not handle a significant volume of wet evidence) for equipment specifically designed for drying evidence generally use low-tech methods. In these cases, it is recommended that an isolated and secure area—such as a locker, shower stall, or room—be designated for this purpose. For example, a metal locker specifically labeled for biohazards is commonly used to dry evidence.

These materials will be used for repackaging the evidence once it has dried. Wet garments should hang with sterilized paper beneath and between them to minimize contamination while drying. After the drying process, the paper should be packaged separately and submitted with the garment, as it may contain trace evidence.

A shower stall is also an excellent, inexpensive way for departments with limited resources to dry evidence. Departments can create this system with a prefabricated fiberglass shower enclosure elevated on a wooden frame to make room for controlled drainage. If possible, there should be an adjacent water faucet on which to attach a cleaning hose for washing the enclosure during **decontamination**.

Any room dedicated to drying evidence should have surfaces that allow for easy decontamination. A locking mechanism should be used to limit access to assigned personnel.

Decontamination

Decontamination of surfaces or items can be accomplished by using a freshly made solution of 10 percent bleach or a suitable substitute. Individuals responsible for decontamination should consult with the laboratory for suitable substitutes (Centers for Disease Control and Prevention, 2012).

LIQUID EVIDENCE AND TISSUE

Certain types of evidence will remain in liquid form or contain fluids. These types require different types of packaging materials as well. Specific storage conditions regarding these and other types of evidence will be discussed later in the section.

Blood samples. Generally, blood drawtubes and vials are collected and submitted in some type of container recommended by the crime laboratory and/or hospital. If the department receives a vial or tube that is not packaged in a readily identifiable manner, it should be placed in an envelope that is easily recognizable, clearly marked as to its contents, and bearing a visible biohazard label. Glass vials of blood should never be frozen because the vial might explode or crack.

Hypodermic Needles. Department packaging protocols should require that any type of needle or other sharp object entering the property room be stored in a container that is closeable, puncture-resistant, leak-proof on the sides and bottom, labeled or color-coded, and breathable. These items should not be commingled in a package with other evidence. Sharps containers also must be maintained upright throughout use.

For employee safety, syringes should be stored in an area designated for such evidence. Commingling packaged syringes with other evidence create a special safety hazard because syringes can accidentally deliver infectious agents directly into the bloodstream (HERC 2012). Filing drawers, bins, or boxes can be used for storing these items.

Breathable Storage Containers

Throughout this text, breathable storage containers are mentioned as a preferred method for packaging. Breathable containers are important because they prevent condensation, which can encourage the growth of bacteria that can attack and degrade DNA samples. Oxygen can provide a protective barrier against these types of bacteria.

Urine Samples. If an agency receives a vial or tube that is not clearly labeled as containing urine, it should be labeled or packaged in an identifiable envelope or box that is clearly marked as to its contents. Employee safety mandates that this type of biohazard, similar to blood, tissues samples, and extracted DNA, be segregated in one centralized location for easy identification and safe storage. Urine should not be frozen in glass jars or vials.

Sexual Assault Kits. State or local crime laboratories, local hospitals, or evidence supply vendors generally supply law enforcement agencies with their sexual assault kits. The contents of these kits can vary by agency. An itemized list of collected items should be submitted with the kit.

Boxes and envelopes of uniform size make storage and retrieval efficient. Given the importance of biological evidence in these cases, sexual assault kits are often retained for decades and must be stored in a manner that prevents degradation and facilitates easy retrieval and identification. Depending on the contents of the kits, a temperature- and humidity-controlled facility may be appropriate.

Extracted DNA. Preservation of **genomic DNA** extracted from biological evidence is an important consideration for any handling, storage, and retrieval procedures, as this DNA may be the only source of material for future testing. Historically, extracted DNA has been stored in a preservative and then frozen or refrigerated. The stability and recovery of DNA extracts is dependent on the quantity and quality of the extracted DNA prior to storage as well as the type of tube used for storage. However, maintaining freezers and refrigerators is costly, which has led to research on room temperature storage of DNA extracts.

Tissue Samples. At times, preservation of tissue samples for the long term may be handled by a property and evidence custodian after the tissue has been sampled and analyzed by a crime laboratory or medical examiner. Tissue samples that are submitted for DNA analysis are usually stored at -20 °C as rapidly as possible to halt the degradation process. In cases of mass casualty disasters, freezing or refrigeration may not be immediately available. The use of preservation reagents used to stabilize tissue samples temporarily at room temperature may be advantageous.

ENVIRONMENTAL CONDITIONS

The proper drying and packaging of biological evidence is the first step toward achieving optimal preservation. The next step is storing it in the proper environmental conditions. Biological evidence must be stored in a fashion that not only safeguards its integrity but also ensures its protection from degradation. The storage of biological evidence may include, but is not limited to, the use of temperature- and humidity-controlled areas or freezers and refrigerators. In all cases, it should be understood that conditions of storage should include protection from moisture, excessive heat, and protection from sunlight.

Biological evidence should be stored in one of the following conditions, depending on the type of evidence, and if known, the type of analysis that will be conducted:

- **frozen**: temperature is maintained thermostatically at or below −10 °C (14 °F)

- **refrigerated**: temperature is maintained thermostatically between 2 °C and 8 °C (36 °F and 46 °F) with less than 25 % humidity
- **temperature controlled**: temperature is maintained thermostatically between 15.5 °C and 24 °C (60 °F to 75 °F) with less than 60 % humidity
- **room temperature**: temperature is equal to the ambient temperature of its surroundings; storage area may lack temperature and humidity control methods

Because of the nature of the evidence storage and management process, it is necessary to distinguish **temporary storage** from **long-term storage**. In many cases, evidence is stored temporarily because the facility handling it does not have the proper conditions to ensure its integrity for a long time. Temporary storage spaces include medical facilities and hospitals, small property rooms at law enforcement headquarters, or vehicles that transport evidence from the crime scene to long-term evidence management facilities. Temporary storage is generally defined to include any location where evidence may be stored for 72 hours or less. Long-term storage is defined as any location where evidence may be stored for more than 72 hours.

REFERENCES AND FURTHER READING

Technical Working Group on Biological Evidence Preservation (2013). *The Biological Evidence Preservation Handbook: Best Practices for Evidence Handlers*.
Available: https://nvlpubs.nist.gov/nistpubs/ir/2013/NIST.IR.7928.pdf

HERC. (2012). *Regulated Medical Waste—Overview.*
Available: http://www.hercenter.org/rmw/rmwoverview.php

SECTION 3.4:

DNA Evidence

In 1996, Gerald Parker-then in a California prison on a parole violation stemming from a 1980 sentence for raping a child--was charged with the rapes and murders of five women between December 1978 and October 1979 and the murder of a fetus during a rape in 1980. DNA samples from the crime scenes were run through California's sexual assault/violent offenders database, and four of the cases were found to have been committed by the same perpetrator. After DNA tests linked Parker to the victims, he confessed to the crimes. He also confessed to a similar, fifth crime for which Kevin Lee Green had been wrongly convicted and had served 16 years in prison.

Just as today's law enforcement officer has learned to look routinely for fingerprints to identify the perpetrator of a crime, that same officer needs to think routinely about evidence that may contain DNA. Recent advancements in DNA technology are enabling law enforcement officers to solve cases previously thought to be unsolvable.

Today, investigators with a fundamental knowledge of how to identify, preserve, and collect DNA evidence properly can solve cases in ways previously seen only on television. Evidence invisible to the naked eye can be the key to solving a residential burglary, sexual assault, or child's murder. It also can be the evidence that links different crime scenes to each other in a small town, within a single State, or even across the Nation. The saliva on the stamp of a stalker's threatening letter or the skin cells shed on a ligature of a strangled victim can be compared with a suspect's blood or saliva sample.

Similarly, DNA collected from the perspiration on a baseball cap discarded by a rapist at one crime scene can be compared with DNA in the saliva swabbed from the bite mark on a different rape victim.

DNA is similar to fingerprint analysis in how matches are determined. When using either DNA or a fingerprint to identify a suspect, the evidence collected from the crime scene is compared with the "known" print. If enough of the identifying features are the same, the DNA or fingerprint is determined to be a match. If, however, even one feature of the DNA or fingerprint is different, it is determined not to have come from that suspect.

WHAT IS DNA?

DNA, or deoxyribonucleic acid, is the fundamental building block for an individual's entire genetic makeup. It is a component of virtually every cell in the human body. Further, a person's DNA is the same in every cell. For example, the DNA in a man's blood is the same as the DNA in his skin cells, semen, and saliva.

DNA is a powerful tool because each person's DNA is different from every other individual's, except for identical twins. Because of that difference, DNA collected from a crime scene can either link a suspect to the evidence or eliminate a suspect, similar to the use of fingerprints.

It also can identify a victim through DNA from relatives, even when no body can be found. Moreover, when evidence from one crime scene is compared with evidence from another, those crime scenes can be linked to the same perpetrator locally, statewide, and across the Nation.

Forensically valuable DNA can be found on evidence that is decades old. However, several factors can affect the DNA left at a crime scene, including environmental factors (e.g., heat, sunlight, moisture, bacteria, and mold). Therefore, not all DNA evidence will result in a usable DNA profile. Further, just like fingerprints, DNA testing cannot tell officers when the suspect was at the crime scene or for how long.

DNA AT A CRIME SCENE

DNA evidence can be collected from virtually anywhere. DNA has helped solve many cases when imaginative investigators collected evidence from nontraditional sources. One murder was solved when the suspect's DNA, taken from saliva in a dental impression mold, matched the DNA swabbed from a bite mark on the victim.

A masked rapist was convicted of forced oral copulation when his victim's DNA matched DNA swabbed from the suspect's penis 6 hours after the offense. Numerous cases have been solved by DNA analysis of saliva on cigarette butts, postage stamps, and the area around the mouth opening on ski masks. A DNA analysis of a single hair (without the root) found deep in the victim's throat provided a critical piece of evidence used in a capital murder conviction.

Identifying DNA Evidence

Since only a few cells can be sufficient to obtain useful DNA information to help your case, the list below identifies some common items of evidence that you may need to collect, the possible location of the DNA on the evidence, and the biological source containing the cells. Remember that just because you cannot see a stain does not mean there are not enough cells for DNA typing.

Further, DNA does more than just identify the source of the sample; it can place a known individual at a crime scene, in a home, or in a room where the suspect claimed not to have been. It can refute a claim of self-defense and put a weapon in the suspect's hand. It can change a story from an alibi to one of consent. The more officers know how to use DNA, the more powerful a tool it becomes.

Evidence Collection and Preservation

Investigators and laboratory personnel should work together to determine the most probative pieces of evidence and to establish priorities. Although this brochure is not intended as a manual for DNA evidence collection, every officer should be aware of important issues involved in the identification, collection, transportation, and storage of DNA evidence.

These issues are as important for the first responding patrol officer as they are for the experienced detective and the crime scene specialist. Biological material may contain hazardous pathogens such as the human immunodeficiency virus (HIV) and the hepatitis B virus that can cause potentially lethal diseases. Given the sensitive nature of DNA evidence, officers should always contact their laboratory personnel or evidence collection technicians when collection questions arise.

Contamination

Because extremely small samples of DNA can be used as evidence, greater attention to contamination issues is necessary when identifying, collecting, and preserving DNA evidence. DNA evidence can be contaminated when DNA from another source is mixed with DNA relevant to the case. This can happen when someone sneezes or coughs over the evidence or touches his/her mouth, nose, or other parts of the face and then touches the area that may contain the DNA to be tested.

Because a new DNA technology called "PCR" replicates or copies DNA in the evidence sample, the introduction of contaminants or other unintended DNA to an evidence sample can be problematic. With such minute samples of DNA being copied, extra care must be taken to prevent contamination. If a sample of DNA is submitted for testing, the PCR process will copy whatever DNA is present in the sample; it cannot distinguish between a suspect's DNA and DNA from another source.

When transporting and storing evidence that may contain DNA, it is important to keep the evidence dry and at room temperature. Once the evidence has been secured in paper bags or envelopes, it should be sealed, labeled, and transported in a way that ensures proper identification of where it was found and proper chain of custody. Never place evidence that may contain DNA in plastic bags because plastic bags will retain damaging moisture. Direct sunlight and warmer conditions also may be harmful to DNA, so avoid keeping evidence in places that may get hot, such as a room or police car without air conditioning. For long-term storage issues, contact your local laboratory.

Elimination Samples

As with fingerprints, the effective use of DNA may require the collection and analysis of elimination samples. It often is necessary to use elimination samples to determine whether the evidence comes from the suspect or from someone else. An officer must think ahead to the time of trial and possible defenses while still at the crime scene.

For example, in the case of a residential burglary where the suspect may have drunk a glass of water at the crime scene, an officer should identify appropriate people, such as household members, for future elimination sample testing. These samples may be needed for comparison with the saliva found on the glass to determine whether the saliva is valuable evidence.

In homicide cases, be sure to collect the victim's DNA from the medical examiner at the autopsy, even if the body is badly decomposed. This may serve to identify an unknown victim or distinguish between the victim's DNA and other DNA found at the crime scene.

When investigating rape cases, it may be necessary to collect and analyze the DNA of the victim's recent consensual partners, if any, to eliminate them as potential contributors of DNA suspected to be from the perpetrator. If this is necessary, it is important to approach the victim with extreme sensitivity and provide a full explanation of why the request is being made. When possible, the help of a qualified victim advocate should be enlisted for assistance.

CODIS

CODIS (COmbined DNA Index System), an electronic database of DNA profiles that can identify suspects, is similar to the AFIS (Automated Fingerprint Identification System) database. Every State in the Nation is in the process of implementing a DNA index of individuals convicted of certain crimes, such as rape, murder, and child abuse. Upon conviction and sample analysis, perpetrators' DNA profiles are entered into the DNA database. Just as fingerprints found at a crime scene can be run through AFIS in search of a suspect or link to another crime scene, DNA profiles from a crime scene can be entered into CODIS. Therefore, law enforcement officers can identify possible suspects when no prior suspect existed.

REFERENCES AND FURTHER READING

Bureau of Justice Assistance. (2018). Utilizing *DNA Evidence To Investigate Cold Case Sexual Assaults Through CODIS.*
Available: https://www.sakitta.org/resources/docs/11664_R1_SAKI_DNA-CODIS_Briefs_Booklet.pdf

Campbell, R., Pierce, S. J., Sharma, D. Feeney, H, Goodman-Williams, R., & Ma, W. (2019). *Serial Sexual Assaults: A Longitudinal Examination of Offending Patterns Using DNA Evidence.* Available: https://www.ncjrs.gov/pdffiles1/nij/grants/252707.pdf

Niedzwiecki, E., Debus-Sherrill, S. & Field, M. B. (2016). *Understanding Familial DNA Searching: Coming to a Consensus on Terminology.*
Available: https://www.ncjrs.gov/pdffiles1/nij/grants/251080.pdf

SECTION 3.5

Hair & Fiber Evidence

During the course of a criminal investigation, many types of physical evidence are encountered. One of the most common is hair evidence. The identification and comparison of human and animal hairs can help demonstrate physical contact with a suspect, victim, and crime scene. Hairs can provide investigators with valuable information for potential leads.

Until recently, the comparison microscope was considered the only reliable tool for the identification and comparison of the microscopic characteristics found in hair. Today, nuclear and mitochondrial DNA (mtDNA) testing can provide additional information that can influence the value of microscopic examinations. When the microscope is coupled with DNA technologies, the combination of these technologies profoundly affects the way forensic scientists, investigators, and prosecutors view hair evidence.

Although DNA technologies may add significant information to hair evidence recovered at a crime scene, the first step necessary in the analytical process is the identification and comparison of human and animal hairs.

A **hair** can be defined as a slender, thread-like outgrowth from a follicle in the skin of mammals. Composed mainly of keratin, it has three morphological regions—the cuticle, medulla, and cortex.

The cuticle is a translucent outer layer of the hair shaft consisting of scales that cover the shaft. Cuticular scales always point from the proximal or root end of the hair to the distal or tip end of the hair. There are three basic scale structures that make up the cuticle—coronal (crown-like), spinous (petal-like), and imbricate (flattened). Combinations and variations of these types are possible.

Animal versus Human Hairs

Human hairs are distinguishable from hairs of other mammals. Animal hairs are classified into the following three basic types.

1. Guard hairs that form the outer coat of an animal and provide protection
2. Fur or wool hairs that form the inner coat of an animal and provide insulation
3. Tactile hairs (whiskers) that are found on the head of animals provide sensory functions

Other types of hairs found on animals include tail hair and mane hair (horse). Human hair is not so differentiated and might be described as a modified combination of the characteristics of guard hairs and fur hairs.

Human hairs are generally consistent in color and pigmentation throughout the length of the hair shaft, whereas animal hairs may exhibit radical color changes in a short distance, called banding. The distribution and density of pigment in animal hairs can also be identifiable features. The pigmentation of human hairs is evenly distributed, or slightly denser toward the cuticle, whereas the pigmentation of animal hairs is more centrally distributed, although denser toward the medulla.

The medulla, when present in human hairs, is amorphous in appearance, and the width is generally less than one-third the overall diameter of the hair shaft. The medulla in animal hairs is normally continuous and structured and generally occupies an area of greater than one-third the overall diameter of the hair shaft.

HUMAN HAIR CLASSIFICATION

Hair evidence examined under a microscope provides investigators with valuable information. Hairs found on a knife or club may support murder and/or assault weapon claim. A questioned hair specimen can be compared microscopically with hairs from a known individual when the characteristics are compared side-by-side.

Human hairs can be classified by racial origins such as Caucasian (European origin), Negroid (African origin), and Mongoloid (Asian origin). In some instances, the racial characteristics exhibited are not clearly defined, indicating the hair may be of mixed-racial origin.

The region of the body where a hair originated can be determined with considerable accuracy by its gross appearance and microscopic characteristics. The length and color can be determined. It can also be determined whether the hair was forcibly removed, damaged by burning or crushing, or artificially treated by dyeing or bleaching.

The characteristics and their variations allow an experienced examiner to distinguish between hairs from different individuals. Hair examinations and comparisons, with the aid of a comparison microscope, can be valuable in an investigation of a crime.

DNA EXAMINATIONS

Hairs that have been matched or associated through a microscopic examination should also be examined by mtDNA sequencing. Although it is uncommon to find hairs from two different individuals exhibiting the same microscopic characteristics, it can occur. For this reason, the hairs or portions of the hairs should be forwarded for mtDNA sequencing. The combined procedures add credibility to each.

Although nuclear DNA analysis of hairs may provide an identity match, the microscopic examination should not be disregarded. The time and costs associated with DNA analyses warrant a preliminary microscopic examination. Often it is not possible to extract DNA fully, or there is not enough tissue present to conduct an examination. Hairs with large roots and tissue are promising sources of nuclear DNA. However, DNA examinations destroy hairs, eliminating the possibility of further microscopic examination.

HAIR RECOVERY METHODS

Because of the nature of trace evidence, when processing evidentiary items, care should be taken to minimize the possibility of contamination and cross-transfer. Examinations should be sequenced to maximize the potential value of the submitted evidence.

Hairs can be recovered from evidentiary items using a number of different techniques. Some of the methods used to collect hairs from clothing and bedding items are scraping, shaking, taping, and picking. Debris from large carpeted surfaces might be vacuumed into a filtered canister. If the specific location of a hair on a clothing item is important, it might be necessary to pick off the hair or tape the item and record where the hair was removed.

Whichever method is used, it should be done in a location designed for that purpose to avoid the possibility of contamination and cross-transfer. Special lighting and magnification may facilitate the location and recovery.

After trace debris has been removed from items of evidence, it is necessary to select the appropriate types and number of hairs for examination. Sometimes when removing a large quantity of debris (e.g., vacuuming), it may be necessary to select only a representative sample. This process includes selecting samples such as hairs of different lengths, racial groups, body area, and color. Another method is to select hairs that are similar in appearance to a target group (e.g., known hairs from a suspect or victim). The combination of random and target sampling ensures a representative sample.

Selecting hairs for microscopic analyses takes place during the initial processing as well as during low-power microscopy at the bench. The microscopic characteristics of hairs are viewed and selected to provide an examiner with a good range of the hair types present.

Head hairs and pubic hairs exhibit a greater range of microscopic characteristics than other human hairs; therefore, head and pubic hairs are routinely forensically compared. An adequate selection of known hair samples includes both random pullings and combings. The number of hairs necessary to represent a suitable known sample varies with the individual. Twenty-five randomly selected head hairs are generally considered adequate to represent the range of hair characteristics of that individual.

It is recommended that the same number of hairs be collected from the pubic region. The selection of hairs to be mounted from a known hair standard may be random, but representative, especially when the known standard consists of many hairs.

The collection of known head hair standards from a suspect might take place many months, possibly years, after the crime. In these instances, the characteristics of the known head hair sample may look quite different from hairs that were shed when the crime occurred. Some hair examiners have indicated that a one-year time span is an outside limit, and environmental conditions or cosmetic alterations could make it shorter. Pubic hairs seem to retain their characteristics for a longer period.

HAIR COMPARISON CHARACTERISTICS

Certain physical features such as sex, size, age, shape, eye color, hair texture, and color can distinguish individuals. None of these features is peculiar to only one individual, but the general appearance and arrangement of these features serves as criteria for identification. There are, likewise, a number of features or characteristics that may be present in a given hair sample that, when considered collectively, provide a basis for association.

There is no criterion for the importance assigned to a particular characteristic. Such a determination can be made only by the individual examiner and must be based on experience. Hair characteristics are not frequently studied because of all the variations in a single sample and the inherent difficulty in assigning standard values for the variations. If, however, particular characteristics are seen in a hair samples that appear with regularity throughout the sample, they must be considered as significant.

The process of identification or association involves distinct stages in the course of an examination. The following 15 different features or characteristics should be considered in the comparison of hair specimens. There are other lists that identify 25 or more hair characteristics, but those lists generally do not disagree in substance with the following, only in the manner of organization.

Race: Features that serve to determine racial origin have been discussed previously. Hairs of a particular racial group can exhibit a significant range in the distribution of microscopic characteristics.

Body area: As a general rule, most comparisons are conducted using head and pubic hair samples. Hairs from other body areas may be of limited comparative value.

Color: There are many variations among individuals in hair color. The particular hue (color shade), value (lightness or darkness), and intensity (saturation) of a specimen are enhanced through microscopy so that even subtle differences may be distinguished. The range in color of a particular hair sample and the variations in color that exist along the length of hairs are important comparison characteristics.

Length: Length is considered, although hairs may have been cut between the time of deposition of the questioned specimen and the collection of a known sample. In addition, there may be a significant difference in the lengths of the shortest and longest hairs on an individual's head.

Tip: The tip can be cut, broken, split, abraded (rounded), or finely pointed. An individual's grooming, hygiene, health, and nutrition can affect these features.

Root: The mature hair root will be hardened, have a bulbous shape, and have little or no follicular tissue adhering to it. Pigment is sparse or absent, and there is frequently an abundance of cortical fusi. A root that has been plucked prior to maturation will be soft, have a distorted appearance, and may have tissue adhering to it. Pigment is present, and there are rarely cortical fusi. A catagen root may exhibit the bulbous shape with a tag attached. Hairs are naturally sloughed from the body after a period of growth. The life cycle includes a growing or anagen phase, a transition or catagen phase, and a resting or telogen phase.

Diameter: The overall shaft diameter can range from very fine (40-50um) to very coarse (110-120um). Consideration is given to the range of variation in a particular sample and the variation in a single hair shaft. Consideration is also given to the degree of shaft diameter variation as well as the rate of change between variations. The phenomenon of abrupt and radical changes is referred to as buckling.

The shape of the hair shaft and how the hair lies on the glass microscope slide influences the apparent shaft diameter variations that exist in hair. What appears to be diameter variation may be different viewing angles of a constant diameter. The twisting of flat to oval hairs on a glass microscope slide also influences the interpretation of diameter variation.

Cuticle: The cuticle is comprised of an outer layer of scales that may vary in thickness and color. There may even be variation in thickness and color throughout the length of a single hair. The inner margin of the cuticle may be clearly defined or may be without a sharp delineation.

Scales: A scale cast is not necessary to observe the features of scales. The scales may be undisturbed and closely aligned with the hair shaft, or they may protrude outward from the shaft. Scale damage and protrusion are associated with mechanical action such as backcombing or harsh chemical action such as dyeing and bleaching. The scales may protrude out from the hair shaft, and then recurve back to the shaft, giving a looped appearance.

Pigment: The pigment granules may be absent as in gray hair or may be so dense that they obscure the inner structural detail of the hair specimen. Granule size can range from very fine to coarse. Consideration is given to local distribution of the pigment across the hair shaft as well as to variations in distribution and density along the shaft from proximal to distal. The granules can be regularly arranged in streaks or clumps, with consideration given to the size, distribution, and density of these groupings.

Medulla: The structure of the medulla can vary from continuous throughout the center of the hair shaft to fragmentary, or absent altogether. It can be opaque, translucent, vacuolated, or completely amorphous in appearance. When the medulla is fragmentary, the cell structures may appear fusiform, or spindle-shaped. The width of the medulla in relation to the overall shaft diameter should be considered.

Cortex: The general appearance of the cortex should be considered. The margins of the elongated cells comprising the cortex may be poorly defined or may be distinct These cells are prominent, particularly in hairs that have been bleached and have resulted in a straw-like appearance.

Artificial treatment: Bleaching removes pigment from the hair and can give the hair a characteristic yellow cast. The cortical cell margins may become more prominent and cortical fusi may develop. In addition, harsh or repeated treatments can make the hair shaft brittle, and the scales will appear disturbed. Artificial bleaching can be distinguished from solar bleaching by a sharper line of demarcation between the bleached and unbleached regions.

To the experienced examiner, dyed hairs possess an unnatural cast or color. In addition, the cuticle will take on the color of the dye. If hair generally grows at the rate of one half-inch per month, the distance can be measured from the root to the line of demarcation of the dyed portion to estimate the time since dyeing. Repeated dyeing or bleaching results in several lines of demarcation. This would serve to further individualize a particular hair specimen.

Damage: Cutting with scissors produces a sheared or square-cut end, whereas a razor cut is angular and very straight or clean. The length of time since cutting is subject to many variables; hence, no reliable determination can be made. Crushed hairs exhibit a widening of the hair shaft, and the cortical cells appear ruptured and separated. Broken hairs exhibit a square tip with elongated fragments. Burned or singed hairs are charred and brittle and exhibit round vacuoles at the point of burning.

SECTION 4

Trace Evidence

When "crime scene investigation" is mentioned, the average person (influenced by Hollywood myths) conjures up images of fingerprints, plaster casts, blood splatters, and copious photographs. These things have an often-shocking visual appeal that draws in the attention of television viewers, but they are only a handful of the broad spectrum of evidence types that detectives use in real cases. Often, minute evidence that can barely be seen by the unaided human eye (if at all) is of critical importance in bringing criminals to justice.

Hairs and other types of trace evidence are not so obvious and are often found through painstaking and methodical searching. Criminals often leave trace evidence, which is less visible evidence such as fingerprints, small particles of glass or dirt, body hairs, or clothing fibers.

SECTION 4.1:

Fiber Evidence

Placing a suspect at the scene of a crime is an important element in a criminal investigation. This can be achieved through the location of textile fibers similar to those from the victim's clothing or the crime scene on the clothing of the suspect, or through the discovery of fibers like those in the suspect's clothing at the crime scene.

Textile fibers can be exchanged between two individuals, between an individual and an object, and between two objects. When fibers are matched with a specific source (fabric from the victim, suspect, and/or scene), a value is placed on that association. This value is dependent on many factors, including the type of fiber found, the color or variation of color in the fiber, the number of fibers found, the location of fibers at the crime scene or on the victim, and the number of different fibers at the crime scene or on the victim that match the clothing of the suspect.

Whether a fiber is transferred and detected is dependent on the nature and duration of contact between the suspect and the victim or crime scene, the persistence of fibers after the transfer, and the type(s) of fabric involved in contact.

A fiber is the smallest unit of a textile material that has a length many times greater than its diameter. Fibers can occur naturally as plant and animal fibers, but they can also be synthetic. A fiber can be spun with other fibers to form a yarn that can be woven or knitted to form a fabric. The type and length of fiber used, the type of spinning method, and the type of fabric construction all affect the transfer of fibers and the significance of fiber associations. This becomes very important when there is a possibility of fiber transfer between a suspect and a victim during the commission of a crime.

Fibers are considered a form of trace evidence that can be transferred from the clothing of a suspect to the clothing of a victim during the commission of a crime. Fibers can also transfer from a fabric source such as a carpet, bed, or furniture at a crime scene. These transfers can either be direct (primary) or indirect (secondary). A primary transfer occurs when a fiber is transferred from a fabric directly onto a victim's clothing, whereas a secondary transfer occurs when already transferred fibers on the clothing of a suspect transfer to the clothing of a victim. An understanding of the mechanics of primary and secondary transfer is important when reconstructing the events of a crime.

When two people come in contact or when contact occurs with an item from the crime scene, the possibility exists that a fiber transfer will take place. This does not mean that a fiber transfer will always take place. Certain types of fabric do not shed well (donor garments), and some fabrics do not hold fibers well (recipient garments). The construction and fiber composition of the fabric, the duration, and force of contact, and the condition of the garment with regard to damage are important considerations.

An important consideration is the length of time between the actual physical contact and the collection of clothing items from the suspect or victim. If the victim is immobile, very little fiber loss will take place, whereas the suspect's clothing will lose transferred fibers quickly. The likelihood of finding transferred fibers on the clothing of the suspect a day after the alleged contact may be remote, depending on the subsequent use or handling of that clothing.

NATURAL FIBERS

Many different natural fibers originating from plants and animals are used in the production of fabric. Cotton fibers are the plant fibers most commonly used in textile materials, with the type of cotton, fiber length, and degree of twist contributing to the diversity of these fibers. Processing techniques and color applications also influence the value of cotton fiber identifications.

Other plant fibers used in the production of textile materials include flax (linen), ramie, sisal, jute, hemp, kapok, and coir. The identification of less common plant fibers at a crime scene or on the clothing of a suspect or victim would have increased significance.

The animal fiber most frequently used in the production of textile materials is wool, and the most common wool fibers originate from sheep. The end use of sheep's wool often dictates the fineness or coarseness of woolen fibers: Finer woolen fibers are used in the production of clothing, whereas coarser fibers are found in carpet. Fiber diameter and degree of scale protrusion of the fibers are other important characteristics.

Although sheep's wool is most common, woolen fibers from other animals may also be found. These include camel, alpaca, cashmere, mohair, and others. The identification of less common animal fibers at a crime scene or on the clothing of a suspect or victim would have increased significance.

MAN MADE FIBERS

More than half of all fibers used in the production of textile materials are man-made. Some synthetic fibers originate from natural materials such as cotton or wood; others originate from synthetic materials. Polyester and nylon fibers are the most commonly encountered synthetic fibers, followed by acrylics, rayons, and acetates. There are also many other less common synthetic fibers. The amount of production of a particular synthetic fiber and its end use influence the degree of rarity of a given fiber.

The shape of a synthetic fiber can determine the value placed on that fiber. The cross-section of a synthetic fiber can be manufacturer-specific: Some cross sections are more common than others are, and some shapes may only be produced for a short period. Unusual cross sections encountered through examination can add increased significance to a fiber association.

FIBER COLORS

Color influences the value given to a particular fiber identification. Often several dyes are used to give a fiber the desired color. Individual fibers can be colored before being spun into yarns. Yarns can be dyed, and fabrics made from them can be dyed. Color can also be applied to the surface of fabric, as found in printed fabrics. How color is applied and absorbed along the length of the fiber are important comparison characteristics. Color fading and discoloration can also lend increased value to a fiber association.

FIBER NUMBER AND LOCATION

The number of fibers on the clothing of a victim identified as matching the clothing of a suspect is important in determining actual contact. The greater the number of fibers, the more likely that contact actually occurred between these individuals.

Where fibers are found also affects the value placed on a particular fiber association. The location of fibers on different areas of the body or on specific items at the crime scene influences the significance of the fiber association.

How a fabric is constructed affects the number and types of fibers that may be transferred during contact. Tightly woven or knitted fabrics shed less often than loosely knit, or woven fabrics; fabrics composed of filament yarns shed less than fabrics composed of spun yarns. Certain types of fibers also tend to transfer more readily.

The age of a fabric also affects the degree of fiber transfers. Some newer fabrics may shed more readily because of an abundance of loosely adhering fibers on the surface of the fabric. Some worn fabrics may have damaged areas that easily shed fibers. Damage to a fabric caused during physical contact greatly increases the likelihood of fiber transfer.

FABRIC SOURCES

When a questioned fiber is compared to fibers from a known fabric source, a determination is made as to whether this fiber could have originated from the known fabric. It is not possible to say positively that a fiber originated from a particular fabric, although the inability to positively associate a fiber with a source in no way diminishes the significance of a fiber association.

The wide variety of fiber types, fiber colors, and fabric types can make fiber associations very significant because the value of a fiber association depends on the type of fiber, the color of the fiber, the number of fibers transferred, the location of the recovered fibers, and other factors.

It could be very helpful to know the frequency of occurrence of a particular fabric and fiber, or how many fabrics with a particular fiber type and color exist, as well as who owns them. Such information, however, is extremely difficult to obtain. If the manufacturer of a fabric is known, the possibility exists that the number of fabric units produced could also be obtained, but this information is not always available.

How many garments like this still exist, and where they are located, are still in question.

Once a particular fiber of a certain type, shape, and color is produced and becomes part of a fabric, it occupies an extremely small portion of the fiber/fabric population. Exceptions to this would be white cotton fibers and blue cotton fibers like those comprising blue jeans. There are other fibers that are common, but the majority of fibers of a particular type and color constitute a very small percentage of the total number of fibers that exist in the world.

SECTION 4.2:

Glass & Soil Evidence

Glass is a material commonly found in our environment. The breakage characteristics of glass under impact forces can produce features that can be used as physical evidence in many types of cases. The various examination techniques described in Scientific Working Group for Materials Analysis documents apply to most types of glass, including the following: flat glass used for windows, doors, display cases, and mirrors; container glass; tableware glass; optical glass; decorative glass; and specialty glass used for headlamps, cookware, and others.

Typically, forensic glass examinations involve a comparison of samples from known and questioned sources to determine if they originated from different sources (e.g., window from a suspect's car compared to glass recovered from the victim's clothing). This comparison involves the recognition and evaluation of class characteristics that associate materials to a group but never to a single source. Conversely, individual characteristics allow the association between two or more items with each other to the exclusion of all other items. For glass examiners, this can only occur when pieces of glass are physically matched.

Due to inherent heterogeneity of physical and chemical properties within a single source of glass, it is essential to emphasize the need to collect and analyze a sample(s) of the known source for comparison to any recovered fragments.

ROCK AND SOIL EVIDENCE

Forensic soil scientists compare soils from crime scenes with natural soils or soils databases in order to locate the scene of crimes the soil samples are obtained from crime scenes by investigators. The soil may be transported by vehicles, shoes, or shovel. The properties of soil are diverse in nature.

Soil samples can be collected in different ways, depending on where the sample is being collected. If samples are being collected indoors or from a vehicle, vacuuming is generally used. If the sample is outdoors, it is collected by placing a teaspoon of soil into a plastic vial. When found on a tool, it is wrapped in plastic and then sent to the lab for testing. Collecting soil samples from a body is not more difficult than collecting a sample from anywhere else, but it takes more work and care so that evidence is not contaminated. When collecting samples from a body, samples should be taken at regular intervals and different spoons should be used each time.

Once the soil samples are collected, they are sent to the laboratory. The examiner will first do a microscopic analysis to perform testing of the mineral content of the soil. Another test used for identification of the origin of soil is a density test. The density test is called the **density gradient tube**. This test consists of adding liquid to two glass tubes. The soil sample is added to both.

After the soil samples become suspended in the liquid, the separation of the bands can then be analyzed to reveal the profile of the soil. Electron microscopes can be used to examine the structure of the minerals in the soil. During examination, an examiner might find that some soil samples may contain biological evidence such as saliva, semen, or blood. If biological evidence is found in the sample, the whole soil sample should be sent to the laboratory for testing.

Collection of Soils

Always use clean tools and individual bindles when collecting soil or rock samples. If an impression, print, body or other evidence is in the area, photograph and document it in notes before collecting nearby soil or rocks. Collect samples from the known crime scene, any "alibi" site(s) (e.g., a site that the victim or accused claims to have visited), or a "representative" site (such as a site where prints that match recovered shoes or tires are found). When soil is firmly attached to a movable object, collect and air-dry the object before packaging it. If it cannot be collected, gently scrape samples from the object onto clean paper.

Never package soil directly into commercially manufactured envelopes or bags. Always package soil in a sealable container: glass or plastic vials, bottles or jars with screw cap lids, self-made envelope, paper bindle, or other container. Collect minimum of three tablespoons of soil from each location. Go a little deeper than at least as deep as the evidence sample appears to have penetrated the ground soil. Usually the top layer of soil is only disturbed for the evidence sample.

Collect a comparison sample close to the suspected or known evidence sample location and at various locations around the evidential sample up to 100 feet, attempting to include varieties of soil in the scene area. Layering of soil can be important to show recent or historical presence at a location. This is particularly true of vehicle collection. Preserve layering whenever possible.

Ensure that the portion of the object with the soil has been photographed and documented in notes and sketching. Include measurements of collected soil (evidence or control/comparison samples) locations.

Label a container for each soil sample with your initials, identification number, the date and time, evidence number, location, and evidence description. Label each bindle, envelope, bottle, or jar with your initials, identification number, evidence number, the date and time, location, and evidence description. Each piece of evidence must have a unique number. This number should correspond to the placard next to the evidence (evidence, control, or comparison) and the evidence log as appropriate.

The evidence description includes:

- Location of each soil sample relative to specific landmarks at the scene
- Whether the soil was wet or dry when collected
- Whether the soil contains any detectable odor or other unusual characteristics or objects
- Estimated amount of sample

When describing soil contents, use the word "apparent" or the phrase "of unknown origin" when the source of the stain/mark is unidentified; e.g., "Soil sample taken from approximately 1 foot north of apparent boot print."

Determine where to begin sample collection depends on the nature of both the crime and the crime scene. In a homicide case, ff a victim died on the ground, and the body has not been removed, collect the sample from as close to the body as possible without disturbing it. Otherwise, prepare to collect a sample from the center of where the body laid and other appropriate locations of the body.

If collecting a series of samples along the path of an impression, determine the start and end points of the path. The starting point is the place where the first impression is made and the first sample must be collected, then along the path traveled by the subject. Be sure to examine the ground for trace evidence that may not have been collected. Dig straight down into the soil/rock to collect a sample of three tablespoons to one cup of the soil. Be sure to start with clean digging tools. Clean the tools after each sample.

Use the mason's tool, gardener's hand trowel, and screwdriver as needed to dig straight into the ground or rocks. Place the soil sample into the container (bottle, jar, vial, bindle). Mix soil as little as possible, keeping in mind the potential for layering of soil. To avoid contamination and leakage, it is critical that each sample is stored in its own sealed container and kept apart from other soil/rock samples and tools that were used.

Collect and package the remaining samples in separate bindles. Take additional samples at distances of 1, 10, 25, and 50 feet from the original impression/impact point. The size of area comprising the scene will determine how far out the samples need to be taken.

Take at least four samples at varying compass points each time the distance from the initial evidence area and sampling location is increased. Ensure that your notes and the label on the container include the compass direction and distance from the previous location, or the initial evidence sample, or permanent markers used for measurement in the scene. Whichever reference point is used, consistently use that point throughout.

If the sample is wet, place it on a clean piece of paper in a secure location used for evidence drying, such as a drying rack, until it is dry. If drugs or ignitable liquids are suspected, the sample must be frozen. Contact a fire investigator or fire debris analyst if ignitable liquids are suspected. Keep the sample as cold/cool as possible helps to slow degradation. Natural components of some soils may degrade the composition of added chemicals in the sample.

Place each initial container (bottle, jar, vial, bindle) into its labeled container. Do not package evidence with comparison/control samples. Close the container and seal the entire opening with evidence tape. Write your initials, identification number, and the date and time across the evidence tape seal.

SECTION 4.3:

Paint Evidence

Paint evidence is documented along the lines of the familiar pattern that has been established throughout this text. Photograph the area in question both with and without a scale. Collection of paint evidence may be accomplished with the use of tape to ensure getting intact pieces of the paint. Known standards may be obtained by chipping the paint to the underlying surface, intact, to ensure layer sequence. Allow these chips to fall into the paper, which is to be folded in the "druggist fold," which in turn is placed in a labeled envelope and scaled. Collect known standards adjacent to the area of interest to be used as a control and package in the same manner as previously mentioned.

LABORATORY ANALYSIS

Crime labs use various processes and resources to conduct forensic paint examinations. The laboratory can use these analyses to source automotive paint that transferred during the commission or crimes.

To conduct this type of analysis, the Chemistry Unit accessed multiple resources used to source automotive paint transfer, including vehicle assembly and paint manufacturing contacts, automotive paint databases, and auto body repair shops' color refinish books.

STRUCTURE OF A PAINT SYSTEM

The paint systems of an automobile typically have three or four layers; a clear coat, over a topcoat, over one or more undercoats. Automotive manufacturers use paint layers from various paint manufacturers, where each layer has a combination of binders and pigments. These variables often create unique combinations that allow forensic scientists to determine the possible make, model, and year range for a vehicle from which a paint chip may have originated.

Each paint layer is separated and placed between two diamonds for infrared analysis. Each component has a characteristic fingerprint known as an **infrared spectrum**.

CASE STUDY

The following case study recounted by Diana Wright (2013) in the *FBI Law Enforcement Bulletin* illustrates how paint evidence can be used in a criminal investigation:

"A recent case demonstrates how the laboratory used these analyses to source automotive paint that transferred during the commission of a hate crime, what information investigators presented at trial, and how law enforcement agencies submitted direct requests to the FBI Laboratory.

In April 2011 a federal grand jury in the western district of Arkansas indicted two men on charges that they committed a racially motivated assault on five Hispanic males. Local law enforcement charged the defendants, aged 19 and 20, with five counts of perpetrating hate crimes and one count of conspiring to do so in violation of the Matthew Shepard and James Byrd, Jr., Hate Crimes Prevention Act, enacted in October 2009.1 The charges resulted from a May 2010 confrontation in which the defendants' racial taunting escalated into a vehicular assault as the five victims in a 1995 Buick LeSabre left a gas station/convenience store.

The defendants, driving a Ford F-250 pickup truck, pursued the green-colored sedan while reportedly hurling racial slurs and repeatedly ramming their truck into the back of the vehicle. The LeSabre's teenage driver lost control of the vehicle, which then rolled, hit a tree, and, ultimately, burst into flames. All five victims survived, with most sustaining life-threatening injuries. Officers recovered the truck less than one-quarter of a mile from the scene where it had run out of gas, thus, enabling evidence collection by local law enforcement officers to occur simultaneously with the crime scene investigation.

The initial investigation resulted in local law enforcement asking the FBI Laboratory's Chemistry Unit to examine green smears on the front tow hooks and bumper of the truck to determine whether they could have come from the sedan. The fire complicated the analysis by destroying all of the paint on the back end of the LeSabre where contact between the two vehicles would have occurred. Therefore, it became necessary to work with the transfer on the truck to determine if it could have originated from a LeSabre of the model-year range represented by the victim's vehicle.

EXAMINATION

To conduct this type of analysis, the Chemistry Unit accessed multiple resources used to source automotive paint transfer, including vehicle assembly and paint manufacturing contacts, automotive paint databases, and auto body repair shops' color refinish books. Combining these tools made it possible to determine if the green paint on the truck bumper could have transferred from a 1995 Buick LeSabre.

The forensic paint examiner presented the results at the trial and described how these resources and the sedan's vehicle identification number (VIN) enabled FBI Laboratory personnel to compile their report. The findings indicated that the victim's vehicle originally was the same general shade of green as the transfer on the truck bumper, the 1995 model was among the vehicles featuring this type of paint, and in 1995 General Motors (GM) produced 6,000 green Buick LeSabres.

A subsequent search of Arkansas Department of Motor Vehicle (DMV) records estimated that there were 25 of those green sedans registered in the state at the time of the incident. The examiner presented the inherent limitations of the results; however, none of these factors provided cause to dismiss the victim's vehicle as the source of the transfer. Ultimately, the federal court convicted the defendants of committing hate crimes against the victims.

EVIDENCE

As outlined in the FBI Laboratory's Handbook of Forensic Services, investigators used a straightedge razor blade to collect green paint scrapings from the front bumper of the defendant's truck. The fire had destroyed any suitable paint available from the victim's vehicle, thus preventing submission of a sample for comparison. Examination in the laboratory revealed that the paint scrapings from the truck's bumper and tow hook contained only a partial-layer structure consisting of a clear coat over a dark-green/emerald-colored base coat. A typical automotive paint-layer system contains a topcoat of clear and base color layers in addition to one or two primer layers between the base coat and sheet metal. Laboratory examinations determined that both of the transferred paint layers were from the original equipment manufacturer (OEM) and could be sourced back to potential vehicle types based on chemical composition and base-coat color.

RESULTS

Because no paint of value was recovered from the victim's vehicle, information reported to investigators did not focus on the LeSabre. Instead, *it helped determine whether that type of vehicle (e.g., make, model, model year) could have paint consistent with that recovered from the defendants' truck bumper.*

Color Information

Due to the damage on the sedan, there was no way to retrieve the original color code or the VIN. However, a traffic citation filed several months prior to the crash noted the VIN and the vehicle color, illegibly recorded as either "gry" (gray) or "grn" (green). Using the VIN from this citation, the FBI Laboratory obtained a vehicle history report for the LeSabre. The statement indicated that the vehicle had four owners over the course of its history. The first and third reported severe damage events, implying that refinish work likely resulted. Neither the areas where damage occurred nor the extent of the repairs were specified in these reports. Only the fourth owner noted the vehicle color as green. Based on the repair history prior to the fourth person's registration of the vehicle, the question of the original color finish remained.

To identify the original vehicle color, an Internet search to correlate color codes to VINs indicated that a local dealership had this information. The first eight digits of the victim's VIN were provided to a Buick dealership located outside of Washington, D.C. The dealership identified the original color as dark-yellow green metallic. This information confirmed that the LeSabre had the OEM green finish. However, because the paint transfer was a smear, rather than a chip, it was not possible to conduct a direct color comparison to the paint color standard. Cross-referencing the code for this color with two independent automotive paint-refinisher pages for GM confirmed that this color was available on Buicks during model years 1994 to 1997, as well as on Chevrolet, Oldsmobile, and Pontiac.6 An Internet search and a GM contact provided some background information on the vehicle's production history. The Buick City assembly plant in Flint, Michigan, produced the LeSabre, the Buick Park Avenue, and the Oldsmobile 88.

Chemical Composition

Using an automotive paint database available only to law enforcement, the lab compared the chemical composition of the transferred paint from the truck's bumper to the clear-topcoat and base-coat layers for vehicles produced at the same plant during model years 1994 to 1995. The chemical composition of the transferred clear-coat layer compared favorably with some of the database samples for model year 1995, while other samples for that year differed.

GM also supplied contact information for the paint manufacturer used at the Buick City plant during this period. The automaker and paint manufacturer independently advised that the clear topcoat for GM's model year 1995 products from the Buick City assembly plant began with a specific paint-chemistry composition. Conversion to a different formulation subsequently occurred between March and June 1995.

This information corroborated the findings from the comparison of the chemical composition of the transferred paint to the database samples. Although the same color code was available at the plant for model years 1994 to 1997, the chemical composition of the transferred clear topcoat was comparable only to the database for model years 1994 and 1995. One of the 1995 database samples had the same color as the victim's Buick LeSabre. The chemical composition of this sample and the transfer paint from the truck bumper coincided.

The FBI Laboratory's GM contact also confirmed use of the paint's chemical composition and color code on the Park Avenue and Oldsmobile 88 produced at Buick City.9 This information was necessary to provide context to the findings presented at trial—the possibility that the victim's LeSabre or another vehicle painted at the same plant with the same *chemical composition could have been the source of the transfer to the suspect's bumper.*

TRIAL

At the trial the examiner presented testimony regarding the automotive paint searches. Statements included the caveat that during the same timeframe, the Buick City plant painted Buick Park Avenues and Oldsmobile 88s using the same color code.

The passenger of the truck pled guilty to committing a federal hate crime and conspiracy. In exchange for his testimony against the driver, he received a sentence of 4 years in federal prison. Four of the victims also testified at the driver's trial. The court convicted the truck's driver of five counts of perpetrating a hate crime and one count of conspiracy and sentenced him to federal prison for 11 years.

CONCLUSION

This article highlights the capabilities and resources of the FBI Laboratory's Chemistry Unit to assist local and state law enforcement agencies with make-model-year investigative lead information in hit-and-run cases. If local or state laboratories have the capability to conduct paint examinations or comparisons but do not have sourcing resources available, the FBI Laboratory will accept cases for automotive paint sourcing."

REFERENCES AND FURTHER READING

Lavine, B.K., Perera, U.D.N., Kwofie, F., & Dahal, K. (2019). *Application of Infrared Imaging and Chemometrics to Facilitate the Forensic Examination of Automotive Paints*. Available:
https://www.ncjrs.gov/pdffiles1/nij/grants/252775.pdf

SECTION 4.4:

Drugs & Chemicals

Perhaps the most diverse classification of forensic science is forensic chemistry. Forensic chemists are called upon to analyze many different classifications of evidence, some of which have already been discussed in this book (e.g., paints and soils). In this section, we will focus on drugs and gunshot residue.

DRUG EVIDENCE

The scientists in the chemistry section of the crime lab analyze items of evidence submitted by law enforcement for the presence or absence of controlled substances. Drug evidence may be in the form of plant material (such as marijuana, synthetic cannabinoids, salvia, and khat), solids (such as methamphetamine, powder cocaine, crack cocaine, and pharmaceutical or clandestine tablets), liquids (such as clandestine laboratory samples), or paraphernalia (such as smoking devices, straws, or spoons).

When suspected drug evidence is submitted to the lab, an initial physical examination is performed. This physical examination includes examining packaging for seals and a macroscopic examination of the evidence. After initial observations are noted (including a weight, volume and/or unit count), a drug chemist typically screens the evidence using chemical spot tests and/or instrumentation. After screening, the scientists use a variety of extractions and instrumentation to confirm the presence or absence of controlled substances as indicated by the preliminary screening tests. Once all examinations are completed, a report is written.

Reports routinely include an amount determination (such as grams, milliliters or units) and a qualitative identification of any controlled substances identified. The lab may also perform **quantitative examinations** to determine the concentration of the controlled substance.

Some state and local forensic laboratories perform quantitative (or purity) analyses, but the majority do so only under special circumstances, such as a special request from law enforcement or from the prosecutor. A smaller number of laboratories perform quantitative analysis on a more routine basis due to state laws that require the amount of pure heroin or cocaine in an item to be determined.

Forensic chemists also provide expert testimony in both state and federal courts. These drug chemists are also a resource for controlled substance information for the courts and other state agencies.

NATIONAL FORENSIC LABORATORY INFORMATION SYSTEM (NFLIS)

NFLIS represents a partnership that includes 263 federal, state, and local forensic laboratories. The information collected through NFLIS supports DEA's mission to enforce the controlled substances laws and regulations of the United States, including tracking the diversion of controlled pharmaceuticals and the diversion of controlled chemicals into illegal markets.

NFLIS provides a unique source of information on the nation's drug problem, providing detailed and timely information on substances secured in law enforcement operations across the country. The NFLIS 2005 Annual Report presents national and regional findings on drug cases analyzed during the past year, including city- and county-level results on drug seizure locations. Among the key findings presented in the NFLIS 2005 *Annual Report*:

- An estimated 1.7 million drug items were analyzed by state and local laboratories in the United States in 2005. Cannabis/THC was the most frequently identified drug (573,904 items), followed by cocaine (570,176), methamphetamine (247,288), and heroin (87,402).

- Nationally, cannabis/THC, heroin, and MDMA declined significantly from 2001 to 2005, while methamphetamine, oxycodone, and hydrocodone items increased significantly.

- Regionally, methamphetamine increased significantly in the South, more than doubling over the 5-year period, while cocaine and heroin declined. Methamphetamine also increased in the Northeast, while heroin declined.

- Among other drugs in the top 25, oxycodone, hydrocodone, and alprazolam, all available in pharmaceutical products, increased significantly in the Northeast between 2001 and 2005. In addition, oxycodone increased in the West and Midwest, hydrocodone increased in the South and Midwest, and alprazolam increased in the Midwest.

- Overall, hydrocodone (39%) and oxycodone (30%) accounted for more than two-thirds of all identified narcotic analgesics, while alprazolam (e.g., Xanax) accounted for 61% of reported benzodiazepines and MDMA accounted for 84% of reported club drugs

DRUG CATEGORIES

The NFLIS also provides a helpful system of organizing illicit drugs into related categories. Interestingly, the degree to which these different "families" of drugs are found varies substantially by region.

Narcotic analgesics are pain relievers available by prescription. According to the 2005 National Survey on Drug Use and Health (NSDUH), approximately 5% of persons aged 12 or older, or 11.8 million, used pain relievers in the past year for non-medical reasons. Among adolescents aged 12 to 17, an estimated 7%, or 1.7 million, reported such use during the past year. A total of 51,432 narcotic analgesics were identified by NFLIS laboratories in 2005, representing nearly 4% of all items analyzed (Table 2.1).

Hydrocodone (39%) and oxycodone (30%) accounted for the majority of all narcotic analgesics reported. The following drugs made up more than one-quarter of narcotic analgesics: methadone (11%), morphine (6%), codeine (5%), propoxyphene (3%), dihydrocodeine (2%), and hydromorphone (2%).

Benzodiazepines are used therapeutically to produce sedation, induce sleep, relieve anxiety and muscle spasms, and prevent seizures. Benzodiazepine abuse is often associated with young adults and adolescents who take benzodiazepines to get "high." During 2005, a little more than 2% of all analyzed drugs, or 33,834 items, were identified as benzodiazepines in NFLIS. Alprazolam (e.g., Xanax) accounted for 61% of reported benzodiazepines. Approximately 17% of benzodiazepines were identified as diazepam, and 16% were identified as clonazepam.

Club drugs. MDMA, ketamine, and GHB/GBL are the most common club drugs. The abuse of MDMA, also known as Ecstasy, has declined in recent years. However, according to the 2005 Monitoring the Future Survey, an estimated 5% of 12th grade, 4% of 10th grade, and 3% of 8th grade students used MDMA during their lifetimes. In NFLIS, 12,473 club drugs were identified in 2005 (Table 2.3). Of these, 84% were identified as MDMA. Among the other club drugs reported, 9% were identified as MDA, 4% as ketamine, and 3% as GHB/GBL. MDMA constitutes the highest percentages for each region, representing 87% of club drugs in the West, 87% in the Midwest, 86% in the South, and 65% in the Northeast. The Northeast continues to report the highest percentages of MDA (19%) and ketamine (14%).

While **anabolic steroids** are legally available in the United States by prescription, many users obtain the steroids illegally through production in clandestine laboratories, smuggling from other countries, or diversion from U.S. pharmacies. The 2005 Monitoring the Future Study shows a significant decline in past year steroid use among 12th grade students, from 2.5% in 2004 to 1.5% in 2005. However, past year steroid use remained relatively the same from 2004 to 2005 among 8th and 10th grade students.3

During 2005, a total of 1,728 items were identified as anabolic steroids (Table 2.4). In NFLIS, the most commonly identified anabolic steroid was testosterone (38%), followed by methandrostenolone (17%), nandrolone (13%), and stenozolol (12%). Approximately 44% of items in the Midwest and South, 31% in the West, and 28% in the Northeast were identified as testosterone (Figure 2.4). Slightly less than one-fifth of items across all census regions were identified as methandrostenolone.

Stimulants. Methamphetamine is a highly addictive stimulant. The number of methamphetamine laboratories seized by law enforcement agencies increased by 25% between 2001 and 2004. Stimulants, including methamphetamine and amphetamine, were involved in 42,538 emergency department (ED) visits, accounting for about 7% of all drug-related ED visits during the last two quarters of 2003.5 A total of 230,769 stimulants were identified in NFLIS during 2005, accounting for about 16% of all items reported. An estimated 97% of stimulants, or 224,605 items, were identified as methamphetamine. An additional 2,888 items were identified as amphetamine, and 1,468 as methylphenidate. Methamphetamine accounted for more than 9 out of 10 stimulants reported in the West, Midwest, and South, and for almost 6 out of 10 stimulants reported in the Northeast. In the Northeast, 24% of stimulants were reported as amphetamine and 12% as methylphenidate.

Drug combinations. Taking multiple drugs simultaneously or mixing substances can be deadly. The typical drug misuse death reported as part of the 2003 Drug Abuse Warning Network (DAWN) involved two or more drugs. Cocaine with opiates/opioids was the most common illicit drug combination involving death.

During 2005, 19,560 items identified in NFLIS, about 1% of all reported items, contained two or more substances. The five most common combinations in 2005—cannabis/THC and cocaine (8%), methamphetamine and MDMA (7%), cocaine and heroin (7%), methamphetamine and dimethylsulfone (6%), and methamphetamine and ephedrine / pseudoephedrine (4%)—accounted for nearly one-third of all combinations reported.

Cocaine, including powder and crack cocaine, was present in 24% of all drug combinations reported during 2005. The most common cocaine combination contained cannabis/ THC (8%). Cocaine/heroin, which is often referred to as a "speedball," represented nearly 7% of cocaine combinations, and cocaine/methamphetamine represented about 3%. Many of the other cocaine-related combinations included excipients used to dilute cocaine. These included non-controlled substances such as procaine (a local anesthetic), inositol, caffeine, boric acid, benzocaine, and lactose.

Heroin was present in 15% of all drug combinations, or 2,899 items, reported in 2005. Almost one-half of the heroin combinations were reported as heroin/cocaine. Among the other substances combined with heroin, many were excipients designed to dilute or adulterate heroin, including procaine, caffeine, mannitol, lidocaine, inositol, and lactose.

Methamphetamine was present in a total of 6,012 items, or in about 31% of all drug combinations. Methamphetamine/MDMA (1,446 items), methamphetamine/ dimethylsulfone (1,131 items), methamphetamine/ephedrine or pseudoephedrine (752 items), methamphetamine/cocaine (577 items), and methamphetamine/cannabis (548 items) were the most commonly reported combinations. MDMA was reported in 7% of methamphetamine combinations, up from 5% in 2004.

HAIR TOXICOLOGY

Forensic testing for drugs of abuse in hair has become a useful diagnostic tool in determining recent past drug use as well as examining long-term drug history through segmental analysis (i.e. identification and quantification of drugs along the length of the hair shaft from scalp hair). The usefulness and the importance of hair analysis depend on the ability to identify and quantify drugs and metabolites in hair that arise from ingestion but not from passive exposure or exogenous application of drugs.

Hair has many beneficial aspects when compared to urine and blood. Since sample collection is non-invasive, hair analysis is commonly used in workplace drug testing and drug treatment programs. Provided the hair has not been cut, it may be easy to obtain a second sample if the results are inconclusive or challengeable. It can be used for establishing personal drug history in situations where classical matrices are not available such as in putrefied bodies; when the full drug use history is unknown; or when time is a factor, for example in drug-facilitated sexual offense (DFSA).

Hair analysis can also assist in drug compliance testing and drug abstinence monitoring. Moreover, drug-hair analysis is becoming a popular alternative to urinalysis since urine samples provide only short-term information about drug use while hair samples provide a larger window of detection as well as the history of use over time. This is because head hair grows at an average rate of 1 cm per month and hence preserves the drug use history of an individual along its length. Due to the cosmetic treatment of an individual, the drugs could be degraded however, not fully eliminated. Therefore, cosmetic history of a person must be considered in such cases while interpreting hair analysis results.

GUNSHOT RESIDUE

Gunshot residue (GSR) collection kit or GSR collection stubs; paper envelopes; paper towels; clean paper; waterproof pen; evidence tape; powder-free protective gloves; face protection. Determine if the suspect(s), victim(s), or witness(es) should be tested; collect the GSR as soon as possible. Do not use tape lifts in place of a GSR kit stub. The instructions included in the GSR kit should always be followed. Sample the hands for GSR using the collection kit as soon as possible. If collection cannot be made immediately on contact with the subject, individually bag the subject's hands using paper bags and not plastic bags (as plastic may cause hands to sweat). Good GSR samples can generally be obtained from the web portions of the hands.

GSR collection kits should contain materials (e.g., carbon-coated adhesive stubs or adhesive-coated discs) required to perform scanning electron microscopy (SEM) residue tests. Do not use GSR kits that have swabs or color tests. Do not allow the suspect(s), victim(s), or witness(es) to wash their hands or subject the hands to any liquids after the shooting, or any rubbing onto other surfaces (e.g., clothing, bag on hand, furniture, etc.). Keep GSR kits away from firearms evidence. Evidence such as vehicles can also be tested for the presence of GSR, by using the same procedure as would be used on hands.

REFERENCES AND FURTHER READING

DEA. (2005). NATIONAL FORENSIC LABORATORY INFORMATION SYSTEM: 2005 Annual Report. Available:
https://www.nflis.deadiversion.usdoj.gov/DesktopModules/ReportDownloads/Reports/NFLIS2005AR.pdf

Gautam, L. & Cole, M. D. (2013). Hair Analysis in Forensic Toxicology. *Forensic Magazine*. Available: https://www.forensicmag.com/article/2013/09/hair-analysis-forensic-toxicology

SECTION 5

Evidence Procedures

SECTION 5.1

Wet Evidence

If an evidence item is wet, place it on a clean piece of paper and allow it to dry before packaging, or transport it for drying at a laboratory facility or a properly outfitted evidence holding area. If you have access to a drying rack, dry the item in it. Place a clean piece of paper on the floor of the drying rack. Hang the item over the paper.

If you do not have a drying rack:

- Lay a clean piece of paper on a clean, flat surface in a secure location where the item will not be disturbed and contamination will be minimized.
- Carefully place the item on the paper.
- Be sure to keep the stain intact in its original form and avoid transferring the stain from one area of the item to another.
- Allow the item to dry naturally. Never expose it to heat, such as from a blow dryer. Avoid exposing the sample to direct sunlight.

Do not place two items in the same container for drying purposes. Clean the surfaces of the drying rack with a disinfectant such as 10% bleach solution after the item has been dried and removed.

DRYING WET DOCUMENTS

To scoop up wet single-page documents, use cardboard sheets (e.g., pieces of manila folders). Wet documents can be dried by placing them on a clean piece of paper towel or a sheet of window screen, and then placed in a secure location for drying. Sheets of clean paper towels or a similar absorbent material should be spread beneath the area used to handle moist documents in order to collect any trace evidence that falls from the documents during handling. The items used to catch trace items may also need to be collected and handled as evidence.

Do not attempt to unfold wet documents, as this should only be done by laboratory forensic document examiners. Documents in a container of water or other liquid may need to be kept in the liquid for transportation to the laboratory and processing by forensic document examiners. Depending on the nature of the investigation, it may be important to avoid potential contamination that results from handling two documents in the same area at the same time.

PACKAGING DRIED EVIDENCE

To scoop up wet single-page documents, use cardboard sheets (e.g., pieces of manila folders). Wet documents can be dried by placing them on a clean piece of paper towel or a sheet of window screen, and then placed in a secure location for drying.

Sheets of clean paper towels, etc., should be spread beneath the area used to handle moist documents in order to collect any trace evidence that falls from the documents during handling. The items used to catch trace items may also need to be collected and handled as evidence. Do not attempt to unfold wet documents, as this should only be done by laboratory forensic document examiners.

Documents in a container of water or other liquid may need to be kept in the liquid for transportation to the laboratory and processing by forensic document examiners. Depending on the nature of the investigation, it may be important to avoid potential contamination that results from handling two documents in the same area at the same time.

Collect and label the paper on which the object was dried. Place the paper into a labeled container, as needed. Carefully pick up and fold the paper on or over which the object was dried. Contain any trace evidence that may have fallen on the paper. Label the folded paper, indicating the evidence number of the item that was dried.

Packaging Dried Documents

Place dried documents between clean sheets of paper, such as paper towels or cardboard sheets, to provide a protective covering before placing them into labeled evidence containers. Label evidence containers before placing objects into them to avoid degrading existing evidence. Handle documents carefully to avoid bending, folding, or otherwise degrading them. Handle documents appropriately to protect any latent prints that may exist. Close the container and seal the entire opening with evidence tape. Write your initials and identification number and the date and time, as required, across the evidence tape seal.

Carefully pick up and fold the paper used as a catch-surface beneath drying documents. Retain any trace evidence that may have fallen onto this catch-surface paper from the evidence, by folding it inward from the corners. Then place the catch-surface paper in a labeled evidence container, as needed. Label the folded paper, indicating the evidence number of the item (e.g., "This paper was used below evidence #36 while it was drying").

Repackage the object using the original packaging and container if possible. Save all original packaging with evidence if it is not used for repackaging. If the original container cannot be reused, label the container indicating the evidence number of the item (e.g., "Original packaging for evidence #36.") and put the labeled, original packaging into a new container with the evidence it was used to collect.

SECTION 5.2

Packaging Procedures

CLOTHING

Label a container that will be used to collect the object. Document the location of the garment with photography, measurement and sketching, where appropriate. If wet, dry according to guidelines. Fold garment and, whenever appropriate, wrap the garment in clean paper.

When folding a garment or large object:

- Do not crumple or wad any portion of the garment.
- Fold the garment only enough so that it fits into the container.
- Do not crease the stained area.
- Make sure, if using paper, that the paper protects trace evidence and prevents transferring the stain to other areas of the garment

Only wrap an item if wrapping the object will not disturb the position of a stain or mark. An item should be wrapped in clean paper when the location or pattern of the stain or mark is significant (such as a handprint or spatter pattern). Position the paper to keep the stain or mark intact in its original form. Avoid transferring any of the stain or mark to another portion of the object. Mark package with appropriate Biohazard cautions regarding contents.

Place the item into the labeled container, such as a paper bag. The container should be large enough to allow air to circulate around the object inside of it. If an object is too large to be packaged in a container, protect the stained area(s) with clean paper during transport. Close the container and seal the entire opening with evidence tape. Write your initials and identification number, and the date and time across the evidence tape seal.

PORTABLE OBJECTS

Label a container that will be used to collect the object. Document the location of the object with photography, measurement and sketching, where appropriate. Dry, if wet, by placing it on or over a clean piece of paper and allowing it to dry before packaging; or dry in place. Whenever appropriate, wrap the object in clean paper. Only wrap an item when wrapping the object will not disturb the position of a stain or mark.

Objects should be wrapped in clean paper when the:

1. Location or pattern of the stain or mark is significant (such as a handprint or spatter pattern).
2. Object is saturated and liquid will leak through the container if not wrapped.

Position the paper to:

· Keep the stain or mark intact in its original form.
· Avoid transferring any of the stain or mark to another portion of the object

Place the object into the labeled container. If an object is too large to be packaged in a container, protect the stained area(s) with clean paper during transport. Close the container and seal the entire opening with evidence tape. Write your initials and identification number, and the date and time across the evidence tape seal.

PARTS OF NON-PORTABLE OBJECTS

Label a container that will be used to collect the object. Document the location of the stain with photography, measurement and sketching, where appropriate. When multiple stains are found, take one or more photographs that show the relationship among those stains. It is important to collect the entire stained area if the shape of the stain is significant (such as a handprint). If possible, cut out the entire stained area using a clean scalpel, utility knife, or scissors, including a large portion of the non-stained area.

If the stain has been absorbed into multiple layers (such as carpet and carpet pad), collect a cutout from each layer. If the entire stained area is too large to collect, cut out a smaller section of the area. Opposite the stained side, mark the orientation of the cutout: for example, mark the area that pointed north, when collected. If the cutout is wet, place it on clean paper and allow it to dry before packaging.

Whenever appropriate, wrap the object in clean paper if wrapping the object will not disturb the position of a stain or mark. Objects should be wrapped in clean paper when the:

1. Location or pattern of the stain or mark is significant (such as a handprint or spatter pattern).
2. Object is saturated and liquid will leak through the container if not wrapped.

Position the paper to keep the stain or mark intact in its original form. Avoid transferring any of the stain or mark to another portion of the object.

A control sample should always be collected. Label a second container with your initials and identification number, the date and time, evidence number, location of the control in relation to the original sample, and description of the control sample.

Each piece of evidence, including the control sample, must have a unique number. A letter or number may be appended to the original evidence number to denote the control sample (e.g., If the original evidence number was #32, the control sample could be #32A or #32.1).

The description of the control sample should include:

- Type of material
- Location of material

- Location of the control sample in relation to the stain

Collecting a Control Sample

Cut out a portion of unstained material. First, locate an unstained area of the same material from which the original sample was taken. Select the least contaminated area possible (such as an unstained area of carpet). Cut out the control sample using a scalpel, utility knife, or scissors. (Use a clean blade; never use a blade that was used to cut another sample.)

If multiple layers (such as carpet and carpet pad) of material were collected in the original sample, collect multiple layers for the control. On the side of the cutout opposite the stained side (of the original non-control sample), mark the orientation of the cutout to north when collected. If the cutout is wet, place it on clean paper and allow it to dry before packaging.

Package the control sample separately from the corresponding stained material. Place the cutout in the container. Close the container and seal the entire opening with evidence tape. Write your initials, identification number, and the date and time across the tape.

Stains on Nonporous Surfaces

Label a container that will be used to collect the item. Document the location of the stain with photography, measurement and sketching, where appropriate. When multiple stains are found, take one or more photographs that show the relationship among those stains. Pre-label with distinguishing markings any swabs that you will use. If the stain is dry, moisten the cotton tip of a swab using two or three drops of distilled water.

If the stain has some residual moisture in it, touch the dry swab tip to the moist area of the stain. To avoid contamination, do not touch the cotton tip of the swab to any surface other than the sample area. Hold the bottle of distilled water, or a one-time use vial of sterile water, above the swab. Use a minimum amount of water to moisten the swab: drop two or three drops of water onto the swab. *Do not touch the tip of the water bottle to the swab.*

Do not saturate the swab. (It should be moist, but not dripping wet.) Swab the stain with the cotton-tipped end of the swab. Touch the swab gently and firmly to the stain. Rotate the swab to ensure that the stain is collected on as much of the cotton tip as possible. Do not smear the stain when swabbing it. Dry the swab in a sterile container, swab dryer or drying box. If necessary, break off the end of the swab so it fits into the drying container.

Place the swab into a bindle; fold the bindle so it seals around the swab. Close the bindle and place it into an envelope large enough to allow air to circulate around the object inside of it. If the swab is thoroughly dried, it can be placed directly into a pre-labeled envelope. If no bindle or swab drying box is available, use another sterile container that can hold the swab while it dries. Ensure that the swab is positioned so that air freely circulates around it.

Close the envelope or other container and seal the entire opening with evidence tape. Write your initials and identification number, and the date and time across the evidence tape seal.

A control sample should also be collected. Label the second envelope with your initials and identification number, the date and time, evidence number, location of the control in relation to the original sample, and description of the control sample. Each piece of evidence, including the control sample, must have a unique number. A letter may be appended to the original evidence number to denote the control sample. The description includes location of the control sample in relation to the original stain.

To collect a control sample, moisten the cotton tip of the second swab using two or three drops of distilled water. Swab an unstained area of the same surface from which the original swab was taken. Dry the swab and package in the same manner as the stained sample.

SECTION 5.3

Trace Evidence

Trace Evidence deals with the collection of all forms of matter, natural or manufactured, usually very tiny materials, but may also be larger forms of matter. Examples are gas from a container (bag or metal cylinder), hair, pollen, stains (non-biological), volatile liquids, fibers, paint, glass, and soil. Trace evidence can be easily destroyed, contaminated, or transferred, so take precautions when approaching the scene. Since trace evidence items are often difficult to see without the aid of magnification, the prudent course of action is to collect items of evidence that may contain trace evidence.

Care should be used when collecting weapons, as improper handling and packaging can compromise the trace evidence. Careful photography, documentation, and sketching are critical for the optimal use and interpretation/reconstruction of trace evidence. Always package items to prevent damage or alteration of the evidence: use packaging that corresponds to the size and type of the item and evidence. Always collect sufficient amounts of the trace evidence when possible.

Do not package evidence if it is wet or damp. Do not package exemplar, standard/reference, or control samples with evidence. Package separately. Use of a bright or alternative light source may help in locating trace evidence. Standard, reference, and control samples should be collected for laboratory comparison, examination, or elimination purposes. Collect enough for multiple analyses. Always wear powder-free gloves while collecting trace evidence to avoid contamination. Change gloves as often as needed to minimize contamination.

DOCUMENTATION AND MARKING

Do not package evidence stained with bodily fluids or other liquids in plastic bags. Avoid altering the trace evidence in any way, other than is necessary for evidence collection (e.g., scraping paint from a metal surface). When possible, when storing evidence, use a freezer/refrigerator that is dedicated to evidence storage to guard against potential biohazard contamination or explosion hazards.

Do not cough, sneeze, talk, or scratch yourself over any sample being collected or to be collected. When using tweezers/forceps, use only sufficient pinching force to collect item to prevent altering or damaging the trace evidence. Keep adhesive tape to be used in lifting evidence in a plastic bag until just before use to prevent contamination of the edges/side of the tape roll. Put unused portion of tape roll back into the plastic bag when finished with tape lifting.

Do not place trace evidence directly into manila envelopes (of any size), paper envelopes, or paper bags without placing the evidence into a smaller, leak-proof container such as a glassine bindle, canister, Teflon-lined screw cap glass vial (or bottle/jar as size dictates), or other container. Keep clear acetate sheet protectors free from contamination by storing in an appropriate size manila envelope or plastic resealable bag. Careful photography, documentation, and sketching are critical for the optimal use and interpretation/reconstruction of the evidence.

To reduce breakage and loss of evidence, secure glass containers (e.g., vials, bottles, jars) in cushioned metal friction lid cans with lids. Cushioning material may be balled-up paper towels. Using a swab to collect a trace evidence sample—whether liquid, powder, gel, or other form of matter, evidential or control—is a last resort.

Ensure that the portion of the object with the stain or other trace evidence has been photographed and documented in notes and sketches. When photographing the object: Include a scale and an identification label. Photograph with and without scale. Take one or more location photographs that show where the object was found in relation to other objects in the crime scene. Show the relationship of the object to other evidence in the photograph.

Label a container for the evidence object with your initials and identification number, the date and time, evidence number, location, and evidence description.

Evidence number: Each piece of evidence must have a unique number. This number should correspond to the placard or identification label next to the evidence and the evidence log as appropriate.

Evidence description: The evidence description includes: Type of evidence (paint, plant stem, glass, etc.) Original location of the trace-evidence-containing object Location of the trace evidence on the object (as appropriate) When describing non-DNA-related stains, use the word "apparent" or the phrase "of unknown origin" when the source of the stain is not scientifically identified; e.g., "Pillow containing a brown stain of unknown origin found on the lower bed sheet on the bed." Label the container just before collecting the object, and seal the container immediately after collection. These actions help to protect the integrity of the trace evidence and the chain of custody.

WET TRACE EVIDENCE

If the item is wet, determine if the liquid is significant or relevant to the case (for instance, acid splashed on a victim). You may not wish to dry the item if the liquid is relevant to the case. If the liquid is not relevant, place item on a clean piece of paper in a secure location used for evidence drying, such as a drying rack, until it is dry. If you have access to a drying rack, dry the item in it. Place a clean piece of paper below the evidence to be dried in the drying rack. Lay the item on or hang it above the paper.

If you do not have a drying rack:

- Lay a clean piece of paper on a clean flat surface (e.g., tabletop) in a secure location where the item will not be disturbed and contamination or loss of the trace evidence due to drafts created by people walking by will be minimized.
- Carefully place the item on or hang it over the paper. If possible, gently fold the paper over the object to cover it from airborne particles (such as hair or fibers) that might land on it.
- Allow the item to dry naturally. Never expose it to heat or significant drafts, such as from a blow dryer. *Avoid exposing the sample to direct sunlight.*

Do not place two items in the same container for drying purposes. If the liquid is relevant to the case, determine if the liquid is related to a fire or explosion and in or on an object (e.g., ignitable liquid in carpet). If so, contact fire investigator or bomb technician or forensic fire debris or explosives analyst as appropriate.

If the liquid is involved in injury or damage to another person or property and on an object, it should be collected as evidence. Proper collection depends on the size of the sample. If the sample is small, secure it in appropriate size glass container with a Teflon-lined screw cap lid or other airtight, non-reactive lid. If the sample is large, document location of wet area by photography, notes, and sketches, then cut or remove the wet area and treat as if small sample.

If the liquid is soaking the object or there are drops of liquid on the surface (non-porous surface), using gloved hands, attempt to squeeze liquid drops into glass container or use swab to collect drops and treat as small sample. If the liquid is forming a large drop or pool of liquid, transfer the liquid using glass Pasteur pipette or plastic transfer pipette into appropriate size glass vial. Consider appropriate hazardous labeling.

When the object has dried, carefully pick up and fold the paper on or over the object that has dried. Contain any trace evidence that may have fallen on the paper. Label the folded paper, indicating the evidence number of the item that was dried (e.g., "This paper was used below evidence #36 while it was drying"). If possible, repackage the object using the original paper and container.

If the original container cannot be reused, save all original packaging as evidence if it is not used for repackaging. Put the labeled, original packaging into a new container with the evidence it was used to collect. Label the container indicating the evidence number of the item (e.g., "Original packaging for evidence #36").

When possible, place glass vials, bottles, and jars into a cushioned metal friction lid container to reduce breakage. To reduce breakage and loss of evidence, secure glass containers (e.g., vials, bottles, jars) in cushioned metal friction lid cans with lids. Cushioning material may be balled-up paper towels.

COLLECTING CONTROL SAMPLES

A control sample is one that the collector knows, that does not appear to have evidence present. It represents the matrix material on which the evidence rests, for instance a piece of wallboard or carpeting. A comparison sample may have evidence present without the collector's knowledge (e.g., fire debris), but represents the matrix material on which the evidence rests or is made of the same matrix material as the evidence (e.g., glass fragments collected from a broken window). It will be compared to the evidential sample. These will be referred to as "control" samples.

Label a second container for the control sample with your initials and identification number, the date and time, evidence number, location of the control in relation to the original sample, and a description of the control sample. Clearly identify this sample as a control (or comparison) sample (e.g., write the words "Control Sample" or "Comparison Sample" in bold print on the container).

Control sample number: Each piece of evidence, including the control sample, must have a unique number. A letter or number may be appended to the original evidence number to denote the control sample (e.g., if the original evidence number was #32, the control sample could be #32A or #32.1.)

Control sample description: Include the type of sample or matrix material (e.g., wallboard), location of the material, and the location of the sample in relation to the evidence sample.

Collect a control sample: Using the appropriate tool, cut out, collect, or remove a portion of the same matrix material on which the evidence sample rests or was part of the evidence sample (e.g., paint smear evidence on paint). Locate an area of the same material from which the original trace evidence sample was taken, but without evidence being present (e.g., undamaged area of paint).

Cut out, collect, or scrape the control or comparison sample using, as appropriate, a scalpel, utility knife, wallboard saw, carpet knife, single edge razor blade, or scissors. (Whenever possible, use a clean blade; never use a blade that was used to cut an evidential or other control sample without changing or thoroughly cleaning.)

If multiple layers (such as carpet and carpet pad or multi-layer paint) of material were observed or collected in the original sample, collect all of the multiple layers for the control or comparison sample. A liquid sample should be collected using a glass or plastic transfer pipette and placed into a glass Teflon-lined screw-cap vial or bottle of the smallest permitted size for the sample. Using a swab to collect a liquid trace evidence sample (evidential or control) is a last resort. Put the swab into an appropriate size screw-cap vial or other airtight container.

REMOVING AN ENTIRE OBJECT

Photograph and document the object with the apparent trace evidence. Whenever appropriate, wrap the entire object in clean (butcher) paper or in a brown paper bag. Only wrap an object when doing so will not disturb the position of a stain or other trace evidence (glass fragment, metal fragment, paint smear, etc.). Objects should be wrapped in clean paper when the location or pattern of the stain or other trace evidence is significant (such as a spatter pattern) or the object is saturated and liquid will leak through the container if not wrapped. Position the paper to keep the trace evidence intact in its original form. Avoid transferring any of the trace evidence to another portion of the object. Place the wrapped object into the brown paper bag or other labeled container.

If an object is too large to be packaged in a container, protect the stain or trace evidence area(s) with clean paper during transport. Close the container and seal the entire opening with evidence tape. Write your initials, the identification number, and the date and time across the evidence tape seal. Ensure that any small openings in the package are also sealed. Place initials over these seals.

If an object is too large to be packaged in a container, protect the relevant area(s) with clean paper during transport. Repackage the object using the original packaging, if possible, and reseal. Store the object in the sealed container. Place the container in a secure, dry storage area. Never expose the container to extreme heat, such as from a heater vent. Avoid exposing the container to direct sunlight.

CUT FROM A NON-PORTABLE OBJECT

Label a container for the object to be collected with your initials and identification number, the date and time, evidence number, location, and evidence description. Photograph, sketch, and take notes on the object with the trace evidence or stain. Collect a larger area than where the trace evidence is observed, especially if the shape or pattern of the trace evidence or stain is significant (e.g., paint spray, broken glass pane, etc.).

If possible, cut out the entire area using a scalpel, single-edge razor blade, utility knife, carpet knife, drywall saw, scissors, or other tool as needed to remove section. If the trace evidence has been absorbed into multiple layers (such as carpet and carpet pad), collect a cutout from each layer. If the entire stained or evidence area is too large to collect as one piece, using the appropriate tool, cut out a smaller section of the area and label to re-assemble the sections later if needed.

On the side of the cut-out opposite the side with a stain or trace evidence, mark the orientation of the cut-out to north when collected. Be careful not to dislodge trace evidence while marking. If the item is "wet," determine if the liquid is water, a biological fluid, volatile, or hydrocarbon.

- If water or biological fluid, place it on or over a clean piece of paper and allow it to dry before packaging.
- If the liquid is volatile, acidic, caustic, or a hydrocarbon, the liquid itself may be significant evidence and must be packaged in an airtight container to prevent evaporation. Contact a fire investigator, fire debris analyst, or bomb technician for instructions.

Whenever appropriate, wrap the cut object in clean paper, glassine bindle, or place in appropriate size glass or plastic container or metal friction lid can. Close and seal the labeled container after having placed the object into it. Write your initials and identification number and the date and time across the evidence tape seal. If an object is too large to be packaged in a container, protect the area(s) with clean paper during transport.

Collect a Control Sample

Using the appropriate tool, cut out or remove a portion of the same matrix material on which the evidence sample rested or was part of the evidence sample (e.g., locate an area of the same material from which the original trace evidence sample was taken but without evidence being present such as an undamaged area of paint). Cut out the control or comparison sample using, as appropriate, a scalpel, utility knife, wallboard saw, carpet knife, single-edge razor blade, or scissors. (Use a clean blade; never use a blade that was used to cut an evidential sample on a control sample without a thorough cleaning or replacement.)

If multiple layers of material (such as carpet and carpet pad or multi-layer paint) were observed or collected in the evidential sample, collect all of the multiple layers present for the control or comparison sample. On the opposite side of the evidential side of the original non-control sample, mark the orientation of the cutout to north when collected.

Whenever appropriate, wrap the control sample in clean paper or other appropriate containment. Place the object into the labeled container. If an object is too large to be packaged in a container, protect the sample with clean paper during transport. Close the container and seal the entire opening with evidence tape. Write your initials and identification number and the date and time across the evidence tape seal.

SCRAPE FROM A NON-PORTABLE OBJECT

Use scraping when the entire object may not be collectable (e.g., quarter panel of car, etc.) Often scraping is used to collect evidence on non-porous surfaces too large to collect, but may be used to collect evidence on porous surfaces (e.g., stain on car seat, furniture fabric, canvas, etc.) Paint transfer is commonly located on the object on the impacted surface. Collect the clothing and shoes of people who have been in the area of the painted surface at the time of and since the impact.

Collect paint control-comparison samples, when the entire item cannot be removed, using the scrape method. Always use clean and/or fresh, disposable scraping tools. Change blades frequently when applicable. Always change gloves and use thoroughly cleaned tools when collecting each new sample (between every evidential or control sample.) The stain or marking should be dry for scraping.

Do not use a commercially manufactured envelope of any kind as they have gaps that permit leakage. If a commercial envelope must be used, seal around all edges of the envelope with tape. Label a container for the object to be collected with your initials and identification number, the date and time, evidence number, location, and evidence description. Photograph, sketch, and take notes on the object with the trace evidence or stain.

Collect as much of the evidence area as possible using a scalpel, single-edge razor blade, utility knife, or other tool as needed to remove section. On vertical surfaces, place or tape a self-made envelope or glassine bindle below the area to be scraped before scraping to capture all of the scraping. By scraping the sample, typically all shape or pattern of the trace evidence or stain is lost.

DOCUMENTING AND MARKING SCRAPES

Label a container for the evidence-scraped object with your initials and identification number, the date and time, evidence number, location, and evidence description. Use a druggist fold to create a glassine paper bindle or self-made envelope. Each piece of evidence must have a unique number. This number should correspond to the placard next to the evidence and the evidence log as appropriate.

The evidence description should include the:

- Type of scrape evidence (paint, apparent vomit, etc.)
- Original location of the object containing the trace evidence
- Location of the trace evidence on the object (as appropriate)

Label an appropriate container just before collecting the scraping, and seal the container immediately after collection. Place a large sheet of clean paper beneath the area that you will scrape. The paper is used to contain any debris that breaks loose while you are scraping. Avoid standing on the paper while you scrape.

Place or tape a self-made envelope or glassine bindle below the area to be scraped before scraping to capture all of the scraping possible. Do not use a commercially manufactured envelope of any kind as they have gaps that risk leakage.

Scrape off as much of the material as possible and go as deep as possible to obtain all layers.

When scraping flakes, attempt to leave the flake as intact as possible as you remove it.

When scraping paint, as when found on a car, scrape down deep to the base material, such as the metal of the car. Collect all layers of paint available (all evidence layers and all matrix layers on which evidence rests) in one scrape. This method applies to all trace evidence to be scraped.

If ample evidence is present, attempt to collect a sample that is at least the size of a quarter when scraping material that is not a flake. Otherwise, scrape and collect all of the evidence present. Scrape the material directly into a paper bindle or self-made envelope. A bindle or self-made envelope is preferred for collection to be able to recover as much of the evidence from inside of it as possible. Close and seal the bindle or envelope to prevent leakage.

Never use staples to seal a bindle containing trace evidence. Place a small section of tape at the point where the top is tucked into the bottom just sufficient to keep the bindle top tucked into the bottom. Do not over wrap the bindle or envelope with tape. Place the bindle or self-made envelope into an appropriate size labeled container.

Take necessary precautions to avoid breaking or damaging larger flakes by affixing the bindle or envelope to a piece of cardboard or other rigid material. Secure the bindle or envelope to keep it from moving with minimum amount of transparent tape (not evidence tape or packing/tape lifting tape). Fold the paper that was below the paint when scraped, and place it into a labeled container.

Keep all evidence from the same scrape together using detailed labeling of the containers and evidence tape. Close the container and seal the entire opening with evidence tape. Write your initials and identification number and the date and time across the evidence tape seal. Consider taking a control sample.

TAPE LIFTS

A tape lift has the advantage over vacuuming by collecting evidence most recently deposited relative to the crime. Suitable types of tape to use are packing or box-sealing tape with a width of 2.5 inches to 4 inches. Do not use fingerprint lift tape, latent print tape strips or lifters unless as a last resort. While excellent for fingerprints, these often have insufficient adhesive for trace evidence. Do not use masking tape, clothing hair-removal tape, duct tape, or other non-transparent tapes. Do not use paper as a backing for tape adhesive. Use acetate page protectors or clear secondary liners.

Hair is frequently located at a crime scene near a weapon, near the point of impact, and below a deceased person, on clothing worn during the crime. Fiber is frequently located at a crime scene on clothing, carpet, furniture, and bedding. Fiber is usually defined as carpet and clothing filaments. Broken glass is frequently found on clothing, shoes, head hair, skin, tools, and weapons.

Paint is commonly located on the object that impacted the painted surface, the area below/around the painted surface that was impacted, and the clothing and shoes of people who have been in the area of the painted surface at the time of or since the impact. Do not freeze the lift. To collect paint samples when the entire item cannot be removed, use the tweezers collection method first, then the scrape method, then the tape lift method. Always use powder-free clean gloves when handling evidence.

Documenting Tape Lifts

Whenever possible, collect the entire item and submit it to the lab. Collect trace evidence (e.g., hair, fiber, paint, etc.) using tweezers when possible, then use tape lifts. Each piece of evidence must have a unique identification number. This number should correspond to the placard next to the evidence and the evidence log as appropriate.

Label the acetate page protector or secondary liner along an edge and a container for the sheet or liner with your initials, identification number, the date and time, evidence number, lift location (e.g., lower, bed sheet, left-front shirt). Label each tape lift with your initials, the date, and identification evidence number. As appropriate (e.g., when collecting a series), add additional specific location information to the tape end.

On the tape, a letter may be appended to the original evidence number to denote the lift. If the original evidence number was #36, for example, the number on the bindle could be #36A or #36.1. If several lifts are from the same evidence item (e.g., shirt) then the same sub-number (e.g., #36A) can be used for all lifts on the same acetate page protector or unique numbers used for each separate lift, according to department preference.

The evidence description should include the:

- Type of evidence
- Location of the evidence
- Description of surface from which lift is taken
- Brief description of evidence, when appropriate, such as "blue-colored glass" or "apparent smokeless powder"

On the envelope, avoid using adjectives, such as "long" or "blonde," to describe hair; e.g., "Hair and other items lifted with tape from green area rug lying across the floor two feet east of the back door." On the bindle, when it is used for debris, refer to the evidence with which the content of the bindle is associated; e.g., "Debris from evidence #36." Label the container just before collecting a sample, and seal the container immediately after collection.

Tape Lifting Trace Evidence

Tape on a roll or as used in sheets are considered "tape." Acetate sheets, page protectors, and release liners will be "backing."

Remove a little longer clear tape from the roll than will be needed to tape lift the intended surface. Fold approximately an inch of tape onto itself on the ends. Place the tape evenly on the surface to be tape lifted. Press repeatedly and firmly along the length of the tape. Peel the tape off the surface carefully to keep evidence from falling off it.

If surface pattern is important, place adhesive side of tape on the backing. If pattern is not important, repeatedly place the tape onto new areas of the surface with potential evidence several times, but before the tape loses stickiness. Place the adhesive side of the tape onto backing.

If lift tape is being used, open the tape lift and remove the protective seal over the sticky part of the lift. If clear tape is being used, remove a piece of tape. While holding the tape over clean paper, close the lift tape or place the piece of clear tape against the sheet of acetate. If lift tape is being used, carefully place the backing over the sticky surface. If clear tape is being used, carefully place the tape on the acetate.

Be sure not to let any evidence fall from the tape lift or clear tape. If the tape lift or clear tape is not sticky enough to securely attach to the backing or acetate, use an additional piece of tape to secure it to the backing. Label the tape with your initials, identification number, the date and time, evidence number, and location as appropriate.

The backing should be labeled along a margin parallel to the direction of the tape with your initials, identification number, the date, evidence number, location and description Packaging Place the tape lift into the labeled envelope. The envelope and tape backing should have identical information on their labels.

Save any debris that fell off of the tape onto the clean paper by folding the paper into a bindle and placing it into an envelope. Take care to fold the paper in such a manner as to contain all debris; using a "druggist fold" to make a bindle is recommended. The container should be labeled in the same manner to match the lift envelope's label.

If a control or comparison tape lift is made, package separately from the evidence tape lift. Close the container and seal the entire opening with evidence tape. Write your initials, identification number, and the date across the evidence tape seal. Store lifts in a secure, dry storage area until they are submitted.

COLLECTING WITH TWEEZERS

Hair is frequently located at a crime scene near a weapon, near the point of impact, and below a deceased person, on clothing worn during the crime.

Fiber is frequently located at a crime scene on clothing, carpet, furniture, and bedding. Fiber is usually defined as carpet and clothing filaments. Broken glass is frequently found on clothing, shoes, skin, tools, and weapons. Paint is commonly located on the object that impacted the painted surface, the area below/around the painted surface, and the clothing and shoes of people who have been in the area of the painted surface at the time of or since the impact. Always use clean, powder-free gloves when handling evidence.

Do not cough, sneeze, talk, or scratch over any sample being collected or dried. Broken glass is frequently found on clothing, shoes, head hair, skin, tools, and weapons. Paint is commonly located on the object that impacted the painted surface, the area below/around the painted surface that was impacted, and the clothing and shoes of people who have been in the area of the painted surface at the time of or since the

Label a container for the bindle or envelope with your initials, identification number, the date and time, evidence number, location, and evidence description. Label the bindle or envelope with your initials, identification number, evidence number, the date, and evidence description. Each piece of evidence must have a unique number. This number should correspond to the placard next to the evidence and the evidence log as appropriate.

Label the bindle and container just before collecting an object, and seal the container immediately after collection. These actions help to protect the integrity of the sample and the chain of custody.

To collect the evidence, gently pick up the evidence using clean tweezers. Use only clean tweezers when collecting a piece of evidence. Grasp the evidence gently and with only sufficient force to securely collect the evidence with the tweezers. When collecting hair, be sure to capture the root of the hair when possible since DNA is contained in the hair root. Continue using the tweezers on all evidence large enough to be collected and place the evidence into the bindle or envelope.

Use and label a different bindle for different apparent types of evidence, different areas of collection (as appropriate), or for other reasons. Close the bindle or envelope to contain the evidence and protect it from contamination or leakage. When closing the bindle, make sure to contain the evidence placed into it. Packaging Place the bindle into an envelope or other container. Close the container and seal the entire opening with evidence tape. Write your initials, identification number, and the date across the evidence tape seal. Store the sealed envelope or container.

SURFACE SWABS

For most trace evidence, all other methods should be considered superior and therefore, the most appropriate ones attempted first before using a swab to collect evidence. Often the swab collects too little of the evidence or embeds the evidence within the fibers of the swab making removal or recovery difficult for analysis. Reasonable uses for a swab exist, however, such as recovery of pepper spray from the face of a subject or dye-pack contents from a vehicle interior or hands of a subject.

Label a container for the swab with your initials, identification number, the date and time, evidence number, location, and evidence description. The evidence description should include whether the stain is wet or dry. When describing stains, use the word "apparent" or the phrase "of unknown origin" when the source of the stain is unidentified; e.g., "Brown stain of unknown origin on bathroom floor." Label the container just before collecting the swab, and seal the container immediately after collection. These actions help to protect the integrity of the evidence and the chain of custody.

If the stain is dry, moisten the cotton tip of a swab using an appropriate solvent depending on the evidence such as two or three drops of distilled water. Do not saturate the swab with solvent, just enough to "dampen" the swab with solvent.

SECTION 5.4

Firearms & Toolmarks

PACKAGING FIREARMS

Avoid altering any stain on the firearm. Firearms should be unloaded and placed in a safe condition at the point of collection. If the collector is unsure of the proper procedure, assistance should be sought from a competent source such as a firearms instructor, departmental armorer, or an on-site firearm examiner. Always follow your department regulations. Ship firearms and ammunition according to your Department and the U.S. Department of Transportation's regulations. Do not cough, sneeze, or talk over any sample being collected or dried.

When photographing the firearm, include a scale and an identification label. Take one or more location photographs that depict the object where it was found in relationship to other evidence at the scene. Turn over the firearm, and photograph the other side if stains, serial number, or safety position is apparent on that side. If no serial number is present, mark the firearm with identifying data, such as your initials and the time and date on at least one component that cannot be removed. Also, place identifying data on removable component(s), such as cylinder, grips or ammunition magazine. When there is no serial number on the firearm due to the firearm's age, or the removal or defacement of the number, mark the firearm on non-removable parts, such as the barrel and the frame. Photograph the firearm to capture any existing stains (such as blowback), the serial number, and the safety position.

Place the mark in a location that will not interfere with existing markings. Label the firearm box or a container for the object with your identifying data, such as initials and identification number, the date and time, evidence number, location, and evidence description. Evidence number: Each piece of evidence must have a unique number or identifying data. This number should correspond to the placard next to the evidence.

The evidence description should include:

- Type of firearm Location of any stains on the firearm
- Whether the stains are wet or dry
- Location of the firearm

Label the container just before collecting an object, and seal the container immediately after collection. These actions help to protect the chain of custody. When handling the firearm, do not touch areas of the firearm where latent fingerprints are likely to be found (such as on smooth surfaces). Handle the firearm by touching only the areas that are checkered or knurled.

REVOLVERS

A revolver is defined as a repeating firearm that has a cylinder containing multiple chambers and at least one barrel for firing.

Mark the cylinder with your initials and the time and date. Put the mark in a location that will not interfere with existing markings. Mark the cylinder position. Document the condition of the firearm. Information needed includes:

- Number of rounds in the chamber
- Type and location of any stains
- Serial number, make, model, and caliber

Protect the barrel, chamber, or other operating surfaces from contact with other objects. Handle the firearm by touching only those areas that are unlikely to contain latent fingerprints, such as areas that are checkered or knurled.

Check your agency evidence submission policy. For firearms that will be analyzed by a trained firearms examiner, a particular agency may require or prefer alternative procedures for submission of evidence to their laboratory. Determine which way the cylinder turns. Cylinder turn can be either clockwise or counterclockwise, from the perspective of the shooter. Create a cylinder diagram.

On the diagram, assign a number to each chamber in the cylinder. The chamber below the hammer/firing pin is number one. From number 1, continue numbering chambers as you move around it in the direction that the chamber turns. The diagram should show the state of each chamber – whether it contains a live or spent cartridge case, or is empty. Document in your notes the type of projectiles/bullets contained in each chamber of the cylinder that you observe. It is important to note the type of projectile/bullet used because more than one type could be in use in the firearm at the same time; e.g., "Chamber one (1) contained .357 caliber "Acme full metal jacket."

Firearms should be unloaded and placed in a safe condition at the point of collection. If the collector is unsure of the proper procedure, assistance should be sought from a competent source such as a firearms instructor, departmental armorer, or an on-site firearm examiner. Remove the cartridge or case from the chamber carefully to avoid disturbing any potential trace evidence or latent prints on it. Mark each cartridge or case with the related chamber number. When labeling the cartridge or case, make all marks in or near the mouth of the casing. Do not label a cartridge or case near the rim, head, or primer.

Mark each cartridge or case with the number of the chamber in which they were contained. The cartridge or case directly below the firing pin is in position number one. Start with number one and move in the direction of the cylinder rotation. Label the container into which you will place the ammunition with the same chamber number as you wrote on the cartridge or case. If necessary, wrap each object carefully so as to protect any potential trace evidence.

Mark each chamber once you have marked the ammunition. On each side of the strap, mark the chamber with the number it was assigned when numbering cartridges and cases. Place the firearm, with available filled ammunition container(s), in the rigid box or container that you prepared for the firearm. If you are collecting multiple firearms, be sure to package each firearm and associated ammunition separately from other firearms. When the firearm is too large to fit into a container, securely attach an evidence tag to it. The evidence tag should include the following firearm information:

- Caliber
- Make
- Model
- Serial number

Place the diagram into the labeled container with the firearm and filled ammunition containers. Make a copy of the diagram for your notes before placing the original copy into the box. Close the container and seal the entire opening with evidence tape.

Write your initials and identification number and the date and time across the evidence tape seal. Consider the possible presence of bodily fluids, latent prints and trace evidence when handling the firearm or submitting it for processing.

OTHER FIREARMS

Document the identity of the firearm or the listed firearm's markings. If no serial number exists, mark the firearm with your initials and the time and date on at least one part that cannot be removed. When the firearm has a bolt, mark the bolt with your initials and the time and date. Information needed includes:

- The safety position: on or off
- Existence of ammunition in the chamber
- Type and location of any stains
- Serial number, make, model, and caliber or gauge

Protect the barrel, slide, chamber, and other operating surfaces from contact with other objects. Handle the firearm by touching only those areas that are unlikely to contain latent fingerprints, such as areas that are checkered or knurled. Firearms should be unloaded and placed in a safe condition at the point of collection. If the collector is unsure of the proper procedure, assistance should be sought from a competent source such as a firearms instructor, departmental armorer, or an on-site firearm examiner.

If removing ammunition, mark each cartridge, case, shell, or magazine as it is removed from the firearm. Some departmental policies allow labels to be placed directly on a cartridge or case. When labeling the ammunition, make all marks near the mouth of the casing. Do not label ammunition near the rim, head, or primer. Mark each cartridge or case with the number of the chamber or position in the magazine in which they were contained, starting with number one, or use another schema that is consistent within your department for the way that the ammunition is stored in the firearm. Document, in your notes, the type of projectile/bullet that you observe in the chamber. It is important to note the type of projectile/bullet used; e.g., "Chamber contained .357 caliber Acme full metal jacket."

Mark each magazine to note where cartridges, cases, or shells are found in it. On each side of the magazine, mark the position in which each numbered cartridge or shell is found. The mark should include the number assigned to the related cartridge, case, or shell. The number reflects the position in the magazine in which cartridge, case, or shell is found. Label a container into which you will place the ammunition with the same number as you wrote on the cartridge, case, shell, or magazine.

The label on the box or container should include the number of the position in the magazine in which cartridge or case was found. If necessary, wrap each object carefully to protect any trace evidence on it. When the firearm does not fit into a container, attach an evidence tag that describes the caliber, make, model, and serial number. The trigger guard is frequently the attachment point for the evidence tag.

Place the firearm and ammunition container(s) in the container that you prepared for the firearm. Close the container and seal the entire opening with evidence tape. Write your initials and identification number and the date and time across the evidence tape seal. Consider the possible presence of bodily fluids, latent prints and other trace evidence when handling the firearm or submitting it for processing.

EMBEDDED AMMUNITION

Gunshot residue and fingerprints are extremely fragile. Collect gunshot residue and fingerprints as soon as possible. When possible, collect the entire object in which the ammunition is embedded.

Always wear protective gear when handling objects that could cut or otherwise cause injury to you. Do not cough, sneeze, or talk over any sample being collected or dried. Documentation When photographing the object: Include a scale and an identification label. Take one or more location photographs that show the object where it was found. Show the relationship of the object to other evidence in the photograph. Use rods or strings to show ammunition entry and exit points.

In your notes, document characteristics of the object in which the ammunition is embedded. Information need Location of ammunition in the object Type of ammunition, when possible Apparent entry angle Collect the object containing the embedded ammunition, when possible. If you were unable to collect the entire object, collect the embedded ammunition: Use available tools (hammer, chisel/screwdriver, forceps, handsaw, etc.) to carefully loosen and remove the ammunition.

Handle the ammunition carefully to avoid destroying marks on it. Pad the tips of the forceps, for example, to protect the extracted item from forceps marks. When fragments and other items related to the embedded ammunition are found in the object or fall from the object, collect them also. During collection, handle the object very carefully to avoid damaging evidence, or dislodging the embedded ammunition or any related residue.

Label a container for the object with your initials and identification number, the date and time, evidence number, location and evidence description. Each piece of evidence must have a unique number. This number should correspond to the placard next to the evidence. The evidence description includes the type of object, color of the object, type of ammunition, and when possible the location of the ammunition in the object, including orientation to key object feature(s); e.g., "Bullet of unknown type in piece of unstained wood beam in garage next to washing machine."

Label the container just before collecting an object, and seal the container immediately after collection. Seal the opening of the container with evidence tape. Write your initials and identification number, and the time and date across the evidence tape seal.

FIRED CASINGS AND WADS

Use a "druggist fold" to create bindles that will be used to hold cases and wads. Always use clean gloves when handling evidence. Do not cough, sneeze, or talk over any sample being collected or dried.

When photographing the object, include a scale and an identification label. Take one or more location photographs that show the object where it was found. Show the relationship of the object to other evidence in the photograph. Label a container for the object with identifying data, such as your initials and identification number, the date and time, evidence number, location, and evidence description. Each piece of evidence must have a unique number. This number should correspond to the placard next to the evidence. The evidence description should include:

- Type of case or wad
- Type of weapon used

- Location where the case or wad was found; e.g., ".357 caliber spent case found lying on the garage floor, beneath the stool."

Label the container just before collecting an object, and seal the container immediately after collection. Pick up the case or wad carefully to avoid damaging or dislodging fingerprints or other evidence. Use tools available to carefully loosen and remove the case or wad when it is difficult to reach and to avoid damaging evidence.

Place the case or wad into the labeled envelope. When multiple cases or wads are collected from the same area, place each case or wad in a separate container. Each container must be individually labeled. Individual, labeled containers with cases found in the same area can be packaged together for transport. Wads should not be packaged with other ammunition or related objects. Close the container and seal the entire opening with evidence tape. Write your initials and identification number, and the date and time across the evidence tape seal.

LOOSE UNFIRED AMMUNITION

Photograph the ammunition and the location where it was found. When photographing the object, include a scale and an identification label. Take one or more location photographs that show the object where it was found. Show the relationship of the object to other evidence in the photograph.

Label an envelope for the ammunition with your initials and identification number, the date and time, evidence number, location and evidence description. Each piece of evidence must have a unique number. This number should correspond to the placard next to the evidence. The evidence description includes:

- Type of ammunition
- Location of unspent ammunition
- Orientation of ammunition relative to firearm or other point of interest, when possible; e.g., "Acme full metal jacket case for a .357 caliber revolver found on garage floor."

Label the envelope just before collecting an object, and seal the envelope immediately after collection. Photograph the ammunition and the location where it was found. When photographing the object, include a scale and an identification label.

Take one or more location photographs to depict the object where it was found in relationship to other evidence in the photograph. Pick up the ammunition carefully to avoid dislodging fingerprints or other evidence. Place the ammunition into the labeled container. Unless departmental regulations state otherwise, do not wrap the casing. Wrapping it could disturb evidence that has not already been collected.

Close the container and seal the entire opening with evidence tape. Write your initials and identification number and the date and time across the evidence tape seal. Collect and package any additional ammunition or related items. When multiple pieces of ammunition or related objects are found in an area, place each object in a separate container. Each container must be individually labeled. Those individual containers can then be packaged together for transport.

TOOL MARK EVIDENCE

A tool mark is any impression, scratch, gouge, cut, or abrasion made when a tool is brought into contact with an item, leaving an impression of the tool. In some cases, tool mark identification may link a person to the tool used in the commission of a crime.

Begin by taking overall photos of the object containing the tool mark to show its nature and relationship to the scene. Take a second set of photos that will show the tool mark specifically so that detail can be seen. Note that as tool marks are three dimensional and photographs are two dimensional, examinations cannot be made from photos alone.

By far, the best method for comparison of tool marks is to secure the actual item containing the mark and submit it to the laboratory along with the suspected tool. Care must be taken to protect the working area of the suspect tool by wrapping it in paper. Under no circumstances should the investigator attempt to fit the tool into the mark as it may destroy the very evidence that is to be examined by the expert.

In dealing with large articles or non-removable articles, the tool mark itself may be cut out of the object bearing it. If this is impossible, the investigator has the option of making a silicone cast to the tool mark. Silicone is recommended for this replica as it will reproduce the necessary detail for examination. Plaster of Paris is *not* recommended for this type of casting.

Silicone kits are commercially available and the individual kit instructions should be followed. The investigator may press the strings of an identification tag into the edges of the casting material in a way that will not affect the cast itself. This tag can then be filled out with the proper identification data.

Photograph the impression before casting it. When making a cast, be prepared to act quickly and methodically. Time is often a critical factor in successfully making a cast. Always use clean gloves when handling evidence. Documentation Photograph the impression. When photographing the object: Include a scale and an identification label.

Make at least one photograph where the camera lens is perpendicular or "orthogonal" to the tool mark surface. Take one or more mid-range location photographs that depict the object where it was found. Show the relationship of the object to other evidence in the photograph. Label a container for the object with identifying data, such as your initials and identification number, the date and time, evidence number, location, and evidence description. Each piece of evidence must have a unique number. This number should correspond to the placard next to the evidence. The evidence description should include:

- Type of item being cast
- Location of the item being cast
- Orientation of the item being cast; e.g. to the north, to a feature of the object with the impression on it, or to a nearby object.

Label the container just before collecting an object, and seal the container immediately after collection. Clean out loose material from the impression, when possible, without disturbing the impression. Never discard a cast, regardless of condition when removed from the impression. Be sure to save and submit all casts to the laboratory.

Close the container and seal the entire opening with evidence tape. Write your initials, identification number, and the date and time across the evidence tape seal. Make sure that the container is also labeled with a description of the item cast, appropriate identifying data, such as your initials and identification number, the date and time, location and, when possible, the evidence number. If the item with the tool mark is collected, it should be packaged separately from a suspect tool(s) to prevent any additional marks, impressions or other damage. Never place the suspected tool(s) into the impression.

REFERENCES AND FURTHER READING

Stevens, B. L. (2017). *Comprehensive Modernization of Firearm Discharge Residue Analysis; Advanced Analytical Techniques, Complexing Agents, and Tandem Mass Spectrometry*.
Available: https://www.ncjrs.gov/pdffiles1/nij/grants/251195.pdf

SECTION 5.5

Impression Evidence

TIRE IMPRESSIONS

A comparison of the accident/crime scene impressions can result in an identification, inclusion, or elimination of a tire. Impression(s) can be found in a variety of substrates including soil and snow, as well as on cement and asphalt. The evidentiary value of a comparison usually depends upon the quality of the impression and the manner in which it is documented and collected.

The decision to cast is affected by the conditions of the substrate that the impression is in or on. Impressions in fine, humus soil, wet sand, and even snow are often excellent candidates for casting. Coarse substrates may not always the best substrate for retaining detail of the tire impression(s). It is recommended that all impressions are photographed and cast, to recover the maximum amount of impression detail.

Photography is a valuable way of collecting impression evidence for later comparison. As with all evidence, overall photographs should be taken using a standard-format lens showing the impressions in relation to the other features of the scene. It is critical that distortions are minimized by adhering to the following: Impression photography requires the use of a tripod and detachable flash. Documentation must include a photograph with a measurement scale. The scale should not be placed over or across the impression. The scale must be level with the bottom of the impression and be approximately the same size as the impression for proper documentation. The scale should contain case identification information. Documentation should indicate the direction of travel, if this can be determined.

The camera should be mounted on a tripod directly over the impression, with the film plane parallel to the impression. The impression should be shaded from direct sunlight. It is recommended that the detachable flash or other light source be at an angle of 45 degree or less depending on the depth of the impression. A variety of flash angles are recommended. These oblique light photographs should be taken with the direction of the flash coming from at least 3 different directions around the impression.

Tire impressions are photographed in an overlapping series that should continue the length of the impression in which detail is present. Each frame should overlap by approximately 20%, and no more than two feet should appear in each frame. A scale or tape measure placed the length of the track will help reconstruct the length of the entire impression from the separate photographs. Single-lens reflex or similar cameras with changeable lenses should be used for capturing impression evidence.

TIRE & VEHICLE MEASUREMENT

Tire Vehicle Measurements The following measurements should be recorded: The track width of a vehicle is the distance between the center of the tire mounted on one side of the vehicle to the center of the tire on the opposite side. The front and rear track widths may be different. The wheelbase of a vehicle is the distance between the center of the front axle and the center of the rear axle.

Measure the track width and wheelbase recorded in the impressions, if possible. The track width may be measured from the inside of one tire track to the outside of the adjacent tire track, if they can be determined to be a pair made by a single vehicle. If the positions of the front and rear tires can be determined where a vehicle stopped, these positions can be measured to determine an approximate wheelbase measurement.

After photography, casting may be performed to document the impression in three-dimensional form. The decision to cast is affected by the substrate conditions and other environmental factors. Impressions should be photographed before casting. Do not remove soil adhering to the cast or attempt to clean the cast after recovery as this may damage cast detail. Place each casting in a protective, breathable container after drying.

Chemicals and/or powders may be used to enhance or optimize impression(s). It should be determined prior to chemical application if a sampling of the blood is required, as the chemicals used to optimize the impression(s) may interfere with DNA analysis.

Forensic light sources may optimize visualization and photography of the impression(s). Examination of the impression(s) using a forensic light source may be conducted prior to applying any chemicals or powders. Blood does not fluoresce, but views as black in infrared (IR) range and may offer contrast between the impression and the substrate of the item it is on.

FOOTWEAR IMPRESSION EVIDENCE

A shoe or boot may be associated or disassociated to a crime scene by footwear impressions. A comparison of the crime scene impressions can result in an identification, inclusion, or elimination of a footwear outsole. Impressions can be found in soil, snow, on counters, tile floors, doors, wood and vinyl furniture, paper items, as well as other surfaces. The decision to cast an impression is affected by the conditions of the substrate the impression is in or on. Impressions in fine, humus soil and even snow are often excellent candidates for casting. Coarse substrates may not always be the best substrate for retaining detail of the tire impression(s).

It is recommended that all impressions are photographed and cast, to recover the maximum amount of impression detail. Photography is a valuable way of collecting impression evidence for later comparison. The evidentiary value of a comparison usually depends upon the quality of the impression and the manner in which it is documented and collected.

Overall photographs should be taken using a standard-format lens showing the impressions in relation to the other features of the scene. It is critical that distortions are minimized by adhering to the following: Impression photography requires the use of a tripod and detachable flash. Documentation must include a photograph with a measurement scale.

The scale should not be placed over or across the impression. The scale must be level with the bottom of the impression and be approximately the same size as the impression for proper documentation. The scale should contain case identification information: Case number Orientation The camera should be mounted on a tripod directly over the pattern, with the film plane parallel to the impression. The impression should be shaded from direct sunlight for flash photographs.

It is recommended that the detachable flash or other light source should be at an angle of 45 degrees or less depending on the depth of the impression. A variety of flash angles are recommended. These oblique light photographs should be taken with the direction of the flash coming from at least 3 different directions around the impression. The entire impression should be captured in one frame unless overlapping photographs are needed to capture sufficient resolution.

After photography, casting may be performed to document the impression in three-dimensional form. The decision to cast is affected by the substrate conditions and other environmental factors. Impressions should be photographed before casting. Do not remove any soil adhering to the cast or attempt to clean the cast after recovery as this may damage cast detail. Place each casting in a protective, breathable container after drying.

TWO-DIMENSIONAL FOOTWEAR IMPRESSIONS

Two-dimensional impressions are usually a deposit or removal of material to or from a surface. These may be found on paper items, doors, counters, tile floors, and other hard surfaces/substrates. There are generally two ways footwear impressions are made: by the removal of dust or other material from a surface by adhering to an outsole leaving a void (negative) impression the deposition of a material or contaminate such as blood, dirt, and oil present on a footwear outsole, transferred to a surface, leaving an impression

If possible, submit the entire item that has the impression on it. If that is not practical, the impressions may be lifted using various techniques such as:

- Electrostatic dust lifter
- Gel print lifter
- Tape or clear adhesive material (if no other material is available)

Chemicals and or powders may be used to enhance or optimize impression(s). It should be determined prior to chemical application if a sampling of the blood is required, as the chemicals used to optimize the impression(s) may interfere with DNA analysis. Forensic light sources may optimize visualization and photography of the impression(s). Examination of the impression(s) using the forensic light source may be conducted prior to applying any chemicals or powders. It should be noted that blood does not fluoresce, but views as black in IR range and may offer contrast between the impression and the substrate of the item it is on.

When making a cast, be prepared to act quickly and methodically. Time is often a critical factor in successfully making a cast. When casting tire impressions, cast as much of the tire impression as possible. Use dental stone for casting in dirt, soil and sand as well as snow. Sulfur may be used for casting in snow. Impression coating materials such as SnowPrint Wax, stabilizers (e.g., hairspray) and highlighters (e.g., paint) may be used depending upon conditions present.

Casts should be marked with the impression identifier, general evidence collection information (date, case number, etc.) and with a directional indicator. Casting material should be allowed to thoroughly harden before removal from surface.

Follow the manufacturer's instructions for preparing the casting material. A sturdy plastic bag is used for mixing dental stone for footwear impressions, a bucket is usually necessary for mixing casting material for tire tracks. The initial pour of the casting material should occur off the impression to avoid damaging detail; the casting material should be allowed to flow into the impression.

CASTING WITH DENTAL STONE

If necessary, prepare impressions for casting. When casting a fragile impression, it may be necessary to apply a fixative. Care should be exercised when applying fixatives to minimize any possibility of damage to the impression. When casting in dense soils, it may be necessary to apply a release agent. Care should be exercised when applying release agents to minimize any possibility of damage to the impression. Add appropriate amount of water to pre-measured amount of dental stone. The average footwear impression requires approximately two (2) pounds of dental stone and approximately ten (10) ounces of water.

The amount of water required may vary depending on the casting product. The resulting mixture should have the viscosity of heavy cream. The viscosity of the mixture may need to be adjusted based upon the nature of the impression. Mix continuously for a minimum of 3–5 minutes so that the powder can thoroughly absorb the water. Pour casting material carefully outside the perimeter of the impression and direct the flow into the impression.

Ensure the impression is completely filled and/or covered evenly. In the event that the casting material does not flow completely into the impression, the top surface of the casting material can be agitated to help it flow. Casts should be of sufficient thickness to avoid breakage. If necessary, additional casting material may be poured over the top of the original cast to complete the cast and/or add thickness.

For fragile and shallow impressions, pour casting material from outside the perimeter so that it rapidly flows over the impression. A thinner mixture of casting material is necessary for this technique. Avoid pouring directly onto the uncovered impression.

Larger quantities of dental stone can be mixed in a bucket to cast large segments of tire impressions. Impressions under water may be cast using dental stone and specialized techniques.

Casting impressions with dental stone and sulfur in snow is possible. If necessary, prepare impressions for casting. It is noted that snow varies considerably in texture and type. Application of highlighting materials (such as Snow Print Wax™ or aerosol paints) may be advantageous during photography.

These materials may or may not be necessary for the casting process. To increase the contrast of the detail, a thin application of highlighting spray may be directed at the impression from an oblique angle. The application of highlighting sprays to the snow impression may increase melting; therefore, the impression may need to be shielded from the sun until it can be photographed and cast. A thick application of SnowPrint Wax™ may be applied if needed before using the dental stone casting material.

To create a casting with dental stone, begin by adding a heaping tablespoon of Potassium Sulfate to the pre-weighed bag of dental stone. Add snow to the water source and place the bags of dental stone in the snow to pre-cool the ingredients. Add the appropriate amount of water to the pre-measured dental stone. A thicker mixture should be used for snow. Pour the casting material from outside the perimeter and direct the flow into the impression. The surface of the casting material can be agitated to help it flow.

Collect and package debris that may have fallen from the cast when it was removed. Store the packaged debris with the cast. Do not clean the cast. Package the debris in a bindle or other container that will securely store it. Label the container with your name, identification number, and the date and time. Place the cast into the labeled container. When necessary, use shock absorbing and protective materials to cushion the cast.

A cast is delicate and can be easily damaged. Package the cast so that it is stable and secure and the face of the impression is up and protected from disturbance during transport. If a cast is too large to box, wrap it in clean paper and shock-resistant material (such as bubble-wrap). The goal is to seal the impression and protect it from damage during transport. Never discard a cast, regardless of condition when removed from the impression.

Be sure to save and submit all casts to the laboratory. Even a broken cast may be useful during the examination process. Close the container and seal the entire opening with evidence tape. Write your initials and identification number, and the date and time across the evidence tape seal. Make sure that the container is labeled with a description of the item cast, your initials and identification number, the date and time, location and, when possible, evidence number.

FOOTWEAR IMPRESSIONS IN DUST

Photograph the impression before collecting or removing it. An electrostatic dust lifter is appropriate to use only when the impression is left in dry dust. Whenever possible to do so without damaging the impression, collect the object containing the impression. Always use clean gloves when handling evidence. Always collect soil/rock samples from the immediate surrounding area when the impression is on the ground.

Properly photograph the impression before lifting. Label a container and an identification label for the developed impression with your initials and identification number, the date and time, evidence number, location, and evidence description. Make sure that the information on the container matches the identification labels. Each piece of evidence must have a unique number. This number should correspond to the placard next to the evidence. The evidence description includes:

- Type of print collected
- Location of the impression
- Orientation of the impression to north, or to a feature of the object with the impression on it, or to a nearby object

Label the container just before collecting an object, and seal the container immediately after collection. Lifting the Impression When lifting impressions, examiners should use the least destructive method first. If in doubt, treat all impressions as dry-origin and apply the methods listed below. If unsuccessful, attempt collection as indicated for wet-origin impressions. All procedures shall be performed when applicable and noted when appropriate. The order and use of these individual techniques is determined by considerations such as substrate, components of the impression, and environmental conditions.

Electrostatic Dust Lifters

Electrostatic lifting is useful for the detection and lifting of dry-origin dust and residue impressions that are the result of tracking from dry, dirty surfaces onto relatively cleaner surfaces. Electrostatic lifting is normally the first technique used, as unsuccessful attempts will not prevent subsequent lifting and enhancement techniques. There are a number of electrostatic lifters available. Consult the manual provided by the manufacturer for specific operating instructions.

All of these devices utilize a film which has a black side and an aluminum-coated side. The black side of the film is placed against the impression, and a high-voltage charge is applied to the film, resulting in the transfer of the dry dust or residue impression. To visualize the lifted impressions, the lifts should be examined in a darkened room with a high-intensity light source held at an oblique angle to the surface of the lift. The lifting film should never be reused.

Smaller lifts can be stored in individual clean file folders. These folders should never be reused. Larger lifts can be stored by carefully rolling with the aluminum side out. After rolling, the edge can be secured with a small piece of tape. Electrostatic lifts are fragile and impressions can be destroyed by any wiping action across the surface of the lift. Consideration should be given to photographing lifts prior to packaging. Electrostatic lifts retain a charge and should never be packaged in cardboard, cardboard boxes, or plastic bags.

Adhesive and Gelatin Lifters

Footwear-size adhesive and gelatin lifters are used for the lifting of dust and residue impressions, wet-origin impressions, as well as impressions developed with fingerprint powder. Gelatin lifters are available in white, black and clear. White lifters provide greater contrast with impressions enhanced with dark-colored powders. Black lifters provide greater contrast with light-colored powders and residue impressions. Clear lifters normally do not provide good contrast. Gelatin lifts of residue impressions should be photographed as soon as possible after collection.

Adhesive lifters are available in white and clear. They include footprint-sized sheets and various widths of rolled tapes. White backgrounds are recommended for clear adhesive. Clear adhesive on a clear background is not recommended for residue impressions, these lifts are normally used for impressions developed with dark-colored powders. Residue or powdered impressions may also be lifted with tape if other lifting material is not available.

Sections of tape may be overlapped and lifted as a single lift to recover the entire impression intact. The tape-lifted impression should be placed on a contrasting or white background. Rolled tapes are available in five-inch widths and are preferred to narrower tapes. Dental Stone can be used to lift impressions such as mud and tire residues from surfaces such as concrete and tile.

A thick layer of dental stone can be poured over the impression area and lifted when dry. Note that a border of cardboard or other material should be placed around the impression to aid the lifting of the dental stone after drying. Mikrosil™ or other polyvinylsiloxane (PVS) casting materials can be used to lift impressions enhanced with powder, from any surface. These products lift the complete powdered impression and are particularly useful on textured surfaces.

Packaging

Insert the lifted impression into the labeled envelope. Do not bend or fold the lifted impression to fit it into the envelope. Close the envelope in which the print is stored and will be transported, and seal the entire opening with evidence tape. Write your initials and identification number, and the date and time across the evidence tape seal.

VEHICLE EXAMINATION PROCEDURES

Process a vehicle with the same caution and detailed approach as you would any crime scene. Obtain warrants as you would other crime scenes if required. Establish well-defined boundaries around the vehicle using boundary markers (such as rope, tape, cones, etc.) to preserve evidence. Photograph the interior and exterior of the vehicle; including the vehicle identification number (VIN). Consider exterior photography from all four corners of the vehicle, towards the center of the vehicle. Collect DNA, fingerprints, or trace evidence before moving the vehicle to avoid damaging or losing it when the vehicle is moved.

Examine exterior surfaces for latent prints including the side mirrors, fenders (when a wheel is missing), and the six-inch-wide areas surrounding the sides, hood, trunk, and roof support post. Examine interior surfaces for latent prints including door handles, rear-view mirror, seat belt buckles, windows and window handles/buttons, stick shift knob, and glove box door. Tow the vehicle to a well-covered, dry, secure area, such as a police compound, when a detailed search for evidence is required. Take steps to ensure that any evidence that can fall from the vehicle during towing can be retained; e.g., placing a tarp below the car or stabilizing bullet holes in glass with tape.

Maintain and continue to protect the boundary around the vehicle until it is towed. Documentation Record critical information about the vehicle before it is moved. Information to record in your notes includes: Odometer reading, gas level, apparent damage, state of windows, head and tail lights, turn signal lights and mirrors, ambient temperature and radiator/hood temperature. Note possible reason for vehicle being at the location. Whenever appropriate, wrap all stray vehicle parts related to the vehicle in clean paper. Lay the object on the paper and fold the paper around it.

Label the container for the object with your initials and identification number, the date and time, evidence number, location, and evidence description. Each piece of evidence must have a unique number. This number should correspond to the placard next to the evidence. The evidence description includes:

- Type of item Location of the item found
- The proximity of the item to the vehicle

Label the container just before collecting an object, and seal the container immediately after collection. Place the wrapped object into the labeled container. Some objects, such as tires, may be transported without placing into another container. If the object will not fit into a container, seal the paper wrapping the object with evidence tape. Close the container and seal the entire opening with evidence tape. Write your initials and identification number, and the date and time across the evidence tape seal.

Seal the openings of the vehicle with evidence tape. It is important to seal the vehicle by taping exterior parts of the vehicle that can be opened with evidence tape. Avoid applying tape to areas that might be or are known to contain evidence that could be damaged when touched. When the weather is inclement, cover the necessary areas with a clean, weather-resistant material, such as plastic.

The vehicle should be accompanied to a secured storage facility. When the vehicle arrives at its destination, sign the evidence log to verify that the vehicle was checked into the storage facility, then check that all seals on the vehicle are intact. When seals are broken, note when the break occurred and reapply evidence tape to secure the vehicle.

REFERENCES AND FURTHER READING

Speir, J. A. (2017). *A Quantitative Assessment of Shoeprint Accidental Patterns with Implications Regarding Similarity, Frequency and Chance Association of Features*. Available: https://www.ncjrs.gov/pdffiles1/nij/grants/251522.pdf

SECTION 6

Information from People

While forensic evidence is extremely valuable, most cases are ultimately resolved because of information that comes from a person who saw the crime happen, who was the victim of the crime, or who perpetrated the crime. This evidence, which is testimonial in nature, comes from *people*. It is important to realize that people make mistakes and can be led by suggestive interview techniques. Well-meaning witnesses can identify the wrong person; they may fail to identify the perpetrator.

The investigator must not only obtain the desired information but must obtain *reliable* information that can be used in court. The courts, recognizing this potential for human error, have instituted legal policies that dictate how police obtain information. In addition to mistakes made by witnesses, the law protects the civil rights of suspects by dictating how interviews and interrogations must be conducted. Ensuring these rights is a major component of the investigator's job when trying to obtain information from people.

INITIAL REPORT OF A CRIME

Nearly every crime begins with a call to the police. These calls are most often routed through the 911 system where a dispatcher takes the call. This is where the information gathering process begins, and dispatchers need to be trained to get it right. The dispatcher is usually the first point of contact with a witness, be they an eyewitness or a victim (or sometimes even the perpetrator). The call-taker should seek to obtain complete and accurate information in a nonsuggestive manner, and then relay that information to officers in the field. This information may include the identity and description of the perpetrator. The actions of the dispatcher can impact the safety of everyone involved in the investigation, as well as impact the overall success of the investigation.

The first order of business is to deal with the exigency of the call, assuring the caller that assistance is on the way. People who call 911 do so because they want help, and they are not likely to calm down and be cooperative if they are not assured that help is coming. Following this, the dispatcher should as open-ended questions. If these open ended questions leave out important information, then it is appropriate to ask closed ended, specific questions. The dispatcher must avoid asking suggestive or leading questions. (e.g., "Was the vehicle a red F150 pickup?"). The dispatcher should follow up by asking if there is anything else that should be known about the incident. Pertinent information should be immediately transmitted to officers in the field, and officers should be updated as more information becomes available.

PRELIMINARY INVESTIGATION

In these days of the CSI Effect, the importance of physical evidence and forensic analysis are at the forefront of the public's imagination, and these effects can rub off on police officers as well. It must be remembered that most crimes are "cracked" by information gathered from people. More often than not, it is "good old fashion" police work that solves cases, not the mere presence of physical evidence. The preliminary investigator's job includes obtaining, preserving, and maximizing the amount of accurate information from the crime scene.

An obvious first step is to try and identify the perpetrator, and, if they are still present at the scene, detain or arrest them. The next step is to determine if a crime has occurred, and, if so, classify it. As soon as new information becomes available, undated descriptions of the incident, perpetrators, and any involved vehicles should be broadcasted to fellow officers.

The identity of witnesses should be verified. Witnesses should be separated and instructed not to discuss the details of the incident with each other. The area should be canvassed for other witnesses.

The manner in which the preliminary investigating officer obtains information from witnesses has a direct impact on the amount of accuracy of that information. Such information forms the foundation of subsequent follow-up investigations, and thus should not be taken lightly.

A first step in any attempt to obtain information from any person is to establish a rapport. A first question should always be concerning the condition of the person. If they are healthy enough to continue the conversation, the officer should begin with open-ended questions and augment those with closed-ended questions. As always, the use of leading questions should be avoided. Any vague or confusing responses should be clarified.

All information obtained from witnesses should be preserved in a written report, always including the identity of the witness. Witnesses should also be encouraged to contact investigators with any further information. Many investigators carry business cards with their contact information on them for this purpose. Witnesses should be encouraged to avoid media exposure to media accounts of the incident. They should also be asked not to discuss the details of the incident with other potential witnesses.

SECTION 6.1

Interviews and Interrogations

Contrary to the Hollywood impression of how criminal investigations work, investigators solve more crimes than scientists. They do so not with forensic evidence, but for the decidedly low-tech reason that "somebody talked." Witnesses, victims, accomplices, and sometimes even the criminals themselves provide testimonial evidence that "cracks" a case. Despite this long standing relationship between interviewing skills and case resolution, the law enforcement community has done a poor job of training officers in the science (some would say art) of interviews and interrogations. Perhaps the cause of this widespread failure to teach officers one of the most valuable skills that they can possess is the enduring myth that getting people to talk requires some sort of innate ability, similar to the "gift of gab."

While it is likely that some officers possess better instinctive communication skills than others, rest assured that the basic skills necessary to conduct successful interviews and interrogations can be learned. Other myths stand in the way of successful interviewing, such as the stereotypical no-nonsense detective that demands "just the facts, Ma'am." Demanding "just the facts" would be convenient for the investigator that is pressed for time, but that simply is not how interpersonal communication works in the real world. Some upstanding citizens will provide information even if an officer seems aloof or officious, but people like that don't often have information about criminal activity. If we view an interview as a "conversation with a purpose," then the need to treat people as *people* quickly becomes evident.

INTERVIEW STRUCTURE

Since no two people are exactly the same, no two interviews (or interrogations) will ever be exactly the same. Even so, there are some generic steps that can provide a framework for conducting interviews that consistently provide a high probability of obtaining information that is useful to an investigation.

Preparation

Preparing for an interview maximizes the effectiveness of witness participation and interviewer efficiency. Prior to conducting the interview, the investigator should: Review available information. Plan to conduct the interview as soon as the witness is physically and emotionally capable. Select an environment that minimizes distractions while maintaining the comfort level of the witness. Ensure resources are available (e.g., notepad, tape recorder, camcorder, interview room). Separate the witnesses. Determine the nature of the witness' prior law enforcement contact.

Performing the above pre-interview preparations will enable the investigator to elicit a greater amount of accurate information during the interview, which may be critical to the investigation.

Introduction

A comfortable witness provides more information. On meeting with the witness but prior to beginning the interview, the investigator should attempt to develop a rapport with the witness. It may be a good idea to inquire about the nature of the witness' prior law enforcement contact related to the incident. It is almost never a good idea to volunteer specific information about the current suspect or case.

Establishing a cooperative relationship with the witness likely will result in an interview that yields a greater amount of accurate information. When introducing yourself to a victim, witness, or suspect, be sure to follow the rules of basic etiquette. There is a lot of truth to the old adage, "you never get a second chance to make a first impression." It is important to remember, however, the difference between being polite and friendly and being subservient and meek.

At this stage, you want to create an atmosphere where it is psychologically easier to cooperate than it is to not cooperate. It is important to not give an interviewee an "easy out" by asking them if they "want to talk." Subtle changes in your word choice can have huge impact on people's psychological state. Don't make a plea, make a statement. "We need to talk because..." is much more powerful than "I'd like to ask you a few questions about last night."

Establishing Rapport

The idea of rapport is rather difficult to define, and most people will use words like *empathy*, *liking*, or *comfort* when they try. In everyday social situations, when two people establish a rapport, we say they "hit it off." The basic idea is a state of harmony between two people where conversation comes easily and spontaneously. This can be difficult when two people are decidedly different. It is especially difficult when an officer is trying to establish rapport with an individual that is uncomfortable or wary about talking to a cop in general, and about recent crime specifically.

Even when a witness is cooperative, the need to establish rapport is not eliminated. Being interviewed by an officer tends to induce anxiety in everyone, and that coupled with the potential trauma of being a victim or witness to a crime can be overwhelming to many. Regardless of the person being interviewed, it is up to the investigator to establish rapport.

One of the quickest ways to destroy rapport with anyone is to appear insincere. This should be somewhat obvious in normal social situations, but when it comes to cops dealing with criminals, the *appearance* of sincerity is what is important. If the interviewee decides that the investigator is trying to "play" them, then much damage has been done. Flattery is certainly a valuable tool in building rapport, but it has to be done in a way that is actually flattering to the person, and it must seem sincere. What a person finds flattering is highly individualistic, so there is no magic formula that can be applied in every situation.

Questions

Interview techniques can facilitate witness memory and encourage communication both during and following the interview. Encourage the witness to volunteer information without prompting. Encourage the witness to report all details, even if they seem trivial. Ask open-ended questions (e.g., "What can you tell me about the car?"); augment with closed-ended, specific questions (e.g., "What color was the car?"). Avoid leading questions (e.g., "Was the car red?"). Caution the witness not to guess. Ask the witness to mentally recreate the circumstances of the event (e.g., "Think about your feelings at the time").

Encourage nonverbal communication (e.g., drawings, gestures, objects). Avoid interrupting the witness. Encourage the witness to contact investigators when additional information is recalled. Instruct the witness to avoid discussing details of the incident with other potential witnesses. Encourage the witness to avoid contact with the media or exposure to media accounts concerning the incident. Thank the witness for his/her cooperation. Information elicited from the witness during the interview may provide investigative leads and other essential facts. The above interview procedures will enable the witness to provide the most accurate, complete description of the event and encourage the witness to report later recollections. Witnesses commonly recall additional information after the interview that may be critical to the investigation.

The record of the witness' statements accurately and completely reflects all information obtained and preserves the integrity of this evidence. During or as soon as reasonably possible after the interview, the investigator should: Document the witness' statements (e.g., audio or video recording, stenographer's documentation, witness' written statement, written summary using witness' own words). Review written documentation; ask the witness if there is anything he/she wishes to change, add, or emphasize. Complete and accurate documentation of the witness' statement is essential to the integrity and success of the investigation and any subsequent court proceedings.

Assessing Accuracy

Point-by-point consideration of a statement may enable judgment on which components of the statement are most accurate. This is necessary because each piece of information recalled by the witness may be remembered independently of other elements.

After conducting the interview, the investigator should: Consider each individual component of the witness' statement separately. Review each element of the witness' statement in the context of the entire statement. Look for inconsistencies within the statement. Review each element of the statement in the context of evidence known to the investigator from other sources (e.g., other witnesses' statements, physical evidence).

Point-by-point consideration of the accuracy of each element of a witness' statement can assist in focusing the investigation. This technique avoids the common misconception that the accuracy of an individual element of a witness' description predicts the accuracy of another element.

The witness may remember and provide additional information after the interview has concluded. During post-interview, follow-up contact with the witness, the investigator should enhance rapport with the witness and ask the witness if he/she has recalled any additional information. It is important not to provide information from other sources.

Reestablishing contact and rapport with the witness often leads to the recovery of additional information. Maintaining open communication channels with the witness throughout the investigation is critical.

DETECTING DECEPTION

Just like most people will tell you that they are an above average driver, most people will tell you that they are a good judge of character. We all like to think that we can "read people" and determine when someone is lying to us. The truth is that we aren't very good at determining when someone is being deceptive, especially when a witness or suspect is a good liar. There are some tested methods, however, that can provide some evidence as to the truthfulness of statements made during interviews and interrogations.

Some officers can naturally "sense" the "symptoms" of a lie, and will tell you that they have a "gut feeling" that a suspect is lying. In reality, there is no sixth sense at work. They are observing the verbal and physical cues that interviewees give off when they are being deceptive. With training, all officers can learn to recognize those symptoms, articulate them, and thus become something of a "human polygraph."

Verbal Cues

When most people think of trying to detect deception in the statements of another person, they immagine "catching them in a lie." By that, we usually mean that some alleged fact is a contradiction of some other alleged fact such that the two statements cannot both be an honest report of reality. Unfortunately, many criminals are really good liars, and good liars seldom contradict themselves. Contradictions, however, are only one type of **verbal cue**. Good investigators will learn to be alert for several different verbal cues.

When people are answering questions about objective reality, certain parts of their brains are working. If you ask someone what they had for breakfast, they activate the part of the brain that holds those memories, and then translate those memories into words that form a statement. When someone is lying, they are using totally different mental processes that rely on totally different sections of the brain. When someone is lying, the are not remembering past experiences, but rather they are creating a narrative. This means that a fabricated story will be constructed differently than a recounted truth, and the way events are described will be different.

Just as the laboratory needs a control sample to provide a "baseline" for comparison for a forensic sample, the interviewer needs a "baseline" of a person's behavior when they are telling the truth. To detect deception, the interviewer is looking for changes from the baseline behavior. This means that good interviewers have to be good multitaskers. During the rapport building phase of the interview, the interviewer is not only building rapport, but carefully observing the behaviour of the interviewee when answering questions about things that already have known answers.

If a suspect knows that they are going to be interviewed about an incident, the chances are they he or she will contrive a story and mentally practice telling the story. Listening is the key to detecting the fabrication. It is important to really listen to what is said, and to what is not said. Obviously, a rehearsed story will sound better than a story created in an instant to respond to an unexpected question. Thus, asking unexpected questions will tend to unnerve a liar and cause a detectable change in their demeanor. Simply put, unexpected questions vex deceivers, and they will telegraph that irritation.

A strategy to take advantage of this fact is to ask about a particular detail that wouldn't likely rehearsed. The question should relate to what the suspect as said; it should make sense in the context. If those two conditions are met, then the suspect will likely respond quite differently than an honest person would under the circumstances.

Honest people may suffer from confusion, and they may not recall details that investigators wish they could, but an honest person will almost never change their story. If a suspect commits to a particular version of a story, a clever investigator can "trap" the suspect by chipping away elements of a fabricated account. While an honest person will get annoyed or confused when what they know to be true is challenged, a liar may well change his account to reflect the new information provided by the interviewer.

Nonverbal Cues

The human central nervous system is designed to deal with danger much more quickly than the "thinking" part of our brain can. When danger is perceived in our environment, a cascade of profound changes occur in the human body. This is often referred to as the **fight or flight response**. It is important to realize that the primitive part of the nervous system that controls this response does not really understand the difference between actual physical danger and a stressful situation.

A stressful situation—whether something environmental, such as becoming a crime victim, or psychological, such as persistent worry about going to jail—can trigger a cascade of stress hormones that produce physiological changes. A stressful incident can make the heart pound and breathing quicken. Muscles tense and beads of sweat appear. For most people, lying is very stressful. A potential problem for investigators is that being involved in a crime and being interviewed by police is also very stressful. That is why establishing a baseline is of such great importance. To detect deception, the investigator isn't merely looking for a stress response. The true "tell" is a *change* in the stress response when moving from truthful statements to lies.

INTERROGATIONS

In court, a cross-examination is the grilling of a witness to bring out the truth for the jury. In the interrogation room, there is no jury to ascertain the truth, so cross-examination techniques do you no good. In other words, cross-examinations don't lead to confessions. A confrontational strategy (what I call the "drill sergeant routine") based on bombarding the interviewee with questions isn't very likely to be successful with the vast majority of criminal suspects.

SECTION 6.2

Eyewitness Identification

The legal system always has relied on the testimony of eyewitnesses, nowhere more than in criminal cases. Although the evidence eyewitnesses provide can be tremendously helpful in developing leads, identifying criminals, and exonerating the innocent, this evidence is not infallible. Even honest and well-meaning witnesses can make errors, such as identifying the wrong person or failing to identify the perpetrator of a crime.

To their credit, the legal system and law enforcement agencies have not overlooked this problem. Numerous courts and rulemaking bodies have, at various times, designed and instituted special procedures to guard against eyewitness mistakes. Most State and local law enforcement agencies have established their own policies, practices, and training protocols with regard to the collection and handling of eyewitness evidence, many of which are quite good.

DISPATCH PROCEDURES

Assure the caller the police are on the way. Ask open-ended questions (e.g., "What can you tell me about the car?"); augment with closed-ended questions (e.g., "What color was the car?"). Avoid asking suggestive or leading questions (e.g., "Was the car red?"). Ask if anything else should be known about the incident. Transmit information to the responding officer(s). Update officer(s) as more information comes in.

FIRST RESPONDER PROCEDURES

Identify the perpetrator(s). Determine the location of the perpetrator(s). Detain or arrest the perpetrator(s) if still present at the scene. Determine/classify what crime or incident has occurred. Broadcast an updated description of the incident, perpetrator(s), and/or vehicle(s). Verify the identity of the witness(es). Separate witnesses and instruct them to avoid discussing details of the incident with other witnesses. Canvass the area for other witnesses.

The preliminary investigation at the scene forms a sound basis for the accurate collection of information and evidence during the follow-up investigation.

Establish rapport with the witness. Inquire about the witness' condition. Use open-ended questions (e.g., "What can you tell me about the car?"); augment with closed-ended questions (e.g., "What color was the car?"). Avoid leading questions (e.g., "Was the car red?"). Clarify the information received with the witness. Document information obtained from the witness, including the witness' identity, in a written report. Encourage the witness to contact investigators with any further information.

Encourage the witness to avoid contact with the media or exposure to media accounts concerning the incident. Instruct the witness to avoid discussing details of the incident with other potential witnesses.

MUG BOOKS

"Mug books" (i.e., collections of photos of previously arrested persons) may be used in cases in which a suspect has not yet been determined and other reliable sources have been exhausted. This technique may provide investigative leads, but results should be evaluated with caution.

In selecting photos to be preserved in a mug book, the preparer should group photos by format (e.g., color or black and white; Polaroid, 35 mm, or digital; video) to ensure that no photo unduly stands out. Select photos of individuals that are uniform with regard to general physical characteristics (e.g., race, age, sex).

Consider grouping photos by specific crime (e.g., sexual assault, gang activity). Ensure that positive identifying information exists for all individuals portrayed. Ensure that photos are reasonably contemporary. Ensure that only one photo of each individual is in the mug book.

In composing a photo lineup, the investigator should include only one suspect in each identification procedure. Select fillers who generally fit the witness' description of the perpetrator. When there is a limited/inadequate description of the perpetrator provided by the witness, or when the description of the perpetrator differs significantly from the appearance of the suspect, fillers should resemble the suspect in significant features. If multiple photos of the suspect are reasonably available to the investigator, select a photo that resembles the suspect description or appearance at the time of the incident.

Include a minimum of five fillers (nonsuspects) per identification procedure. Consider that complete uniformity of features is not required. Avoid using fillers who so closely resemble the suspect that a person familiar with the suspect might find it difficult to distinguish the suspect from the fillers. Create a consistent appearance between the suspect and fillers with respect to any unique or unusual feature (e.g., scars, tattoos) used to describe the perpetrator by artificially adding or concealing that feature.

Consider placing suspects in different positions in each lineup, both across cases and with multiple witnesses in the same case. Position the suspect randomly in the lineup. When showing a new suspect, avoid reusing fillers in lineups shown to the same witness. Ensure that no writings or information concerning previous arrest(s) will be visible to the witness. View the spread, once completed, to ensure that the suspect does not unduly stand out. Preserve the presentation order of the photo lineup. In addition, the photos themselves should be preserved in their original condition.

COMPOSITE IMAGES

Composite images can be beneficial investigative tools; however, they should not be used as stand-alone evidence and may not rise to the level of probable cause.

The person preparing the composite should:

1. Assess the ability of the witness to provide a description of the perpetrator.
2. Select the procedure to be used from those available (e.g., artist, kit, computer-generated images).

Unless part of the procedure, avoid showing the witness any photos immediately prior to the development of the composite. Select an environment for conducting the procedure that minimizes distractions. Conduct the procedure with each witness separately. Determine with the witness whether the composite is a reasonable representation of the perpetrator.

The use of composite images can yield investigative leads in cases in which no suspect has been determined. Use of these procedures can facilitate obtaining from the witness a description that will enable the development of a reasonable likeness of the perpetrator.

Instructing Witnesses & Documentation

Instructions to the witness prior to conducting the procedure can facilitate the witness' recollection of the perpetrator.

An investigator conducting a mug book examination by a witness should provide some basic instructions. The investigator/person conducting the procedure should: Instruct each witness without other persons present. Describe the mug book to the witness only as a "collection of photographs." Instruct the witness that the person who committed the crime may or may not be present in the mug book. Consider suggesting to the witness to think back to the event and his/her frame of mind at the time. Instruct the witness to select a photograph if he/she can and to state how he/she knows the person if he/she can. Assure the witness that regardless of whether he/she makes an identification, the police will continue to investigate the case. Instruct the witness that the procedure requires the investigator to ask the witness to state, in his/her own words, how certain he/she is of any identification.

An investigator developing a composite should provide the witness with some basic instructions. The investigator/person conducting the procedure should: Instruct each witness without other persons present. Explain the type of composite technique to be used. Explain to the witness how the composite will be used in the investigation. Instruct the witness to think back to the event and his/her frame of mind at the time.

Documentation of the procedure provides an accurate record of the results obtained from the witness. The person conducting the procedure should:

Document the procedure employed (e.g., identikit-type, mug book, artist, or computer-generated image) in writing. Document the results of the procedure in writing, including the witness' own words regarding how certain he/she is of any identification. Document items used and preserve composites generated.

Documentation of the procedure and its outcome improves the strength and credibility of the results obtained from the witness and can be an important factor in the investigation and any subsequent court proceedings.

SHOWUPS

When circumstances require the prompt display of a single suspect to a witness, the inherent suggestiveness of the encounter can be minimized through the use of procedural safeguards. The investigator shall employ procedures that avoid prejudicing the witness.

When conducting a showup, the investigator should determine and document, prior to the showup, a description of the perpetrator. Consider transporting the witness to the location of the detained suspect to limit the legal impact of the suspect's detention. When multiple witnesses are involved: Separate witnesses and instruct them to avoid discussing details of the incident with other witnesses. If a positive identification is obtained from one witness, consider using other identification procedures (e.g., lineup, photo array) for remaining witnesses.

Caution the witness that the person he/she is looking at may or may not be the perpetrator. Obtain and document a statement of certainty for both identifications and nonidentifications. The use of a showup can provide investigative information at an early stage, but the inherent suggestiveness of a showup requires careful use of procedural safeguards.

The record of the outcome of the field identification procedure accurately and completely reflects the identification results obtained from the witness. When conducting a showup, the investigator should document the time and location of the procedure. Record both identification and nonidentification results in writing, including the witness' own words regarding how certain he/she is.

Preparing a complete and accurate record of the outcome of the showup improves the strength and credibility of the identification or nonidentification results obtained from the witness and can be a critical document in the investigation and any subsequent court proceedings.

LINEUPS

Fair composition of a lineup enables the witness to provide a more accurate identification or nonidentification.

In composing a live lineup, the investigator should include only one suspect in each identification procedure. Select fillers who generally fit the witness' description of the perpetrator. When there is a limited/inadequate description of the perpetrator provided by the witness, or when the description of the perpetrator differs significantly from the appearance of the suspect, fillers should resemble the suspect in significant features. Consider placing suspects in different positions in each lineup, both across cases and with multiple witnesses in the same case. Position the suspect randomly unless, where local practice allows, the suspect or the suspect's attorney requests a particular position. Include a minimum of four fillers (nonsuspects) per identification procedure. When showing a new suspect, avoid reusing fillers in lineups shown to the same witness.

Consider that complete uniformity of features is not required. Avoid using fillers who so closely resemble the suspect that a person familiar with the suspect might find it difficult to distinguish the suspect from the fillers. Create a consistent appearance between the suspect and fillers with respect to any unique or unusual feature (e.g., scars, tattoos) used to describe the perpetrator by artificially adding or concealing that feature.

The above procedures will result in a photo or live lineup in which the suspect does not unduly stand out. An identification obtained through a lineup composed in this manner may have stronger evidentiary value than one obtained without these procedures.

Instructions given to the witness prior to viewing a lineup can facilitate an identification or nonidentification based on his/her own memory. Prior to presenting a photo lineup, the investigator should instruct the witness that he/she will be asked to view a set of photographs. Instruct the witness that it is just as important to clear innocent persons from suspicion as to identify guilty parties. Instruct the witness that individuals depicted in lineup photos may not appear exactly as they did on the date of the incident because features such as head and facial hair are subject to change.

Instruct the witness that the person who committed the crime may or may not be in the set of photographs being presented. Assure the witness that regardless of whether an identification is made, the police will continue to investigate the incident. Instruct the witness that the procedure requires the investigator to ask the witness to state, in his/her own words, how certain he/she is of any identification.

Prior to presenting a live lineup, the investigator should instruct the witness that he/she will be asked to view a group of individuals. Instruct the witness that it is just as important to clear innocent persons from suspicion as to identify guilty parties. Instruct the witness that individuals present in the lineup may not appear exactly as they did on the date of the incident because features such as head and facial hair are subject to change.

Instruct the witness that the person who committed the crime may or may not be present in the group of individuals. Assure the witness that regardless of whether an identification is made, the police will continue to investigate the incident. Instruct the witness that the procedure requires the investigator to ask the witness to state, in his/her own words, how certain he/she is of any identification.

Instructions provided to the witness prior to presentation of a lineup will likely improve the accuracy and reliability of any identification obtained from the witness and can facilitate the elimination of innocent parties from the investigation.

The identification procedure should be conducted in a manner that promotes the reliability, fairness, and objectivity of the witness' identification. When presenting a simultaneous photo lineup, the investigator should confirm that the witness understands the nature of the lineup procedure. Avoid saying anything to the witness that may influence the witness' selection. If an identification is made, avoid reporting to the witness any information regarding the individual he/she has selected prior to obtaining the witness' statement of certainty. Record any identification results and witness' statement of certainty.

Document in writing the *photo lineup* procedures, including identification information and sources of all photos used. Names of all persons present at the photo lineup. Date and time of the identification procedure. Instruct the witness not to discuss the identification procedure or its results with other witnesses involved in the case and discourage contact with the media.

When presenting a *sequential photo* lineup, the investigator should provide viewing instructions to the witness. Provide the following additional viewing instructions to the witness: Individual photographs will be viewed one at a time. The photos are in random order. Take as much time as needed in making a decision about each photo before moving to the next one.

All photos will be shown, even if an identification is made; or the procedure will be stopped at the point of an identification (consistent with jurisdictional/departmental procedures). Confirm that the witness understands the nature of the sequential procedure. Present each photo to the witness separately, in a previously determined order, removing those previously shown. Avoid saying anything to the witness that may influence the witness' selection.

If an identification is made, avoid reporting to the witness any information regarding the individual he/she has selected prior to obtaining the witness' statement of certainty. Record any identification results and witness' statement of certainty as outlined in subsection D, "Recording Identification Results." Document in writing the photo lineup procedures, including identification information and sources of all photos used. Names of all persons present at the photo lineup. Date and time of the identification procedure. Instruct the witness not to discuss the identification procedure or its results with other witnesses involved in the case and discourage contact with the media.

When presenting a *simultaneous live lineup*, the investigator/lineup administrator should provide viewing instructions to the witness. Instruct all those present at the lineup not to suggest in any way the position or identity of the suspect in the lineup. Ensure that any identification actions (e.g., speaking, moving) are performed by all members of the lineup. Avoid saying anything to the witness that may influence the witness' selection. If an identification is made, avoid reporting to the witness any information regarding the individual he/she has selected prior to obtaining the witness' statement of certainty.

Record any identification results and witness' statement of certainty. Document the lineup in writing, including identification information of lineup participants. Names of all persons present at the lineup. Date and time the identification procedure was conducted. Document the lineup by photo or video. This documentation should be of a quality that represents the lineup clearly and fairly. Instruct the witness not to discuss the identification procedure or its results with other witnesses involved in the case and discourage contact with the media.

When presenting a *sequential live lineup*, the lineup administrator/investigator should provide viewing instructions to the witness.

Individuals will be viewed one at a time. The individuals will be presented in random order. Take as much time as needed in making a decision about each individual before moving to the next one. If the person who committed the crime is present, identify him/her. All individuals will be presented, even if an identification is made; or the procedure will be stopped at the point of an identification (consistent with jurisdictional/departmental procedures).

Begin with all lineup participants out of the view of the witness. Instruct all those present at the lineup not to suggest in any way the position or identity of the suspect in the lineup. Present each individual to the witness separately, in a previously determined order, removing those previously shown. Ensure that any identification actions (e.g., speaking, moving) are performed by all members of the lineup. Avoid saying anything to the witness that may influence the witness' selection. If an identification is made, avoid reporting to the witness any information regarding the individual he/she has selected prior to obtaining the witness' statement of certainty.

Record any identification results and witness' statement of certainty. Document the lineup procedures and content in writing, including identification information of lineup participants. Names of all persons present at the lineup. Date and time the identification procedure was conducted.

Document the lineup by photo or video. This documentation should be of a quality that represents the lineup clearly and fairly. Photo documentation can be of either the group or each individual. Instruct the witness not to discuss the identification procedure or its results with other witnesses involved in the case and discourage contact with the media.

Preparing a complete and accurate record of the outcome of the identification procedure improves the strength and credibility of the identification or nonidentification results obtained from the witness. This record can be a critical document in the investigation and any subsequent court proceedings.

REFERENCES AND FURTHER READING

National Institute of Justice. (1999). *Eyewitness Evidence: A Guide for Law Enforcement*. Available: https://www.ncjrs.gov/pdffiles1/nij/178240.pdf

SECTION 6.3

Fingerprint Evidence

The skin is both the largest organ and the first line of protection in the human body. Completely covering the body from head to toe, the skin is primarily consistent in nature everywhere except for the areas covering the palmar surfaces of the fingers and hands and the plantar surfaces of the toes and feet. The skin on these areas is referred to as friction ridge skin. Obtaining legible recordings of these areas of skin is crucial for subsequent comparisons to latent impressions recovered from crime scenes, for comparison against previous records, or for input into automated fingerprint identification systems (AFIS). Inked prints, record prints, standards, and exemplars are all terms that are used to describe the recording of these unique details.

Various types of equipment, inks, scanning devices, and techniques are used to record friction ridge detail. Although the concept of recording friction ridge detail seems basic, care and determination should always be exercised in order to obtain the best quality recordings because complete and legible recordings are a necessity in latent print examinations.

PROCESSING LATENT FINGERPRINTS

Prints on evidence are fragile. The slightest amount of handling can degrade a print. Whenever possible, collect the object on which you find prints. Photograph the powdered print before collecting it. Always use clean gloves when handling evidence. Remember: Your prints and DNA may be transmitted by gloves when you touch anything, such as when you scratch your nose. Identify the object that needs to be dusted.

Smooth surfaces yield the best latent prints. When looking for latent prints, examine windows, mirrors, glasses, door handles, doors, etc. Position the print powder, brush, and lifting tape within reach of the object.

Use a powder color that contrasts with the background of the item from which the print is being collected. The color of the backing material must contrast with the color of the print powder used. Gently brush the powder onto the object. When available, follow manufacturer's development process instructions.

Pour a small amount of powder on a clean piece of paper or jar lid. Lightly dip the brush into the powder. Tap the brush lightly to cause excess powder to fall off the brush onto the paper. Carefully and gently, brush the object being printed using curved strokes that follow the natural lines of the print.

Note: Don't ever blow on the surface since it can contaminate the surface with DNA.

Be sure to photograph the developed print. Also, be sure that each photograph shows the scale and identification label. Always shoot location photographs as well as one-to-one/close-up photographs.

Label a lift card for the print with your initials and identification number, the date and time, evidence number, and evidence description. Record the information on the back of the card holding the lifted print. Each piece of evidence must have a unique number. This number should correspond to the placard next to the evidence. The evidence description includes:

- Type of print being collected
- Location of the print
- Orientation of the print to north or to a prominent nearby object; e.g., "Fingerprints found on telephone receiver."
- A brief diagram of the location of the print on an object, depicted with an "X."

Lifting a Developed Print

Remove a piece of lifting tape. If a premade tape lift is being used, open the tape lift and remove the protective seal over the sticky part of the tape. If contact paper is being used, remove the protective backing that covers the adhesive side of the paper. Press the sticky side of the lifting tape to the developed print. Use firm but gentle pressure taking care not to smear the print. Place the sticky side of the lifting tape onto the card stock.

Packaging Lifted Prints

Protect the print by pressing the lifting tape to the card stock while taking care not to smear the print. Place the print lift in a container. Multiple print lifts can be placed in the same container. Submit all print lifts to the laboratory. Do not attempt to determine which lifts are suitable for comparison purposes. Close the container and seal the entire opening with evidence tape.

Write your initials and identification number, and the date and time across the evidence tape seal. If printing a surface that may contaminate the fingerprint brush or powder with physiological fluids or controlled substances, do not use them on subsequent items until they have been decontaminated.

If possible, collect the item on which the print was found. If the print is still moist, allow it to dry before collecting it. When packaging an item with a developed print on it, be sure the transport container is made of paper and large enough to hold the item without damaging the print. Place the item with the print, print side up, into the container while protecting the print from being touched. Secure the item so that the print will not move or be disturbed during transport. Seal the container with the evidence tape. Label the evidence tape.

PROCESSING PATENT FINGERPRINTS

Patent is another word for visible.

Prints on evidence are fragile. The smallest amount of handling can degrade a print. Always photograph the print before collecting it. Always use clean gloves when handling evidence. Your prints may be transmitted through your gloves when you touch anything, such as when you scratch your nose. Documentation Photograph the visible print.

When photographing the print, ensure that each photograph shows the scale and identification label. Always shoot location photographs as well as one-to-one/close-up photographs. Collection If possible, collect the item containing the visible print. If the print is still moist, allow it to dry before collecting it.

Select a suitable container to transport the print. Make sure it is made of paper and is large enough to hold the item without damaging the print. Place the item with the print on it, print side up, into the transport container while protecting the print from being touched. Secure the item so that the print will not move or be disturbed during transport. Seal the container with the evidence. Label the evidence tape.

CHEMICAL PROCESSING OF PRINTS

Chemical processing is best performed in a laboratory or controlled environment. Chemical processing involves safety considerations since the chemicals used may constitute a hazard. Chemical processing should only be performed by someone trained in the use of the process in the field.

Ninhydrin: Used on porous surfaces such as wood, wallboard, and paper.

Caution: If ninhydrin is used at the crime scene, proper safety precautions must be taken. Solvents used in the preparation of ninhydrin can be flammable or deplete oxygen.

Cyanoacrylate (Super Glue): Used on non-porous surfaces such as glass, metal, and glossy or coated surfaces.

Small particle reagent: Used on wet surfaces.

Crystal Violet: Used on the sticky side of adhesive tapes.

Sudan Black: Used on plastic baggies, coated drinking cups and plates, food stuff-contaminated non- and semi-porous items, and cyanoacrylate-processed items.

Latent prints can also be enhanced by the use of a forensic light source in combination with the following processing chemicals and powders: DFO Indanedione Rodamine 6G, RAM, Basic Yellow, etc. Redwop, Greenwop.

INKING PRINTS FOR COMPARISON

The equipment that is needed to record friction ridge detail includes an ink roller, an inking plate (constructed of glass or a smooth metal, such as stainless steel), fingerprint or palm print cards for recording the prints, and a quality black ink formulated for this purpose. These items can be obtained from various forensic or printing supply companies.

Only inks formulated for forensic purposes should be used, because other types of inks (printer's ink, writing ink, or rubber stamp ink) are too light, too thin, or do not dry quickly enough on the recording cards; this retained moisture could cause subsequent smearing of the prints. An alternative to the ink-and-roller method is the use of micro-reticulated thermoplastic resin pads or ceramic inking pads, both of which are impregnated with special permanent and nonfading inks.

A fingerprint stand is also useful. The fingerprint stand can be placed at a height that is necessary to comfortably record friction ridge detail while conveniently holding within its built-in storage bins all of the equipment needed for this purpose. The standard cards that are used to record prints are 8" x 8". This size has space for two rows of five rolled fingerprints and space for plain or flat prints of the fingers under the rows of rolled prints. These cards are white and are usually lightweight cardboard or heavy paper stock. Fingerprint cards are handled countless times and may be stored in files for many years. For these reasons, the texture and strength of the card must be such that it will withstand frequent handling.

In addition to the spaces for the fingerprint impressions, there is room on the card to record information about the person being printed (e.g., name, date of birth), information about the agency, and space for the date and signatures of the subject and technician.

Livescan technology replaces the process of using ink to record friction ridge detail. The friction ridge surfaces to be recorded are placed on a scanner that records the detail in a matter of seconds. High-resolution scanners can produce images that rival the quality of ink recordings, and the digital images are easily reproduced and distributed electronically. The process of rolling the finger impressions (and plain impressions) on the scanner platen is the same as for the actual recording of inked impressions on a card, but without the ink.

The basic method of recording friction ridge detail on the hands or feet can be accomplished by applying a thin coat of black ink directly to the skin's surface using a roller or by coating an inking plate with the ink and rolling the fingers onto the plate. Next, the inked skin is pressed on a surface of contrasting color, such as a white piece of paper or a fingerprint card. The difference in elevation between the ridges and the furrows of the friction ridge skin leaves a print that is a recording of the unique detail of the friction ridge skin.

To begin this process, if using the ink-and-roller method, a small amount of ink is deposited at the edge, center, and opposite edge of a thoroughly cleaned inking plate. The ink is then rolled and smoothed out. The ink should look black, not gray. A gray color means that there is not enough ink on the plate. The ink should not look wet. If the ink looks wet, too much ink has been placed on the plate, and this could result in a smearing of the print. After the proper amount of ink has been rolled onto the plate, the next step is to ink the fingers.

Before any ink is applied to the fingers, the fingers must be inspected to ensure that they are clean and dry, because contaminants can interfere with proper recording. If the subject's fingers are too dry, a moisturizing hand lotion may be applied sparingly to soften the fingers. If the subject's fingers are too moist, they must be dried individually or, in case of excess moisture, wiped with an alcohol wipe and then dried.

Regardless of what method of recording is used (ink and roller, Porelon Pad, or scanning device), the fingers should be rolled away from the body, and the thumbs should be rolled toward the body (thumbs in, fingers out). This procedure allows the fingers and thumbs to be rolled from an awkward position to a more relaxed position and is less likely to produce smeared recordings.

To completely roll each finger, with the subject standing in front of and facing the cardholder, the hand should be firmly grasped in such a manner that the finger is extended and the other fingers are out of the way. The inking plate and the cardholder should be side by side, with the cardholder nearest the operator. The hand is then rotated so that the side of the finger can be placed on the inking plate. While one of the operator's hands grasps the hand of the subject, the operator's other hand holds the end of the finger or thumb being printed to keep it from slipping, to apply light pressure, and to guide the roll.

Two key factors to remember are control and pressure. For best results, the subject should not help with the process and should be asked to remain in a relaxed posture. The finger or thumb is then rotated 180° (i.e., nail edge to nail edge) and is immediately lifted from the plate and rolled in the same manner in the appropriate box on the fingerprint card that has been previously placed in the cardholder.

The plain (i.e., flat or simultaneous) impressions are recorded by grouping the fingers from each hand and pressing them on the inking plate. The grouped fingers, numbers 2–5 and 7–10, are then pressed on the fingerprint card or scanning device in the appropriate boxes, taking care not to superimpose these impressions over the rolled impressions. The thumbs are inked and recorded separately in the same manner. The fingers and thumbs that are recorded in these boxes should not be rolled from side to side. As the fingers and thumbs are lifted from the card or scanning device, they should be rolled toward the tips of the fingers by keeping pressure on the fingers and lifting the subject's wrists so as to record as much friction ridge detail as possible toward the top of the pattern area.

Palmprints are recorded in much the same manner as fingerprints; however, a cylindrical device is often used to facilitate the process to ensure complete recording of all friction ridge detail. The palms are not pressed on an inking plate. Rather, the roller is loaded with ink from the inking plate and the ink roller is used to apply a thin coat of ink directly to the hands from the base and edges of the palms to the tips of the fingers. Care must be exercised to ensure complete coverage of ink to all areas containing friction ridge detail.

To record palmprints, a standard 8" x 8" card or heavy plain white bond paper is attached to a cylinder approximately 3" in diameter. Removable adhesive tape or rubber bands may be used to attach the paper to the cylinder. (Some technicians prefer to let the paper "ride" across the cylinder without attaching it, taking care to prevent slippage.)

The inked palm is then rolled either from the base of the palm toward the fingers or from the fingers to the base of the palm. Either way is acceptable and is generally left to the discretion of the technician. Most technicians prefer beginning at the base of the palm and rolling toward the fingers because this gives the technician more control over the subject and position of the print on the card.

The hand can simply be pulled rather than pushed across the surface, which also tends to help prevent lateral movement of the subject's hand. The palm must be recorded in one smooth, unceasing motion to prevent smudging or distortion. Light pressure should also be applied while rolling in order to maintain completeness and to adequately record the centers of the palms. (Extending the thumb to the side will also help eliminate voids in the center of the recorded palm.)

The thumbs are recorded separately because of their position on the hand. The extreme side of the palm, opposite of the thumb, referred to as the "writer's palm" (i.e., the edge of the hypothenar area), is also recorded separately on the palmprint card. The card is removed from the cylinder and placed on a hard flat surface.

This area of the palm is then pressed on the palmprint card, with the little finger extended, to the right of the previously recorded palmprint for the right hand and to the left of the previously recorded palmprint for the left hand, if space allows. The thumb area of the palm is then recorded in the same manner and placed to the left side of the previously recorded right palmprint and to the right side of the previously recorded left palmprint, again, if space allows. If adequate space does not allow for the thenar and hypothenar areas to be recorded on the same card, separate cards should be used for these recordings.

Major case prints (also referred to as major criminal prints) are a recording of all the friction ridge detail covering the hands. If necessary, this may also include a recording of all the friction ridge detail on the feet. In addition to legible and completely recorded fingerprints and palmprints, major case prints include a legible and completely recorded set of the tips of the fingers, from just below the nail to the center of the fingers, rolled from one side of the nail to the other, as well as completely recorded lower joints of the fingers, including the extreme sides. Major case prints are often required for comparison to unknown impressions that have been collected from crime scenes, and these impressions may include areas of friction ridge detail that are not routinely recorded.

To begin, a complete set of the subject's fingerprints should be recorded as previously described. Next, all of the remaining friction ridge detail on the phalangeal areas of the thumbs and fingers is recorded using 8" x 8" cards or white bond paper firmly attached to the edge of a table. Beginning with the right thumb, a thin coat of ink is applied to all of the friction ridge detail with an ink roller, from the base of the thumb to the tip, including the extreme sides of the finger. Usually beginning at the lower left corner of the paper, the extreme left side of the thumb is firmly pressed on the paper. The thumb is removed by lifting from the base of the thumb to the tip. This will record the extreme left side of the thumb and tip.

Next to this impression, the center of the thumb is placed on the paper and is removed in the same manner, thus completely recording the friction ridge detail from the base of the thumb to the tip. The extreme right side of the thumb is then placed to the right of the center portion, thus recording the extreme right side of the thumb and tip.

Lastly, above the three recorded areas of the thumb, the extreme left side of the tip of the thumb is placed on the paper and rolled to the extreme right side with one continuous motion. This group of recorded friction ridge details of the thumb should be labeled "#1", or "right thumb", above the rolled tip. This process should be repeated with the remaining four fingers of the right hand, moving counterclockwise around the paper.

RECORDING FOOTPRINTS

On occasion, it may become necessary to record a subject's footprints. The same basic procedures as with recording palmprints are used; however, because of the large size of an adult foot, a larger cylinder and paper must be used. The cylinder used for this process should be approximately 5" in diameter and should hold an 8.5" x 14" (legal size) sheet of heavy white bond paper attached to the cylinder, as previously described. The foot should be rolled across the paper in the same manner as the palmprints, in one smooth, continuous motion from the heel of the foot toward the toe, with the toes passing completely over the cylinder.

Recordings of the feet may also be obtained by applying ink to the bottoms of the subject's feet with a roller and instructing the subject to walk across paper that has been laid out on the floor. This, however, requires cooperation from the subject and may not produce satisfactory recordings, because excessive pressure and movement of the feet may blur or smear the impressions. Another method is to mount a card or paper on a flat board. With the subject in a sitting position and with the leg elevated and supported, the paper is pressed against the subject's inked foot.

PRINTS FROM A DECEASED PERSON

Coordinate with the Medical Examiner or Coroner before attempting to collect prints from a deceased person. Protect a deceased person's hands and feet by covering them with paper bags that are secured at the victim's wrist and ankle. Never use plastic bags to protect these areas of a body. Elimination prints can be collected after evidence collection has occurred. The preferred method for collecting comparison/elimination prints is using ink. Finger, palm, hand, toe, heel, feet, and major case prints can be inked and rolled. Always use clean gloves when handling evidence.

Before collecting prints, ensure that the hands are photographed to document any trace material or physiological fluid which may be present, and collect the material before proceeding. Set up the location where prints will be taken, preferably on a flat surface. Ensure that fingerprint supplies are easily accessible and ready for use. Instruct the person to clean their hands before rolling the prints if applicable. Complete as much of the information requested on the print card as possible. Critical information includes your name and identification number, the name of the fingerprinted person, the date and time, and which hand was printed. Insert the print card into a cardholder.

Position the person being printed so that the hands are easily accessible to you without your firearm side being exposed if you are wearing a firearm. Just before rolling prints, put on clean gloves to ensure that you have eliminated the possibility of transferring your prints to the card. The person being printed should stand facing the print card. You can stand, being sure to safeguard your firearm if you are wearing one, to the side of the hand being printed or in front of the person.

Hold the person's thumb tip and wrist gently, and press the thumb onto the ink strip. Roll the thumb on the ink from the edge of the nail on one side to the edge of the nail on the other side. Be sure to ink the tip of the thumb (or finger) well so that the developed print is as clear and complete as possible. Gently and with steady force, press the inked thumb to the card and roll it from the edge of the nail on one side to the edge of the nail on the other side. Repeat the inking and rolling process for all fingers on one hand, starting with the index finger. Print the fingers in this order: index, middle, ring, and little.

When a print is smudged or otherwise defective on the card, take another print on a new card for that finger only. Label the card so that it clearly corresponds with the card containing the smudged print. Never discard a print card; do not cover the print with a fingerprint tab designed for this purpose. When print impressions are not clear due to a skin condition or other circumstance, write "Best print possible due to (reason)" in the space nearest the print on the card. When a finger is injured or missing, note the condition in the space for that finger. When necessary, obtain a new card for the prints from the other hand. When using a ten-print card, use the space provided for the other hand. Package to protect the completed card.

FLEXIBLE LIFTERS

Finger, palm, hand, toe, heel, and feet prints, and major case prints can also be developed using this method. Always use clean gloves when handling evidence. Prepare to take the prints by setting up the location where prints will be taken and instructing the person to clean their hands if they are very soiled. Before collecting prints, ensure that the hands are photographed to document any trace material or physiological fluid which may be present, and collect the material before proceeding.

Complete as much of the information requested on the print card as possible. Critical information includes your name and identification number, the name of the fingerprinted person, the date and time, and which hand was printed. Avoid touching the lifter in the area where the person's prints will be developed.

Cut a sheet of flexible plastic lifter into 1½"×8" strips to record fingers. Rub a small amount of fingertip moistener onto the subject's fingers. Any excess may be wiped off with a paper towel. Lightly dust palm side of the hand with black fingerprint powder. Separate release paper from the flexible plastic lifter. Spread fingers and press hand on the adhesive side of the lifter. Lift hand. Press the lifter along the length of each finger, and around the sides of the fingertips. Press around thumb as much as possible. Larger pieces of lifter can be used to capture palm detail.

Prepare a backing material, such as clear acetate, and cover the adhesive side of the lifter with the acetate. Write identifying information on the back of the lifter. Trim and add to a ten-print fingerprint card, if applicable. When print impressions are not clear due to a skin condition or other circumstance, write "Best print possible due to (reason)." in the space nearest the print on the card. When a thumb or finger is injured or missing, note the condition of the thumb or finger in the space for the print. Repeat the rolling and dusting process to collect the thumb and fingerprints from the person's other hand. Place the print cards in the container.

REFERENCES AND FURTHER READING

Office of Justice Programs. (2018). *Defining the Difficulty of Fingerprint Comparisons*.
Available: https://nij.gov/topics/forensics/evidence/impression/Pages/defining-difficulty-of-fingerprint-comparisons.aspx

SECTION 6.4

Surveillance

For police managers, time is money. Every hour officers are tied up doing a particular task, means that something else isn't getting done. When officers are on a "stake out" or conducting other types of surveillance, they often spend a great deal of time waiting and watching and not much else. For this reason, surveillance and undercover assignments are usually employed when other methods of continuing an investigation have failed. In other words, surveillance is usually used as a last resort.

The term surveillance means "to watch over." In practice, it means the covert watching of people and places by officers. **Surveillance,** then, is the act of keeping persons, premises, and vehicles under observation with the view towards acquiring knowledge of the identities and activities of persons, and of the use of vehicles and premises. The term "surveillance" has commonly used synonyms such as "tailing," "shadowing," "covering," and "observing." The most obvious reason to conduct surveillance is to gather information to support a criminal complaint. Surveillance can also be used to corroborate witness statements, provide probable cause for search warrants, and identifying suspects and their associates.

The **surveillant** is the officer that is making the observations. At times, it is valuable to have multiple officers form a surveillance team. This sort of patient watching is a notorious challenge to the ability of officers to withstand tedium and remain alert during long periods of intense boredom. Officers conducting surveillance must be resourceful and be able to devise adequate cover for the operation. This can be actual concealment such that the officers presence is not detected, or it can be a strategy of blending in by playing the roles of average citizens going about their routine activities. Either way, a lapse in cover can equate to disaster for the investigation.

Surveillance is an extremely important investigative method, and at times the only available method, of obtaining factual information during an investigation. The success of a surveillance operation usually depends upon the experience and professional ability of the surveillants.

The **subject** is the person (or place or thing) that is being observed. People under surveillance are most often suspects or the associates of suspects. Places are usually surveilled when officers suspect that the place is harboring a suspect, or the place is used for criminal activities such as selling drugs, gambling, and prostitution. Since 9/11, places that are suspected of serving as the headquarters of terrorist organizations are commonly under surveillance.

CHARACTERISTICS OF SUCCESSFUL SURVEILLANTS

Due to the nature of surveillance and its importance as an investigative method, the surveillant should possess certain basic qualifications and attributes.

Patience. Although largely inherent, patience can be developed through practice, self-discipline and determination. The surveillant who is able to remain patient under arduous conditions and through long hour~, increases the likelihood of a successful surveillance.

Adaptability. The successful surveillant must be able to adapt to unexpected developments, whether they be caused by the actions of the subject, third persons, the weather, or the environment, and to chart and pursue a new course of action.

Perseverance. This quality involves a determination to bring about the successful conclusion of the surveillance in the face of long hours and arduous conditions. It includes a capacity to "stick" to the subject under prolonged and adverse circumstances.

Alertness. The above stated qualities are of little use if the surveillant fails to give her full attention to all activities in the area under observation. Where alertness is lacking, the surveillance may be uncovered, or significant actions of the subject may pass unnoticed. Alertness involves the concentration of all of the surveillant's senses directed toward the subject.

Attitude. The surveillant's attitude will influence the performance of his assignment. The dedicated Surveillant, with a sincere interest in his profession and a desire for a successful performance, will contribute greatly toward a successful investigation.

Keen Perception. The surveillant should not only be able to observe the activities of the subject, but he should be able to understand and interpret such activities in relation to the suspected crime. He must weigh the importance of what he sees.

Good Memory. The ability, to accurately retain mentally that which the eyes observe is essential to the current surveillance and to future operations. Memory can be improved by practice and concentration.

Good judgment. In the face of unexpected developments, the surveillant must exercise good judgment and common sense, oftentimes quickly, in adjusting his course of action to the changing situation.

Resourcefulness. The surveillant cannot always rely upon past methods and techniques in a given situation, and should have the ability to adapt new methods to a new situation by the use of whatever means or materials are at hand.

TYPES OF SURVEILLANCE

The most general classification of surveillance types consists of **stationary surveillance** and **moving surveillance**. Stationary surveillance often involves the classic Hollywood stakeout. This type of surveillance is used when officers are relatively sure that a suspect will come to the location being surveilled.

Officers wanting to observe a particular place have two basic options. Either they can attempt to remain unseen, or they can attempt to blend into the environment and appear to be something other than law enforcement. The choice often comes down to the environment. In a rural setting where vegetation offers ready concealment, officers may choose to use camouflage and terrain to remain undetected. In urban environments, officers may choose to "hide in plain sight" by pretending to be painters, carpenters, or other service professionals.

The subject of surveillance can also be divided into three major categories:

1. surveillance of premises
2. surveillance of vehicles
3. surveillance of persons

Although each category will be presented as a separate and distinct type of surveillance, it must be emphasized that a particular surveillance may entail observation of vehicles, persons, and premises concurrently.

OBJECTIVES OF SURVEILLANCE

All types of surveillances have a purpose and an objective. The objective may be singular or multiple, and may be changed during the course of the surveillance due to unexpected developments. The objectives of surveillance operations are to:

1. Determine whether a violation exists or will exist.
2. Secure probable cause for a search warrant.
3. Secure evidence for prosecution.
4. Determine identity of violators.
5. Determine activity of violators and suspects.
6. Secure information as to the vehicles and types of materials used in a violation.
7. Learn the physical layout and use of the premises.
8. Gather information as to identities and activities of associates of violators.
9. Aid in appraising reliability of an informer.
10. Determine ownership and use of a vehicle in a violation.
11. Determine destination of vehicles.
12. Determine location of a "drop" or "stash" of illicit whiskey or alcohol, or cache of contraband firearms or illegally possessed firearms or explosives.
13. Determine location of illicit distillery, or pickup point for the illegal distribution of firearms or explosives.
14. Determine the methods of operations of the violators.

OBSERVATION POSTS

As the name implies, an observation post is a position or point from which the surveillant or observer watches the activity of a subject, premises, or a vehicle. It is usually hidden from the view or knowledge of the subject. There are two general types of observation posts: Indoor posts and outdoor posts. Examples of indoor posts are:

- Private houses
- Apartment buildings
- Factories, warehouses, and other manufacturing premises
- Stores and other commercial buildings
- Office buildings
- Farm houses, barns, and out-buildings
- Schools and other public buildings
- Fire towers
- Automobiles and other vehicles

Examples of outdoor posts are:

- Wooded areas
- Hills, cliffs, and other high points
- Ravines, gullies, and depressions
- Trees
- High weeds and vegetation
- Foxholes or dugouts

Certain requirements or standards must be met in all types of observation posts. Failure to observe these requirements may endanger the success of the surveillance operation. The observation post must afford an adequate view of the premises or activity under observation. If the post is too far away from the observer to identify persons or vehicles or discern activity taking place, or the field of vision is acutely limited to only a small portion of the area of suspected activity, the observation post should be changed to a better location.

The observation post must protect the observer against discovery by the subjects. If the surveillants are exposed to either visual or audio detection by the subject or his friends and associates, the post is inadequate. The avenues or means of entering and leaving the observation post must be inconspicuous, or at least unlikely to attract unwanted attention to the surveillants. In this regard, consideration must be given to the time of day the post will be entered as well as the physical means of entering.

For example, entering the front door of a public school at a late hour of the night might easily attract the attention of the police and neighbors in the area. In such a case, the school would probably be adequate if a rear or basement entrance was available. In other types of observation posts, the best means of entrance might be a direct approach through the front door. In addition to the requirement of an inconspicuous entrance and exit, the observation post itself, as well as the presence of the observers, must not attract suspicious attention from the subject or persons in the immediate area.

To meet this requirement, it may be necessary for the surveillants to wear a disguise or carry the equipment of workmen, painters, and so forth into the observation post. In any event, the attire of the surveillants should be consistent with either the undercover role or the inhabitants of the area. For example, a surveillant dressed in an expensive suit, white shirt, and tie would appear out of place in an observation post located in a cheap hotel or rooming house.

Another item to be considered in selecting an observation post is the cost of obtaining and maintaining it. Such cost might be out of proportion to the nature and seriousness of the crime or the potential revenue loss to the Government. Good judgment should be exercised under these circumstances.

The selection of a suitable observation post can best be accomplished through an inspection of the area of operation. Topography and street maps of the area may be used, but visual inspection must be employed to select the actual observation position. Usually several locations will be considered and the position that best meets the requirements selected. If a building is to be used as an observation post, consideration must be given to the use of the building and to the trustworthiness of the occupants.

In some instances, the owner or manager of the building should be contacted in person and advised in confidence as to the Government's interest in using the building in an investigation. Unless unusual circumstances dictate otherwise, the owner should not be advised of the subject or premises to be observed. The nature of the surveillance, the type of neighborhood, and the known or probable reliability of the owner will dictate the amount of discretion needed.

Regardless of the approach used, the person contacted must be requested to maintain in complete confidence the identity and purpose of the surveillants. An outdoors observation post presents different problems as to selection. In most cases it is not necessary or even advisable to contact the owners or occupants of land through which the surveillants might need to travel to reach an observation post.

The fewer persons who are aware of the surveillant's presence in the area, the better. There are times when a particular landowner is friendly with or a source of information to the Special Agents, and the use of his land is ideal for observation of a suspected premises.

GENERAL SURVEILLANCE GUIDELINES

There are some common general principles common and essential to all types and methods of surveillance. Once the surveillance begins, the surveillant's ability to apply these principles probably determines the success of the operation.

Secrecy of surveillance

As stated earlier, the surveillant's mission is to observe the activities of the subject or premises without revealing the existence of the surveillance. The best way of maintaining secrecy, of course, is to remain out of the subject's view. At times, this is not possible, and 'the surveillant's ability to act naturally and fit in with the neighborhood will usually prevent detection. Above all, the surveillant should not behave in a suspicious or "cloak and dagger" manner.

Recording observations

The observer should record in his notes all activity possibly relating to the suspect crime as soon as possible after occurrence. Improper or inadequate note taking may result il1 failure of prosecution of the violators due to insufficient evidence. Even activity which might seem insignificant at the time should be recorded as its value may become apparent at a later time. The notes should specifically include the identity or detailed description of persons and vehicles, the activity occurring, and the time and place of occurrence

In addition, they might include the weather conditions, the distance between the observation post and the site of activity, and other factors affecting the surveillance. Such information may be helpful to the United States Attorney in evaluating evidence for future prosecution. The notes should be of such accuracy and completeness that Hie surveillant can refer to them months later and recall in detail the activity observed. The investigator should not embellish the facts when transcribing notes or testifying in court, but report the facts as recorded in the original notes. Each observer should record her own observations.

During the surveillance of a vehicle, the route taken, as well as the location of any stops or contacts, should be recorded. In view of recent court decisions which allowed the defense to examine the original notes of Special Agents, under certain circumstances, the notes of each separate surveillance or special investigation should be kept consolidated and isolated from those of other investigations. This can best be accomplished by using a loose-leaf notebook, or one from which the pages can be removed, such as a stenographer's notebook, or by using separate sheets of paper. Thus, the pages pertaining to a particular surveillance or investigation can be removed and kept together in a file after the completion of the investigation.

Comfort of Surveillants

The physical comfort of the surveillants should not be minimized as it aids mental alertness, physical endurance and good health. The degree of comfort will depend upon· the circumstances and nature of the observation post. The act of standing for long periods can tire an observer quickly. This can be alleviated by using a chair, table, crate, log, or any other such item available upon which the observer can sit.

The surveillants should bring food and water to their posts, unless relief is to be provided for such purposes. If toilet facilities are lacking, the observer would be wise to carry a relief can with him. This is particularly true when observations are made from a "peep-truck." Other items such as sunglasses, insect repellent, blankets, sleeping bags, and mosquito netting can be indispensable at times in bringing comfort to the observer.

Even reading material has its place at times on a surveillance. It may be used as a diverting cover when the surveillant is exposed to view, and it may be an aid to relaxation for an observer when there are more than one stationed at a post. However, such materials should never be allowed to interfere with the attention and alertness of the observer.

The clothing worn on surveillance is important not only as an aid to comfort, but also as a means of blending the appearance of the observer into the surroundings. When observing out of doors, the clothing should be suitable for inclement weather. In rainy weather, water repellent outer clothing, including proper foot and headgear, should be worn. In cold weather, besides keeping the body warm, it is important that the feet and head are adequately protected. More heat is lost through the extremities, especially the uncovered head, than from the body proper. Even inside an unheated building, it would be wise for the observers to be adequately clothed.

When observing outdoors, the clothing worn should blend as much as possible with the natural surroundings. In the summertime, clothing of a grey or dark green color has been found to be the least conspicuous. In the fall or winter seasons, clothing of grey or tan shades blends into the background. Contrasting and obvious colors, whether light or dark, should not be worn unless the surveillant has a particular purpose for doing so, such as appearing as a hunter, etc.

Another requirement of clothing is that it should be consistent with that worn by the local inhabitants. This would particularly apply to surveillances in urban and commercial areas. In some areas, wearing of a suit might cause alarm and suspicion, and the same might be true of work clothes in another type of area. The nature of the surveillance area, as well as the role or disguise of the surveillant, will dictate the clothing worn.

Nighttime Observations

Observations during night hours present problems different from those daytime operations. The major problem is limited vision. The observation post or position must be closer to the premises or activity under observation. When first selecting a position of observation, this fact should be considered if nighttime observations are contemplated. The identification of persons and vehicles is made questionable due to the restricted vision. Colors, in particular, are often indiscernible or misleading at such times.

The surveillants should bear in mind that the public's activity in anyone area is usually different at night than during the daytime. In some areas, there may be few persons on the streets after dark, while in other areas, cities in particular, there may be considerable pedestrian and vehicular traffic until the late hours of the night. Some buildings may be occupied after dark. This, of course, would have a bearing upon the selection of the observation post or position.

Observers should bear in mind that a light, even a match or cigarette, may be seen at a great distance at night. The use of lights should be held to a minimum, and when needed, the light should be shielded by a cover.

Although observations at night present problems to the observer, the cover of darkness may aid the observer in moving closer to the scene of activity and thereby possibly acquiring information that he could not learn otherwise. It should be kept in mind that the subject is also at a disadvantage at night in that he cannot easily detect a surveillance.

Technical Equipment

The use of technical equipment can be helpful and often essential to a surveillance, but only when the equipment is working efficiently. It is the responsibility of the surveillance personnel using the equipment to protect it from damage and misuse. This is especially true ill inclement weather. Binoculars and cameras, for example, are useless if moisture gets into the lenses.

SURVEILLANCE OF PREMISES

The surveillance of a premises may be accomplished by several methods of observation: from an indoors observation post, from an outdoors observation post, from a vehicle, or by using an undercover means of observation. The circumstances will dictate which methods will best accomplish the purpose.

Observation Post is a Building

After a building has been selected as the best available post, the success of the surveillance depends largely upon the ability and actions of the surveillants assigned to the post. It is desirable that two observers, if possible, be assigned to a post. Each observer can corroborate the observations of the other. Such an arrangement also permits one observer to rest while the other maintains observation. In the event of unexpected trouble such as the illness of an observer, the other surveillant can give emergency aid.

The first concern of the surveillants is to enter the observation post without causing undue attention. If possible, they should be dropped off in the immediate vicinity by other Special Agents. If a Government vehicle must be driven to the observation building, it should be unknown to the violators, inconspicuous in appearance, and should not be parked in the immediate vicinity.

If equipment is to be carried into the building, it should be disguised in some manner. Unnecessary fraternization with other persons present in the building must be avoided. If the observation post is in a secluded or segregated part of the building, the observers should remain in that portion. Arrangements should be made to secure the portion used from unwanted intrusion by others.

When camera equipment is used, it should be set up and prepared for immediate operation. The camera should be on a tripod, or other steady rest, and the appropriate exposure, distance, and lens settings correctly adjusted. When the activity of the suspects or violators begins, the surveillants will have little opportunity to prepare the camera. Therefore, it must be ready for instant use.

Notes should include the subject matter of each picture and the identification number of the picture, when still cameras are used. This data will be valuable for proper identification of the film or photographs if they are used as court exhibits.

However, when testifying, the Special Agent should refrain from discussing any technical aspects of the photographic process, such as the camera settings used, unless he is questioned about them. Usually, he will testify only that the film or photograph is an accurate portrayal of the scene in question.

Binoculars should be focused on the immediate area under observation. Radios, if used, should be in contact with the receiver sets in the area. The volume should be set as low as possible and still be audible. Radio noises can be heard for quite a distance at times, and care must be used.

As discussed earlier in the text, the surveillants should make themselves as comfortable as the conditions will permit, using a chair or table. Care must be used when observing from a window. If shades or venetian blinds are on the window, they will provide excellent cover. Shades should be drawn to within a few inches of the bottom.

The observers should not peek around the edge of the shade or otherwise disturb its condition. The same would apply to curtains or other types of window coverings. If the window is bare or uncovered, it may be necessary for the observers to take positions far back in the room to avoid exposure to view, or to improvise some type of blind or camouflage at the window. Any movement at a window may be easily seen from the outside.

The behavior of the surveillants should be such as to avoid attracting attention to their presence either from persons inside or outside the building. Unnecessary noises, such as loud talking and laughing, and banging and scraping sounds must be avoided, especially when others are in the building, or within hearing.

Care should be exercised in smoking, particularly near windows and other openings or under circumstances which might be detrimental to the surveillance. Observations at nighttime are especially vulnerable to detection from a carelessly used match or lighter. It should be remembered that odors, such as tobacco smoke, and noises can be carried for a surprising distance by the wind, especially at night.

While making observations, the surveillants should be alert to all activity within their view, regardless of how insignificant it may seem. This does not mean that the observers should allow their attention to wander unnecessarily from the premises under observation to the extent that important activity might be missed, but rather that the surveillants be aware of the general activity of the area, some of which might later prove to be important.

In this way, the surveillants might notice conditions potentially capable of uncovering the surveillance. During periods of inactivity, the surveillants would be wise to study the premises and area under observation, giving particular attention to the position and physical structure of all buildings concerned. Avenues of escape for the subject should be noted as well as the best means of approach by a raiding party. In this respect, a sketch made of the area would be helpful.

The surveillants must remain alert, and not be lulled into a false sense of security because they are hidden in a building. They should be on the alert for any activity or indication by the subject that the surveillance has been noticed. It should be remembered, though, that while the subject's behavior might tend to indicate that he is aware of a surveillance, it does not mean that he has actually detected the observation post or the surveillance. Many times the unintentional presence of a third party in the area, such as Special Agents from another Government agency, police detective, or any unknown persons, will temporarily alarm the subject. Actually, such an occurrence will often be advantageous to the surveillants as the subject will probably be lulled into a false sense of security upon realizing the intruders are not interested in his activity.

At times, activity might occur at such an angle from the window that the surveillants would have to expose themselves to view in order to observe. This can be remedied by placing a mirror at the proper angle at the side of the window. In doing so, caution should be used to avoid a reflection that might be noticed by the subject or other persons.

If the surveillance is to be continuous or for an extended period, the surveillants on duty should be relieved by other personnel. Such relief should be accomplished quickly and quietly with disturbance kept at a minimum. The relieved observers must advise the next team of any unusual conditions or occurrences. All trash, such as lunch bags and wrappings, cigarette butts, etc., should be disposed of or removed from the post. The relieved surveillants should then leave without loitering in the observation post unnecessarily.

At times, it may be necessary for the relieving team or other personnel, to use a signal or means of communication with the observation post to advise of their intended entrance. This would be especially true if the doors of the observation room or the building were locked, necessitating unlocking from within.

If the observation post is to be left unoccupied for a period, all evidence of the surveillant's presence must be removed, especially technical equipment. Not only will such measures prevent detection of the observer's purpose, but will avoid creating criticism of the Government by the building owner or occupants. In this respect, the surveillants should always remember that they are guests in the building as well as representatives of the Government and must act accordingly.

OUTDOORS OBSERVATION POST

An outdoors observation post differs greatly from the indoors post in that the observers must utilize whatever natural cover is available to shield their activity. They are subject not only to inclement weather conditions, but to detection by other persons in the area while moving to and from the observation post. To insure the security of the surveillance, the Special Agents must take precautions essential to this type of operation.

When moving to and from the observation post, the surveillants should avoid crossing open fields providing little cover. If it is necessary to cross such areas, it should be done so by using natural depressions in the land contour, and by keeping close to the ground, even crawling if necessary. Fields of corn, tall weeds and brush, etc., usually provide good cover for crossing, but care should be' exercised to avoid leaving telltale signs which might attract the attention of anyone nearby. Before any open area is crossed, the surveillants should study the area carefully for the presence of persons working or walking nearby.

Soft ground, such as sand and mud, should be avoided, if possible. If it is necessary to cross these areas, walking on the toes will lessen the appearance of footprints. The banks of streams are particularly difficult to walk on without leaving prints. Walk as much as possible on gravel rocks, or any hard surface that prevents leaving obvious tracks.

At times, walking in the streambed itself, particularly when the surrounding area is muddy or marshy, will enable the covering of a large distance without leaving a trail. This should not be done, though, if the condition of the stream is such that walking will disturb the bottom, and thereby muddy the water, leaving evidence of a person's passing.

When traveling through the woods, the surveillants must also use caution, especially in the vicinity of the suspected premises. Broken branches, trampled grass, discarded papers and cigarette butts will leave distinct evidence of the surveillant's presence in the area. Usually the special agent should avoid moving fast through the woods, thereby creating a disturbance and leaving an obvious trail. With practice, he can learn to move stealthily but steadily.

Surveillants should not walk on paths that they may be following, but rather to one side. While doing this, they should be alert for trip wires, delicately placed branches that will fall if brushed, and other traps that the violator may install to detect the presence of intruders. Whenever possible and appropriate, movement through woods should be made in daylight.

Farm and domestic animals should be avoided if at all possible. When a dog, horse, or other farm animals detect a surveillant, the best course is usually to pacify them rather than attempt to chase them away. Scraps of food will often accomplish this purpose. Horses are particularly troublesome in that they possess keen eyesight and a curious nature. They will often stand and stare at men moving in the area, and even trot over for a closer look. Under such conditions, a surveillant's position may be disclosed inadvertently.

The greater the familiarity the surveillant has with the area, the easier it will be for him to move through that area undetected. Besides having knowledge of the terrain, it is advantageous to know which fields are being cultivated, what buildings are occupied or empty, and what other persons might be working in the area, such as timber crews, etc.

As with the indoors observation post, it is desirable that two observers be assigned to the outdoors post for two additional reasons. First, it allows one observer to watch for surprise intrusion or accidental discovery by strangers in the area. Secondly, if the circumstances warrant, one observer can move temporarily to a closer or more advantageous position.

Movement of the observers should be held to a minimum at the observation post. They may find it necessary to conceal their position with brush' gathered in the area. It should be remembered, though, that the leaves of .freshly cut branches will turn brown after a short time, and thus could create an obvious area of dead foliage against a green background. Blankets, the color of the background, are useful as camouflage and to break up the outline of the observers movements, especially at night. By holding the blanket in front of his body, an observer may be able to move to a closer position at night without fear that his body will be silhouetted against the background. The blanket also serves as a shield under which a flashlight, if necessary, may be used.

Trees make excellent observation posts at times, and should be given definite consideration. Not only is the observer provided cover by the foliage, but the added height may increase the field of vision. The danger of detection, provided the observer remains quiet, is minimized as few persons look up in the trees as they walk in the woods.

When making observations from a position on a hill, with the danger of becoming silhouetted against the skyline must be considered by the observers. They should remain below the crest, if possible, or take a position with a rock, tree, or other obstacle behind them. When used properly, hills, like trees, provide observation positions with an advantageous view of a large area.

While making observations, the surveillants should remain as quiet as possible. Loud talking and laughing may be heard at a surprising distance. The same holds true for coughing and sneezing, and every precaution should be used to avoid such noticeable sounds. Special Agents afflicted with colds and similar ailments should not be assigned to the post. Any sidearms worn by the observers should be covered by clothing in the event of accidental discovery in the area.

Under some circumstances, it may be appropriate for surveillants to disguise their identity and purpose by carrying equipment and assuming certain roles consistent with the area. Some of the typical roles or disguises that might be used: fisherman, hunter, survey crewman, Fish and Wildlife Service employee, and timber cruiser. The type of disguise used would depend upon the supporting equipment available, the season of the year, and the nature of the terrain, etc.

If the observers on duty are to be relieved by other personnel, definite plans covering the procedure should be made in advance. It may be necessary for one observer to meet the relief team at a prearranged point and direct them to the observation position. This will be particularly true if the relief team is unfamiliar with the area, or if the location of the observation post has been changed. It is important that the relief team arrive at the time they are expected (to avoid causing confusion or alarm to the observers at the post). It may be necessary to arrange for a signal or method of communications with the observation post.

If the observation position is to be abandoned for a period, it is important that as much evidence as possible of the observer's presence be removed, including materials used for camouflage. This would minimize the possibility of discovery of the site during the observer's absence.

VEHICLES AS OBSERVATION POSTS

Many times vehicles are used as observation posts in the surveillance of premises. Although such use is usually of a temporary nature, they are particularly adaptable when other types of observation posts are unavailable or inadequate, and when it is necessary to follow suspected vehicles from the premises.

Generally, the observation vehicle should be parked or located at a safe distance away from the premises in the daytime, moving closer at night. As in any observation post, the observer must be near enough to the premises or subject for clear discernment of activity, and yet at a distance that minimizes detection, from persons on the premises.

The greatest danger of detection, particularly when using automobiles, comes from neighbors and friends of the subject becoming aware of the observer's' presence. For this reason, the position of the vehicle should be changed at intervals, if practical. The observers must appear as natural as possible. To do this they may find it advisable to employ diversionary tactics such as:

1. Simulate motor trouble by lifting the hood
2. Pose as traffic survey team
3. Pose as highway surveyors
4. Appear to be testing commercial radio equipment

The imaginative surveillant may simulate many other types of occupations that will be appropriately applicable for the particular area.

When using the car radio, care should be used to avoid holding the microphone in obvious sight, especially when passersby are near. The volume should be set as low as possible and still be audible. At nighttime, it would be wise to cover the radio's receiver signal light with a piece of tape to prevent telltale illumination.

Observation by "Peep Truck"

One of the most effective means of observation from a vehicle is through the use of the observation or "peep truck." Generally this vehicle is of more use in a commercial area, but it is often valuable in other areas if equipped with appropriate signs or lettering. If it is parked for long periods in a residential area though, attention attracted to it could bring police investigation. With respect.to the signs or lettering on the truck, it should be kept in mind that the violators may attempt to verify the company or services advertised.

If the truck is equipped with a radio, the antennae should be of the normal broadcast radio type rather than the whip type. Many "peep trucks" are equipped with one-way glass in the rear door, but often such glass is quite noticeable from the outside. To alleviate this, some trucks use two-way or transparent rear windows, and by arranging a blind of boxes, crates, or other merchandise, create a realistic appearance of a commercial vehicle as well as providing cover for the observers. Camouflaged peepholes, placed strategically in the blind, allow ample field of vision for the observer.

When the surveillance begins, the truck should be driven to the desired location with the observers secreted in the rear. The driver should lock the truck and leave the area on foot. The observers must remain in the truck while it is parked. This may entail long periods of seclusion, and for this reason, the observers should be prepared with food, water and relief cans.

Activity of the observers within the truck must be held to a minimum, conversation or noises from within the truck may be quite apparent to anyone close by. Even though the truck may be equipped with one-way glass, a light or face held close to the glass can be seen from the outside.

At times, the circumstances make it impossible or inadvisable to locate an observation post that will hide the surveillants from the view of persons at the subject premises. Usually the surveillant will not be able to loiter on foot in the area, except for a short period, without establishing a reason for his presence. In such instances, he will have to improvise a position of observation by assuming a role or disguise to explain his presence. The following are some of the undercover roles that may be used, although investigators in various parts of the country may assume other roles more appropriate to their area.

- Telephone company lineman
- Sewer inspector or worker
- Gas line repairman or worker
- Highway and roads repair crew
- Traffic survey team
- Geographical survey team
- Good Humor truck driver and other types of vendors
- Fire safety inspector
- Panhandler
- Painter

The types of roles and disguises to be used lire limited only by the extent or the Special Agents imagination and resourcefulness. Local and state government agencies will often prove helpful in providing equipment and advice concerning an undercover role, but good judgment must dictate the extent to which outside aid is sought.

SURVEILLANCE OF VEHICLES

Although vehicles are often used in the surveillance of premises, as discussed earlier in the text, their primary value and use is the surveillance of "tailing" of suspected or known violation vehicles. This type of surveillance can be, for the purpose of discussion, generally divided into two main categories: using two or more surveillance vehicles and using one surveillance vehicle.

If possible and practical, at least two surveillance vehicles should be used in tailing of suspect vehicles. If they are used properly, the probabilities of avoiding detection by the subject are greatly increased and the chances of losing the subject, due to traffic problems or mechanical trouble such as a flat tire, are minimized.

The vehicles to be used on a surveillance operation should be particularly suited for the purpose. They should be of such inconspicuous appearance that they will not noticeably stand out among other vehicles. It is preferable that the vehicles be of subdued, rather than bright, colors. The colors may be further subdued, and often made indistinguishable at a distance, by allowing a light coat of dust and road grime to accumulate on the vehicle.

Official papers, books, handcuffs, clipboards, and other such matter, should be removed from the seats or the rear window shelf where they might be exposed to outside view. The inside dome light and the license plate light should be removed to avoid possible identification at night. The vehicles should be radio equipped in order to obtain the maximum benefit from using more than one surveillance vehicle. The result otherwise, could be general confusion as to each vehicle's position. The radio antennas should be of the normal broadcast radio type rather than whip antennas.

Two surveillants should be assigned to each vehicle. The driver must give his full attention to the operation of his vehicle, while the passenger acts as observer, operates the radio, and records the activity. There may be times when the passenger observer will be required to leave the vehicle and follow the subject on foot, or take up a position from which he can observe the subject's parked vehicle.

During the surveillance, the vehicle that is the closest to or immediately behind the subject vehicle will generally act as the "lead" vehicle, and as such will radio directions and information to the other cars. The lead position will change from one car to another during the surveillance. Radio transmissions must be as short and concise as possible, giving accurate and essential information. All surveillants should use the radio only to acknowledge orders or give essential information. This will reduce the possibility of two or more vehicles transmitting at the same time.

he surveillant's knowledge of the streets, roads, and traffic conditions in the area may make the difference between success and failure of the operation. The surveillant may be able to anticipate the route and direction to be followed and, in the event of loss of contact with the subject, the "tail" may be resumed at a further point on the route. Such familiarity with the area may also prevent the surveillant from being led into a "detection trap," such as dead end street or road.

Usually the surveillance operation will begin in the area where the subject vehicle is parked. The lead vehicle should be in position from which the subject vehicle can be viewed, with the other cars deployed strategically in the area covering anticipated routes of travel. As the subject drives away, the leader will direct the most appropriate car to assume the lead position, and the other cars to take positions to the rear or on a paralleling course. The subject will be more likely to check for a "tail" at the beginning of his trip, and when near his destination, than at any other times. Therefore, the surveillants must be especially careful at these times.

During the surveillance, the lead car must use every means possible to avoid a prolonged appearance within the rear view vision of the subject. This may be done by keeping one or two unrelated vehicles between the subject and the lead car. In heavy traffic, the lead car should not be more than two or three vehicles behind the subject. The other surveillance cars should follow at reasonable distances, with the second car possibly about one-half block behind the lead car. When traveling in sparse traffic, such as on a rural road or highway, the distance between all vehicles will be greater, particularly between the subject and the lead car. The lead car should avoid following the subject for an unreasonable length of time, and may need to pull off the road at an appropriate place to allow the second car to assume the lead position.

Although the surveillance personnel should he alert to any indications by the subject that he is suspicious or aware of the surveillance cars, they should bear in mind that the subject's rear view vision is limited and, unless he has noticed the same vehicle on two or three different occasions during the tail, he will have no particular reason to be suspicious.

She may make precautionary checks for a "tail" as a general method of operation. On the other hand, a subject who is aware that he is being followed will not go anywhere of importance to the surveillants unless he thinks he has lost the "tail." If the subject is not "burned," the tail may be resumed at another time. Just when to discontinue a "tail" is a matter of judgment for the surveillants, which experience will help to develop.

There are several other methods of conducting a surveillance with two or more vehicles, other than following directly behind the subject.

Parallel tailing. With this method, the surveillance vehicles travel a route parallel to the subject's arriving at each cross street at the same time as the subject. This method is usually limited to residential type areas where the traffic is light and the streets are parallel. The obvious danger to success lies in the possibility of the subject stopping, slowing down, or increasing his speed, thereby disrupting the timing of the tailing cars and causing them to lose sight of the subject at the next cross street.

If there is a third tail car available, this danger may be eliminated by placing the car sufficiently to the rear of the subject from where it can advise the other cars of the subject's location. If the subject turns left or right at a cross street, each surveillance vehicle will assume new positions.

Progressive tailing. This method is of particular advantage in rural areas and when part of the subject's route of travel is known. When used properly, it avoids the possibility of the subject noticing a tailing vehicle. By this method, the surveillance cars are stationed and hidden if possible, at various points along the suspected or known route, preferably at intersections. The distance between the surveillance cars will depend upon the number of intersecting roads. The cars may be stationed at every intersection or alternate intersections. When the subject fails to reach a particular position covered, it is possible to determine where he turned off after his last known position, and the next surveillance will be resumed at that point.

Lead tailing. One surveillance vehicle may actually lead the subject while the other surveillance cars follow behind the subject at a discreet distance. The particular advantage of this method lies in the fact that the subject will pay little attention to vehicles ahead of him. It is of value only when the subject continues on a relatively straight course for a reasonable distance.

Using one surveillance vehicle. Surveillance under these conditions is far more difficult as the subject must be kept in view and followed constantly by the same vehicle. This, of course, greatly increases the chances of detection by the subject. The lone surveillance vehicle must use all available traffic cover in remaining out of the subject's rear vision. In heavy traffic, the tail car must remain close to the subject or run the risk of losing him. On rural roads and highways, greater distance must be allowed between the two vehicles, even to the extent of losing sight of the subject at times.

The surveillants should make every effort to alter the appearance of their vehicle so that it does not present the same picture to the subject each time it is in view. This may be accomplished by:

1. Changing seating arrangements within the surveillance vehicle.
2. Donning and removing hats, coats, and sunglasses.
3. Changing license plates of vehicle.
4. Turning off into side streets or roads, and then resuming the tail.

In the one car surveillance. the observer will travel on foot many times to take up a position of observation after the subject has turned a corner or parked. From his position, he can give further directional signals to the driver as to the subject's activity.

Surveillance of Vehicles at Night

Nighttime surveillance presents unusual problems that counterbalance the advantage of darkness screening the surveillants. The subject is able to view any vehicles following him due to their headlights. He can also use the advantage of darkness to elude suspected tailers by cutting off his lights and turning off the road.

Under medium to heavy traffic conditions, though, the surveillants gain an advantage in that the subjects' field of vision in the rear view mirror is restricted. Due to the glare of headlights, he is unable to distinguish objects clearly. Generally, at night the subject must be followed closer than during the daytime. This is particularly true in heavy traffic.

The surveillants must be familiar with any identifiable features the subject vehicle may present from the rear. The taillights may be of unusual shape or brilliance, or present some pattern that might distinguish that vehicle from others at night. Such identification may be aided, if the opportunity presents itself, by loosening the taillight bulb, replacing the taillight bulb with a brighter one, or other means of discreetly marking the subject vehicle. There have been times when a small hole has been punched in the taillight lens or the lens broken, but this procedure is not recommended.

REFERENCES AND FURTHER READING

Hollywood, J. S., Vermeer, M. J. D., Woods, D., Goodison, S. & Jackson, B. A. (2018). Using *Social Media and Social Network Analysis in Law Enforcement.*
Available:
https://www.rand.org/content/dam/rand/pubs/research_reports/RR2300/RR2301/RAND_RR2301.pdf

Balkovich, E., Prosnitz, D., Boustead, A. & Isley, S. C. (2015). *Electronic Surveillance of Mobile Devices: Understanding the Mobile Ecosystem and Applicable Surveillance Law*.
Available:
https://www.rand.org/content/dam/rand/pubs/research_reports/RR800/RR800/RAND_RR800.pdf

https://www.ncjrs.gov/pdffiles1/Digitization/60130NCJRS.pdf

SECTION 6.5

Reports & Testimony

The world's most talented and brilliant investigator is completely useless to the justice system if that investigator can't write high quality reports. In the justice system, "if it ain't on paper, it didn't happen" always applies. Investigative reports written by police officers aren't that different than those written by journalists: Both seek to answer the who, what, when, where and why questions.

In a police report, the who, what, when, where and why questions are concerning a matter that has come to the attention of the police. The amount of effort and detail that goes into answering these questions largely depends on the seriousness of the matter and an officers estimation of what will be relevant later. Departments also have report writing policies, and the particulars of forms, formatting, and content may be dictated to some degree by departmental policy.

Reports represent the department's official and complete record of how officers responded to an incident as well as the particulars of an incident. They provide a critical record for other officers conducting follow up and continuing criminal investigations. They supply the courtroom workgroup important information on which to base decisions about searches, seizures, arrests, and prosecutions. They also supply critical information for criminal justice databases and planning at all levels of government.

EXCULPATORY EVIDENCE

Exculpatory evidence is evidence favorable to an accused. It includes not only evidence which tends to exonerate an accused, but also evidence which may diminish his culpability or mitigate punishment should he be convicted of a crime. It also includes impeachment evidence such as evidence that may undermine the credibility of a witness for the prosecution.

The duty to disclose exculpatory evidence by the prosecutor applies irrespective of whether or not there has been a request by the accused. Impeachment evidence as well as exculpatory evidence must be disclosed to a defendant.

Non-disclosure of evidence favorable to an accused by the State violates the discovery law irrespective of the good faith or bad faith of the investigator or prosecutor. Law enforcement agencies and prosecutorial agencies may be ordered by a court to make their complete files available to a defendant. The term file includes the defendant's statements, the co-defendant's statements, witness statements, investigating officer's notes, results of tests and examinations, or any other matter of evidence obtained during the investigation of the offenses alleged to have been committed by the defendant.

Once the State provides discovery, a continuing duty exists to disclose the existence of additional evidence. The prosecutor must be made aware of any such additional evidence immediately and written notification should be made as soon as possible. This continuing duty to disclose applies before, during, and after trial.

INTERVIEW NOTES

Interviews should be paraphrased, written in the third person, and in the past tense. Verbatim quotations may be used if deemed essential to the investigation and can be attributed to a specific source. Copies of written statements should be incorporated into the report as an attachment. Question and answer reporting should only be used if it is critical to the investigation that the report contains the precise wording used by two or more parties.

Notes are defined as any initial written documentation of investigative activity created as part of a criminal investigation. This would include, but not be limited to, initial documentation of crime scenes, interviews, surveillance, record searches, analytical notes regarding evidence or records examined or seized, or any other matter of evidence obtained during the investigation of the offense. Additionally, notes would include written documentation of investigative processes such as development of lead sheets and completion of pertinent forms utilized during the investigative process.

There are various methods and procedures for note taking. Some Agents use complete sentences, some use key words and phrases, many use abbreviations. You as the interviewer should use the method that you are most comfortable with and meets your needs in report preparation.

With the exception of quotes, statements made by interview subjects do not have to be recorded in the exact language used by the subject. The meaning of the statement as recorded must hold true to the meaning of the statement as given.